SCRAPBOOK MEMORIES OF THE POTTERVERSE

An Unofficial Oral History of the Harry Potter Films

Edward Gross

Scrapbook Memories of the Potterverse: An Unofficial Oral History of the Harry Potter Films

Copyright 2023 – Edward Gross

No part of this book may be used or reproduced, stored in a retrieval system, or transmitted in any form or by any means, electronic, mechanical, photocopying, recording, or otherwise, without the prior written permission of the author except in the case of brief quotations embodied in critical articles or reviews.

This book was not prepared, approved, licensed, or endorsed by Warner Brothers, J.K. Rowling, or any other entity involved in creating or producing Harry Potter books, movies, or television series. The opinions expressed are solely those of the author or those interviewed.

ISBN: 978-1-949802-32-0

Published by Black Pawn Press

First Edition

Previous Books by Edward Gross

The Fifty-Year Mission: The Complete Oral History of Star Trek: The First 25 Years
(Thomas Dunne Books)
The Fifty-Year Mission: The Next 25 Years, from The Next Generation to J.J. Abrams
(Thomas Dunne Books)
Slayers & Vampires: The Complete Oral History of Buffy & Angel
(Tor Books)
So Say We All: The Complete Oral History of Battlestar Galactica
(Tor Books)
Nobody Does It Better: The Complete Oral History of James Bond
(Forge Books)
Secrets of the Force: The Complete Oral History of Star Wars
(St. Martin's Press)
They Shouldn't Have Killed His Dog: The Complete Oral History of Gun Fu, John Wick and the New Age of Action Films
(St. Martin's Press)
Above & Below: A 25th Anniversary Beauty and the Beast Companion
(BearManor Media)
All in This Together: The Unofficial Story of High School Musical
(ECW)
Rocky: The Complete Guide
(DK Books)
Spider-Man: Confidential
(Hyperion)
Planet of the Apes Revisited
(Griffin Books)
Voices from Krypton: The Unofficial, Unauthorized Oral History of Superman
(Nacelle Books)
Chevrons Unlocked: The Unofficial, Unauthorized Oral History of Stargate SG-1
(Nacelle Books)

Contents

A Personal Journey to Hogwarts and Back	7
Harry Potter and the Sorcerer's Stone	11
Harry Potter and the Chamber of Secrets	49
Harry Potter and the Chamber of Secrets Behind-the-Scenes Interview	73
Harry Potter and the Prisoner of Azkaban	76
Harry Potter and the Goblet of Fire	97
Harry Potter and the Goblet of Fire Behind-the-Scenes	122
Harry Potter and the Order of the Phoenix	129
Harry Potter and the Order of the Phoenix Behind-The-Scenes Interview Section	151
One on One with Dumbledore's Army	151
The Ministry of Designers	160
Bringing Action to the Potterverse	164
Harry Potter Takes Flight	167
Harry Potter and the World of Visual Effects	170
Daniel Radcliffe: Harry Potter and Beyond	173
Harry Potter and the Half-Blood Prince	178
Harry Potter and the Half-Blood Prince Behind-the-Scenes Interviews	193

Daniel Radcliffe: Coming to Terms with Harry Potter	193
Emma Watson Returns as Hermione Granger	199
Life With and After Ron Weasley	203
Tom Felton and the Two Sides of Draco Malfoy	209
The Wright Stuff	213
Dressing the Hogwarts Student Body	217
Animal Trainer of Hogwarts	222
Harry Potter and the Deathly Hallows Parts 1 and 2	227
Harry Potter and the Deathly Hallows Behind-the-Scenes Set Visit	256
Harry Potter and the Deathly Hallows Behind-the-Scenes Interviews	276
Daniel Radcliffe and the Role of a Lifetime	276
The Other Side of the Coin: Tom Felton Reflects on Draco Malfoy	283
Appendix: Odds and Ends from the Potterverse	287
About the Author	323

A PERSONAL JOURNEY TO HOGWARTS AND BACK AGAIN

Do you believe in magic? It's actually been a part of me for most of my life as I've been swept up in its wake and transported from one wondrous place to another in what feels like a blink of an eye — despite the fact that decades have actually passed. And this was happening long before Harry Potter was an inkling in J.K. Rowling's imagination.

In the time when there wasn't yet a Hogwarts — at least that we were aware of — I was battling SPECTRE agents inside hollowed-out volcanoes alongside James Bond, going where no man had gone before with Captain Kirk and the crew of the starship *Enterprise*, journeying to a planet of talking apes, making my way to a galaxy far, far away; having no doubt that a man could fly, heading back to the future with Marty and Doc Brown, climbing into the boxing ring with Rocky Balboa again and again, encountering Jurassic beasties in a park of their own, becoming part of the ring's fellowship, and most recently saving half of all life in the universe with the help of Earth's Mightiest Heroes.

In between all of *that*, the collective we finally *did* become aware of Rowling, Hogwarts and, of course, young Mr. Potter, first through the novels and then via films adapted from them. And by the time of that first movie, *Harry Potter and the Sorcerer's Stone*, in 2001, I'd already spent considerable time taking all of that collective magic from throughout my life and somehow turned it into a career as an entertainment journalist. I'd been on editorial staffs, written quite a few behind-the-scenes books and even made a couple of (very) small sales to Hollywood in terms of scripts.

In 2000, I was brought on as Executive Editor of a series of one-shot magazines devoted to a specific subject — most of them teen-related — like the Backstreet Boys, Britney Spears, 'N Sync and, later on, Justin Bieber, Selena Gomez, One Direction and many others. But about a year into the job, we watched in amazement as Harry Potter grew in popularity and was revealing itself to be a true phenomenon. Our response was to do a one-shot largely focused on exploring what it was all about. That special led to a second, then a third and, 10 years later, we had done a total of 15 issues featuring Harry Potter on the cover, during the course of which we were able to lift the curtain on all eight films, taking readers behind-the-scenes of each entry.

Along the way, I became friendly with many of the cast and crew, speaking on occasion to Daniel Radcliffe, Emma Watson, Rupert Grint and Tom Felton, among others. Just as importantly, though, were the more frequent conversations with crew members, ranging from producers David Heyman and David Barron to production designer Stuart Craig (with whom we had the running joke about his determination to get the cameras into the upper areas of Dumbledore's office to showcase his craft, but somehow it never happening), and directors Chris Columbus, Alfonso Cuaron, Mike Newell and (especially) David Yates, who it seemed like I was talking to every couple of months — and who was the calmest, most even-keeled human being I have *ever* spoken to. Even when he was working on three *Harry Potter* films simultaneously!

And insofar as Columbus was concerned, back in the '80s, when he had become a screenwriting wunderkind, having penned the scripts for *Gremlins*, *The Goonies* and *Young Sherlock Holmes*, and with my just getting started as a journalist, I called New York information and found his number "in the book" (an expression many people reading these words may not be familiar with). He answered the phone, I introduced myself and we did an interview, which became one of my first sales to *Starlog* magazine and was key to getting my career off the ground (thanks again, Chris!).

It all culminated with my traveling to England for a set visit to the final film in the Potter series, *Harry Potter and the Deathly Hallows Part 2*, at Leavesden Studios. I'd actually been to Leavesden a little more than a decade earlier for the filming of Pierce Brosnan's first James Bond film, *GoldenEye*, the official magazine for which I was serving as editor and writer, so there was something extra special about being there again for me.

A lot's happened in the years since the Potter films concluded — both good and terrible, as many can attest — and somehow, I've been lucky enough to continue writing, with my focus being primarily on oral histories of such subjects as *Star Trek* (the two-volume *The Fifty-Year Mission*), *Battlestar*

Galactica (*So Say We All*), James Bond (*Nobody Does It Better*), *Star Wars* (*Secrets of the Force*), John Wick (*They Shouldn't Have Shot His Dog*) and *Stargate SG-1* (*Chevrons Locked*). All of which has led to the book you're reading now; a book that started as kind of an experiment to see if all of those encounters I had with people from the Potterverse could be woven into an oral history for the films' recent 20th anniversary. As such, this is a kind of oral scrapbook taking you inside the *Sorcerer's Stone, Chamber of Secrets, Prisoner of Azkaban, Goblet of Fire, Order of the Phoenix, Half-Blood Prince,* both parts of *Deathly Hallows* and even a brief look on the stage sensation, *Harry Potter and the Cursed Child*.

I genuinely hope you enjoy this return to the adventures of the Boy Who Lived.

Edward Gross
July, 2023

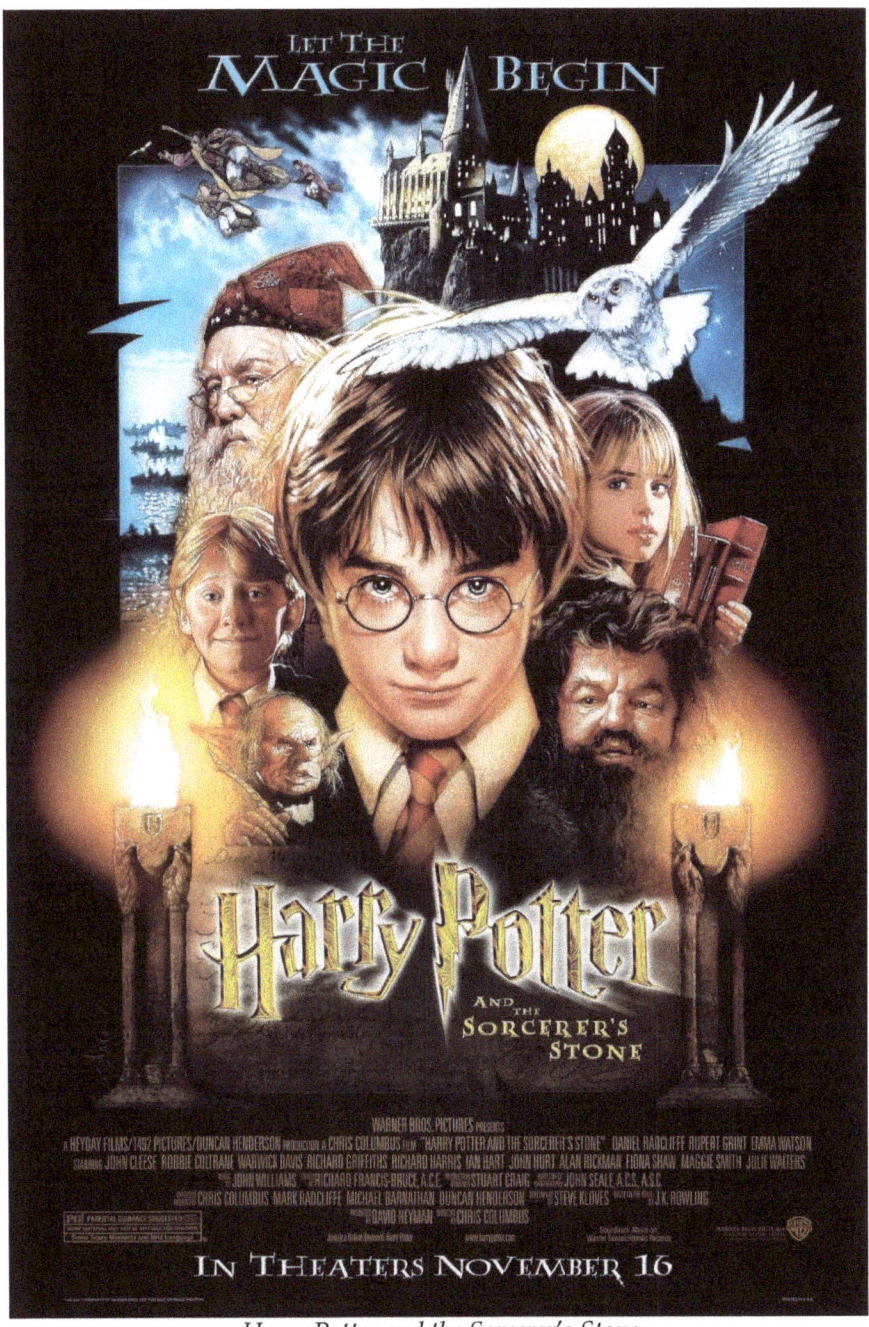

Harry Potter and the Sorcerer's Stone
Copyright and Trademark Warner Bros. Discovery

CHAPTER 1: *HARRY POTTER AND THE SORCERER'S STONE (2001)*

Harry's epic adventure begins on a quiet suburban night. Wizard Albus Dumbledore and Professor Minerva McGonagall await the arrival of Hagrid, groundskeeper of the Hogwarts School of Witchcraft and Wizardry. Flying down on his special motorbike, Hagrid, along with headmaster Dumbledore and Prof. McGonagall, deliver to Petunia and Vernon Dursley baby Harry Potter, the Dursley's being Harry's only living relatives. They are to raise Harry until the time comes for him to attend the wizarding school 10 years hence.

The Dursley's, though, treat Harry as a burden and force him to live in a cupboard under the stairs for the first 10 years of his life. As Harry's eleventh birthday approaches, owls begin to appear trying to deliver the boy's invitation to join Hogwarts. The Dursley's, however, do everything in their human power to keep Harry from getting the messages, knowing full well what happened to his parents. The Dursleys are among the few human beings, or muggles (non-magical humans) who know of the wizarding world and want their charge to have nothing to do with it. As the messages keep coming, the Dursleys keep them from Harry by destroying them. Then they take him where they think they won't be found and won't have to deal with the letters any more. Then giant Hagrid comes in person and delivers the last invitation, at which point the Dursleys argue about it but finally back off and Harry is off to wizarding school.

From here, Harry enters a world hitherto unknown to him; the secret wizarding world where magic and monsters dwell. To get him started, Hagrid takes Harry to the famous Diagon Alley for school supplies, which Harry buys with part of the fortune his parents left him at Gringott's Wizarding Bank years before. Harry also goes to Ollivander's to get a wand, but the wand must pick you. Interestingly, the wand that picks Harry is the brother of the wand that killed Harry's parents. The boy is shocked to learn that he is famous--the only one to survive the death curse that he-who-must-not-be-named, namely Lord Voldemort, used to kill Harry's Parents. But when the curse hit Harry, thanks to the love of his mother, the curse bounced back to Voldemort, destroying the evil wizard's body, and leaving Harry with a lightning bolt shaped scar on his forehead.

To get aboard the Hogwarts Express, Harry had to find platform 9 and 3/4, which was nowhere to be found. He finally heard someone say 'muggles' and went to find who it was. Mrs. Molly Weasley was leading her kids to go to Hogwarts. Harry gets to where they are just in time to see Fred and George go through the portal to the platform. Molly tells Harry what he needs to do to get onto the platform, and he's amazed when it works and he walks right through bricks. Once aboard the Express, he sits in a car by himself and Ron Weasley joins Harry in the mostly empty car. Together they meet Hermione Granger on the train. Hermione is born of non-magic parents, which the racists call a mud-blood, the most terrible name you can call someone in the wizarding world. Harry learns this thanks to the egotistical Draco Malfoy, who is more than pleased with himself and his pure wizard blood. Nobody can stand Malfoy and he and Harry become immediate enemies.

Once in the most-amazing Hogwarts school Harry encounters its living portraits, the friendly but unnerving Nearly-Headless Nick, and stairways that change direction on a whim, no matter where you're headed.

Once in the castle, first year students have to go through the sorting hat ritual, a magical hat that, once placed on a student's head, will tell them which House of Hogwarts they will be assigned to after reading the person's deepest thoughts. There are four Houses; Gryffindor, Hufflepuff, Ravenclaw and Slytherin. Everyone is quickly sorted into their proper houses, until the hat comes to Harry; it reads the nobility that could place him in Gryffindor, but also something else. The hat believes the magic house of Slytherin would also be a good fit, but eventually, Harry is placed in Gryffindor alongside Ron and Hermione, with elitist Malfoy appropriately placed in Slytherin.

It's discovered that there was a robbery at Gringott's in the very vault Hagrid and Harry visited earlier. While that's being investigated, the kids start their classes, but it's not enough for Harry, Ron and Hermione. They get caught-up in the moving stairs and accidently find themselves on the forbidden third floor and run to avoid being caught by Filch. Hermione unlocks a door so they can hide until Filch leaves so they can make their way back to safe ground. What they discover behind that door is a terrifying three-headed dog, Fluffy, the sort-of pet of Hagrid and the guardian of something through a trap door in the floor. Since Fluffy isn't the playful type, they barely get out of there and make it back to the Gryffindor common room.

Their first class the next day is broomstick flying. Harry discovers a natural talent for riding that's so impressive Professor McGonagall takes him to meet the Gryffindor quidditch captain telling him that Harry is their new seeker. He is the youngest seeker in over a century.

Everyone is in the Great Hall eating dinner when the Dark Arts teacher, Quirinus Quirrell, slams open the door and informs everyone that a troll, a huge, dumb, destructive creature, has broken into the Gryffindor dungeon. Angry and hurt at Ron for embarrassing her, Hermione had spent all that afternoon crying in the girls' bathroom. Harry and Ron run to warn her about the troll and find it going into the girls' bathroom. They manage to save her and their bond of friendship starts growing when Hermione realizes that the boys aren't that bad after all, and the boys realize she isn't that bad either.

There have been glimpses of a hooded figure that turns out to be what's left of Lord Voldemort. Hagrid accidentally tells this figure and the kids how to get past Fluffy, music puts him right to sleep. Harry, Ron and Hermione believe that Potion's teacher of Slytherin House, Severus Snape, wants to get the stone, at first for himself and then to give to Voldemort to bring him back to normal life. They plan to get to the stone before Snape does. When they get there, Fluffy is already asleep with a harp playing soothing music. When the harp stops playing Fluffy wakes up and they barely get through the trap door. At this point they have to get past three perilous traps – one being a deadly plant called the devil's snare, another being a bizarre room of living keys, and a deadly life-size chess game that Ron beats within an inch of his life.

When Harry gets into where the stone is instead of Snape, he finds Quirinus Quirrell to know what the mirror does. Then demanding the stone. Voldemort wants to talk to Harry so Quirrell removes his turban to reveal the ruined face of Voldemort barely surviving, having grown onto the back of Quirrell's head. Turns out that Snape and Dumbledore are protecting the stone, with Dumbledore's spell that only let someone that wanted the stone, but not use it, helping to get the stone in Harry's pocket. Despite enticements to bring his parent's back to life with the stone, Harry resists Voldemort and is attacked by Quirrell. A touch from Harry burns Quirrell to ashes and Voldemort's soul escapes and passes through Harry, who passes out with the stone safely in his possession.

Harry comes to in the school infirmary and learns the stone has been destroyed lest someone else try to possess it. With the end of the school year, the point totals for each House that they were given for grades and proper behaviour and this year Slytherin is in the lead, one hundred and sixty points ahead of Gryffindor, who is in last. That is, until Dumbledore awards Harry sixty points, Ron fifty points and Hermione fifty points for their bravery. He also awards Neville ten points for standing up to his friends, giving Gryffindor that year's House Cup. And with that the school year is over and Harry must return to the Dursleys' over summer vacation, knowing he has friends and a place where he fits in.

Harry Potter and the Sorcerer's Stone was published as a novel (under the name, in England, Harry Potter and the Philosopher's Stone) on June 26, 1997, with its movie adaptation being released on

November 16, 2001. It immediately touched the literary and film worlds, becoming a best-seller and global theatrical hit. All of it, of course, sprung forth from the imagination of author J.K. Rowling, who found inspiration in the strangest of places.

J.K. Rowling (creator, Harry Potter): Where the idea for *Harry Potter* actually came from, I really couldn't tell you. My boyfriend was moving to Manchester and wanted me to move, too. It was during the train journey back from Manchester to London, after a weekend of looking for a flat, that *Harry Potter* made his appearance. I have never felt such a huge rush of excitement. I knew immediately that this was going to be so much fun to write. I didn't know then that it was going to be a book for children, I just knew that I had this boy, Harry. I also saw it as a series which would follow Harry to the end of his school days at Hogwarts, which would be seven years. So, in the final book, Harry will have come of age in this wizarding world.

It was the weirdest feeling. I was on the train and it seemed like the idea was just floating in my head; it was like the idea had been floating around, waiting for someone to write it, and it chose me. It was like an explosion in my head, like magic. I know that sounds corny, but it was like pure inspiration. You can always tell when you have a good idea when you are writing, because you get this physical response to it; a surge of excitement. I never felt such excitement. And during that journey, I not only discovered Harry, but also Ron, Nearly Headless Nick, Hagrid and Peeves. But with the idea of my life careening round my head, I didn't have a pen that worked. And I never went anywhere without my pen and notebook. So rather than trying to write it, I had to think it. And I think that was a very good thing. I was besieged by a mass of detail, and if it didn't survive that journey, it probably wasn't worth remembering.

For wont of a better word, life has been "magical" for Harry Potter's creator, despite the fact that in more recent years she's mired herself in controversy with many of her online comments. She's not only become one of the wealthiest women in the world, but someone who has seen her creativity genuinely touch the imagination of children of all ages around the globe. And it seems that with every corner she's turned, she's been met with one surprise or another, though none more so than the way fans connected with her creation.

J.K. ROWLING: I remember that a boy asked me in San Francisco, "Where did Scabbers come from? What's Scabbers' history?" And Scabbers, for people who don't know, is a rat who subsequently was revealed not to be a rat at all. I found it quite spooky that he honed in on Scabbers, because, of course, I'd known from the first book that Scabbers wasn't really a rat, but nobody else did. That kind of thing keeps cropping up and I think it's that children are reading the novels, like, 12 times or whatever it might be, and they really started knowing the way my mind works.

The creativity in Rowling, who was born Joanne Kathleen Rowling in England on July 31, 1965, was evident from an early age. Growing up, she took on the "responsibility" of entertaining others, particularly her young sister Di. In fact, it was for Di that she wrote her first story, which was called "Rabbit," the subject matter of which is pretty obvious, with Rowling saying, "Rabbits loomed large in our early storytelling sessions; we badly wanted a rabbit."

According to Rowling, from that moment on she wanted to be a writer, though it wasn't something she would readily admit as she was afraid others would be dismissive of her dreams. In fact, when she entered Exeter University, she studied French. After graduation, she took her French degree and headed off to Portugal, where, ironically enough, she taught English. The way she structured her days was that she would teach in the afternoon and evenings, and write in the mornings. During that time, she wrote a pair of incomplete novels when she turned her attention to writing about this child wizard named Harry Potter.

At about the same time, Rowling married a Portuguese journalist and together they had a young daughter named Jessica. Unfortunately, the marriage didn't work out and she and Jessica headed to Edinburgh, Scotland to be near Di. Working as a French teacher — and taking advantage of Jessica's nap times to get some writing done — she was lucky enough to get a grant from the Scottish Arts Council to finish her novel. However, things weren't always easy, as her job was phased out and she began to struggle as a single mother. In fact, this was the image that the media widely portrayed when she eventually did sell Harry Potter and the Philosopher's Stone *(renamed* Harry Potter and the Sorcerer's Stone *in the U.S.) to Bloomsbury in the U.K.*

J.K. ROWLING: I wasn't a struggling single mother all the time that I was writing the first Harry book. It was only during the final year of writing that I found myself poorer than I'd ever been before. For six months I lived exclusively on welfare. That was horrible. I got myself a part-time clerical secretary job. I mean, really part-time, like a couple of hours a week. The grant certainly helped. Obviously, continuing to write was a bit of a logistical problem: I had to make full use of all the time that my then-baby daughter slept. This meant writing in the evenings and during nap times. I used to put her into the pushchair [carriage] and walk her around Edinburgh, wait until she nodded off and then hurry to a cafe and write as fast as I could. It's amazing how much you can get done when you know you have very limited time. I've probably never been as productive since, if you judge by words per hour. But I look back on myself then and I'm very proud. I was the only bread-winner and I was being mother and father. If anyone thinks that's easy, try it sometime. *And* I was writing a novel.

Shortly thereafter, her problems quickly began to vanish. She finished the first Harry Potter novel, which was roundly rejected until it found a home at Bloomsbury. The publishing advance was enough to keep her going as a writer, but things really began to change when the book went to auction with American publishers (ultimately picked up by Scholastic).

J.K. ROWLING: Three months after British publication, my agent called me at about eight one evening to tell me there was an auction going on in New York for the book. They were up to five figures. I went cold with shock. By the time he called back at 10PM, it was up to six figures. At 11PM, my American editor, Arthur Levine, called me. The first words he said to me were, "Don't panic." He really knew what I was going through. I went to bed and couldn't sleep. On one level I was obviously delighted, but most of me froze. The stakes seemed to have gone up a lot, and I attracted a lot of publicity in Britain for which I was utterly unprepared. Never in my wildest imaginings had I pictured my face in the papers — particularly captioned, as they almost all were, with the words, "penniless single mother." It is hard to be defined by the most difficult part of your life. But that aspect of the story, thankfully, receded. The books are now the story, which suits me fine.

The rest, of course, is history, with seven Harry Potter novels in print, eight feature film adaptations and a phenomenon that has touched the world, including theme parks, the Fantastic Beasts *spinoff films and the Broadway production of* Harry Potter and the Cursed Child.

J.K. ROWLING: I would have been crazy to have expected what has happened to Harry. The most exciting moment for me was when I found out Harry was going to be published. It was my life's ambition to see a book I had written on a shelf in a bookshop. Everything that happened since has been extraordinary and wonderful, but the mere fact of being able to say I was a published author was the fulfillment of a dream I had had since I was a very small child. If someone asked me for my recipe of happiness, step one would be finding out what you love doing most in the world and step two would be finding someone to pay you to do it.

Given the success of the Harry Potter novels, it's not surprising that there was some concern about adapting them to the big screen. After all, even with today's technology — or the technology that existed at the turn of the century — how do you take a written work that has touched so many imaginations and translate it into a visual piece? It's a challenge that didn't seem to faze producer David Heyman, whose career started when he was hired as a production assistant on David Lean's 1984 film A Passage to India. *Two years later he became a creative executive at Warner Bros and, later still, a vice president at United Artists. In 1997 he returned to his native London where he began his own production company, Heyday Films.*

DAVID HEYMAN (producer, the Harry Potter film series): Success has many partners. The story is that I came back to London to start my company, where I wanted to focus on books. I'd been looking for a subject matter that would appeal to audiences in both Europe and the United States. Having a brother and sister who were 10 and 14 at the time, I was very interested in finding a children's film that I could enjoy as much as they would. My team at Heyday was aware of this and my head of development, Tanya Seghatchian, read an article about a new children's book by a then-unknown author. The agent sent her a copy and my assistant Nisha read it over the weekend. Nisha reported that it was a curious book about a young boy who goes to wizard school. I thought it was a wonderful idea and read the novel that evening. What I thought was a great idea turned out to be an even more remarkable book, and so much richer than the idea that initially attracted me. I realized this was something very special and began pursuing the rights the following morning.

J.K. ROWLING: We were inundated with offers from film companies, and I said no to all of them. Even Warner. But they kept coming back. I wasn't against the idea of a film. I love films. The vital thing for me was that it would be true to the book. The decision to go with Warner wasn't about money or power, it was because I believed in them.

Rowling was a little leery of the idea, fearing that, like most adaptations, the films would be little more than an excuse to exploit a popular book title. Assurances from Heyman that the film would remain true to her original vision began to convince her it might not be such a bad idea. Even more exciting to her were some of the names being bandied about in terms of directing, including Steven Spielberg. Ultimately, chosen to helm the project was Chris Columbus, whose previous credits include the first two Home Alone *films,* Mrs. Doubtfire, Bicentennial Man *and* Step Mom. *Prior to directing, he wrote the screenplays for the original* Gremlins, The Goonies *and* Young Sherlock Holmes *(which actually seems to be more than a little inspirational to the world of young Mr. Potter).*

CHRIS COLUMBUS (director, *Harry Potter and the Sorcerer's Stone*): My daughter Eleanor was reading the book at the time and insisted that I read it as well. I started reading it, finished it in one day and couldn't stop thinking about turning it into a film. But at that point the film was already in the hands of another director. A few months later, I received a call from my agent, telling me the book was available. There was only one problem: *several* directors were now also interested in making the film. Warner Bros. and David Heyman began a lengthy process of interviewing the potential candidates. Nevertheless, I wasn't intimidated by this. I felt that if I could articulate my passion and obsession with the material, if I could clearly specify how I would make the film, David and the studio would realize that I was the man for the job.

Over the years, people — particularly the media — have implied that I've gone soft, because I've directed some sentimental films. But based on my own personal life at the time, I felt that those were films I needed to make. Once I got those stories out of my system, I wanted to go back to where I was when I started out as a writer, which is a much darker place. I've always been a big fan of British cinema, everything from David Lean, comedies like *Kind Hearts and Coronets* [1949] and particularly the Hammer Horror films, which I adored. I found them very atmospheric and evocative. I grew up watching these films and they influenced my early writing. *Young Sherlock Holmes* [1985] was set in a British boarding school and involved two pre-teen boys and a girl who solve a supernatural mystery. It was sort of preparation for directing *Harry Potter*.

DAVID HEYMAN: There was a lot of interest from numerous directors who wanted to be involved with *Harry Potter*, but Chris emerged as the person with the greatest passion and understanding of the books and the desire to remain faithful to Jo's vision. I thought he would be the right person for the film. He worked with children before and had a great sense of humanity. We knew that would be necessary for this kind of movie, plus he had a great passion for the books.

CHRIS COLUMBUS: I'd heard these horrendous and actually amusing stories about how certain directors had wanted to adapt the book, like changing the locale to a Hollywood high school or turning Harry, Ron and Hermione into American students or making the entire film as a computer animated picture. I was stunned by some of these notions. I mean, it all feels painfully obvious to me. There's a reason why millions of children and adults have fallen in love with the Harry Potter books. To destroy the foundation of this world and these characters would alienate our audience. So I was adamant about being incredibly faithful to the books.

J.K. ROWLING: They made me two promises. That it would be an all-British cast, and that Chris Columbus would keep it as true to the book as was possible within the constraints of film. And they kept both promises.

DAVID HEYMAN: There is no stipulation from Jo other than my promise to her. I'm a man of my word and that's important. Second, the very fact that the books have been so successful encourages fidelity and responsibility. And third, Jo is the most wonderful collaborator. She's not a person who says, "No, you can't do this." She's incredibly reasonable and very clear.

CHRIS COLUMBUS: At first I was nervous, being such a big fan of the books, but I immediately felt comfortable with Jo. I explained that I would protect the integrity of the book. I told her how I wanted to keep the darkness and the edge of the material intact. I also think Jo was excited by the fact that I wanted her to be involved in the creative process, and she was an invaluable collaborator. Her inspiration and ideas were absolutely wonderful. To me, the movie is a companion piece to the book. My goal was to involve Jo Rowling as a collaborator. People would say, "Well, isn't that going to interrupt your vision and isn't that going to get in the way of what you want this film to look like?" I thought, "If I were doing *Dracula* and had access to Bram Stoker, I would certainly want to know what he was thinking." If I were doing a World War II movie, I would hire a consultant who had been in the war and knew what was happening in terms of reality. Jo was a very willing collaborator. She never came in with a sledgehammer and said, "This must be done *this* way, you need to do *this*." That never happened, so I just found it a joy to work with her.

STEVE KLOVES (screenwriter, *Harry Potter and the Sorcerer's Stone*): What would happen with a writer like me is that I would get an envelope with a half a dozen synopses of books. The last one was something called *Harry Potter and the Philosopher's Stone*. The title was interesting, but the synopsis didn't do it justice. I decided to go into a bookstore about a block from my office, I bought it and I was about ten pages in when I called my agent and said, "I think I'm going to want to do this movie called *Harry Potter and the Philosopher's Stone*." Little did I know it was going to be the next 11 or 12 years for me. It was just one of those things that was meant to happen. I just felt this weird kinship with this material. **(Hero Complex)**

J.K. ROWLING: Steve and I were introduced, in L.A., by David Heyman and we almost immediately went into a lunchtime meeting with a big studio executive. Steve turned to me while food was being ordered and said quietly, "You know who my favorite character is?" I looked at him, red hair included, and I thought, "You're going to say Ron. Please, please don't say Ron. Ron's so easy to love." And he said, "Hermione." At which point, under my standoffish, mistrusting exterior, I just melted, because if he got Hermione, he got the books. He also, to a large extent, got me. **(reported by Patrick Keating)**

STEVE KLOVES: I think for some reason, from that moment on she sort of trusted me. The thing about Jo, though, which is remarkable for someone who had no experience with the filmmaking process, was her intuition. We had a conversation the very first day I met her where she said, "I know the movies can't be the books. I just ask you to be true to the characters, that's all I care about." And that was always my watchword. **(Hero Complex)**

CHRIS COLUMBUS: Some of the best experiences that I had on the movie were with Jo Rowling, Steve Kloves, David Heyman and myself. We laughed, we had fun, we talked about what would work on screen, what wouldn't work on screen, we got the script to where we wanted it to be, we talked about the design, about the look of the Troll and all of those things, and Jo was just a collaborator. Sometimes we would say, "Well, how can we make this work? We need to change it from the book," and the perfect example is the kids on the book cover who were wearing rugby shirts and jeans and sneakers with a wizard cloak over them. Well, we tested that look and it looked like a bad Halloween costume. So we said to Jo, "Since this is steeped in British boarding school tradition, we need to get this to look like it exists in a real place," and that's why we came up with the uniforms and she was all for that. I asked Jo at one point, "Wizard hats, do the kids wear wizard hats at all time?", and she said, "Yeah, and most of them wear wizard hats through most of the book." I said, "Well, I can't justify that. I think that it will start to feel a little odd if they wear wizard hats throughout the film. Can we just use wizard hats for special occasions, for the sword ceremony and the final piece?" And she agreed to that. So, that's the kind of conversations that you could have with Jo. She's never in your face, never gets in your way.

Interestingly, back in 1985 Columbus saw his screenplay of Young Sherlock Holmes *adapted to the big screen as a Steven Spielberg production, and it's highly recommended that all Harry Potter fans see it as there is, as previously noted … common ground.*

CHRIS COLUMBUS: First out of the gate for me is *Young Sherlock Holmes* in 1985, then when I got involved with Harry Potter, I'd be a fool not to notice the similarities between *Young Sherlock Holmes* and *Harry Potter*. I guess it's just the kind of stuff I'm attracted to. After seeing the new Sherlock Holmes movie, and the opening was kind of the end of *Young*

Sherlock Holmes, I turned to my wife and asked, "Does this look familiar to you?" I never had the balls to ask J.K. Rowling if she ever saw *Young Sherlock Holmes*.

The next biggest challenge was finding the right cast to bring Rowling's various characters to life. Most important, of course, was that of Harry Potter himself.

DAVID HEYMAN: It was not easy to find a boy who embodied the many qualities of Harry Potter. We wanted someone who could combine a sense of wonder and curiosity, the sense of having lived a life, having experienced pain; an old soul in a child's body. He needed to be open and generous to those around him and have good judgment. Harry is not great at academics; he has flaws. But that's what makes him so compelling, so human — that he's not perfect. Harry has an "everyman" quality, yet he is capable of great things. He makes us all believe that magic is possible.

J.K. ROWLING: We'd know him when we found him. I was walking around in London and Edinburgh, looking at kids as I passed them, just thinking, "Could be, you never know." I could have lunged at a kid and said, "Can you act? You're coming with me. Taxi!"

CHRIS COLUMBUS: We literally auditioned hundreds of actors for the role of Harry, but with little luck. Then, the first casting director, in a fit of total frustration, threw up her arms and said, "I just don't know what you want!" Sitting on a shelf in the office was a video copy of *David Copperfield*, starring Daniel Radcliffe. I picked up the video box, pointed to Dan's face and said, "This is who I want! *This* is Harry Potter." The casting director said, "I've told you before, he is unavailable and his parents aren't interested in him doing this film."

A couple of months later, Heyman and Kloves decided to check out a play, and ran into an agent Heyman knew named Alan Radcliffe, whose son turned out to be the actor that Columbus was so interested in.

DAVID HEYMAN: It was all the clichés. Lightning struck, the skies opened! All through the second half of the play, I couldn't concentrate. The Radcliffes left before I had a chance to speak to them, so I had a very sleepless night before calling Alan the next morning.

DANIEL RADCLIFFE (actor, "Harry Potter"): I went to go see a play with my mom and dad called *Stones in the Pockets*. In the row in front of us were David Heyman and Steve Kloves, the producer and writer of the film. David introduced himself to us during the break. He was a really nice guy and my dad knew him from work. I was only introduced to them as a producer and writer; I didn't know they were doing *Harry Potter*. Then we got a call asking if we would meet with David and I went.

DAVID HEYMAN: We met the next morning and Daniel's parents expressed their concerns. I completely understood their reticence and caution in allowing their child to play a role that would inevitably change his life. But we arranged a meeting over tea that afternoon with Dan. We talked for an hour and a half. His energy and enthusiasm were wonderful. I had a feeling then that this was our Harry.

CHRIS COLUMBUS: To the Radcliffes' credit, they were totally aware of the enormity of this project and for the sake of their child, were not going to make this decision lightly. We made it very clear to them that we would protect their son. We knew from the start that Dan was Harry Potter. He had the magic, the inner depth and darkness that is very rare in a twelve-year-old. He also had a sense of wisdom and intelligence that I haven't seen in many other kids his age.

DANIEL RADCLIFFE: Now, I never thought of me as being Harry, although when a friend of mine told me they were holding auditions, I was dead keen. Later, we got a call asking me to do another audition and it just went from there. I had to go on three auditions and two or three screen tests.

CHRIS COLUMBUS: We knew we had made the right choice after sending Jo a copy of Daniel's screen-test. Jo's comment was something to the effect, "I feel as if I've been reunited with my long-lost son." Dan was a 12-year-old with a 35-year-old heart. There is so much depth, so much going on behind his eyes and you realize, "This is a kid who has lived a life. This is a kid who can appear haunted and troubled by his past. Yet he's charming." That kind of maturity is hard to find in a 12-year-old.

DANIEL RADCLIFFE: I remember getting the news that I'd passed the audition. I remember thinking, "There are a million boys auditioning and I know I won't get it. I was in the bath at the time and my dad picked up the phone. I heard him say, "Hello, David." David Heyman was the only David that we knew at the time, so I was pretty sure it was him. My dad came upstairs and told me and I just sat there for a while to let it sink in. I just started to cry, because I was so happy. There are no words for it, really. I just sat there, wiped out for a while. Then I woke up at 2 a.m. and woke my mum and dad up and asked them, "Is it real? Am I dreaming?" I was so excited.

When word of Radcliffe's casting was made public, there were a number of rumors that made their way through the media, among them that his parents weren't very supportive of his trying to get on the film.

DANIEL RADCLIFFE: The story that they were frightened of the effect it might have on me wasn't really true. They were just afraid I would be disappointed if I auditioned and didn't get the part.

CHRIS COLUMBUS: Daniel's parents were another reason why he was so perfectly cast. Back in the early 1990s I directed the first two *Home Alone* films, which starred Macaulay Culkin. I'd had about 10 years away from *Home Alone* and I've learned from that experience. I learned as a director that you have to "cast" the parents, too; you have to see what kind of environment the kid lives in. You also have to realize that Dan really seems to love doing his work. That's one of the things you look for as well — kids who are interested in the job, interested in being there and also that the parental relationship is a good and healthy one. With Macaulay, I just think he was more interested, to be honest with you, in being a little kid, which I think is incredibly healthy.

For the most part, most of the kids on *Harry Potter* had never even been on a film set before. For me, that was important in terms of getting their performances to be real. They don't come in with stage mothers or stage parents telling them how they should act. It's all very real and, psychologically, that's important. These kids come in and they realize that they're doing a job. The British tradition — particularly with stars like Richard Harris and Maggie Smith — is not about how big your trailer is, "Do I have a trainer? Do I have a cook," and all that star stuff that is sometimes upsetting to me when I work in Hollywood.

While the casting of Harry was a top priority, it was equally important that the right actors be found for Harry's best friends, Hermione Granger and Ron Wesley. It was Rupert Grint who scored the latter part. Born on August 24, 1988 in Hertfordshire, England,

Grint, like his young costars, didn't have much of a professional career prior to being cast in Harry Potter. *That being said, he had nonetheless had a chance to test the acting waters. In school he played a character called Mystic Meg in a talent show and was cast as Rumpelstiltskin in* Grimm Tales. *Wanting an opportunity to explore the idea of acting a little more, he joined a local theater drama group, through which he appeared as the gangster named Rooster in* Annie *and in a production of J.M. Barrie's* Peter Pan.

RUPERT GRINT (actor, "Ron Weasley"): I was Harry's biggest fan before I even knew it was going to be a movie. When I was reading the books, I always thought I could relate to Ron, because we both have red hair, we both like sweets, we're both scared of spiders and we both have lots of brothers and sisters.

Grint wasn't aware that a film version of Rowling's first novel was being prepared until he caught an item on the British television series Newsround, *which basically made mention of the fact that the producers and director were auditioning young actors for the starring role in not only* Harry Potter and the Sorcerer's Stone, *but the planned sequels as well.*

RUPERT GRINT: I decided to do my own video, pretending to be one of my drama teachers. I dressed up like my teacher, who's a girl, so it was kind of scary. Then I made up this rap song about how much I wanted to be in the film.

CHRIS COLUMBUS: We immediately fell in love with Rupert Grint. He's extremely funny and has such an incredibly warm presence.

RUPERT GRINT: It was so cool and amazing when I was cast. It was the coolest moment in my life. I'd just been doing, like, school plays and stuff. One time, I was a fish in *Noah's Ark*. Then I was in *Harry Potter* – that's a big step.

Although she was only 13 at the time of the first Harry Potter, *actress Emma Watson, who was signed to play Hermione Granger, had accomplished quite a lot in her young life. Born on April 15, 1990 in Oxford, England, she discovered her attraction to the world of acting while at school, starring in productions of* Arthur: The Young Years *and* The Happy Prince. *At age seven, she won the Daisy Pratt Poetry Competition, and ultimately made her professional acting debut in* Harry Potter and the Sorcerer's Stone.

EMMA WATSON: It's the scariest thing that's ever happened to me and it was the biggest thing that ever happened to me. And it's the *best* thing that ever happened to me.

DAVID HEYMAN: We'd been simultaneously looking to fill the other roles, but the casting of Harry was the peak of the triangle. Without him, none of the rest would make sense. We brought in several children for screen tests, but it soon became apparent who we wanted.

EMMA WATSON: Some people came around to my school in Oxfordshire and said, "Do you have anyone who would like to audition?" So I had an audition at my school. I think I ended up doing over five auditions. My dad told me, "You do realize there are going to be, like, a thousand girls auditioning, right?" And I was kind of, like, "Oh, okay ... I'll keep that in mind." I tried to enjoy it instead of desperately trying for it. I found out that I had gotten the part when David Heyman invited Rupert Grint and me to come in. We sat down in his office — all very casual — and he said, "You've got the part." I was so shocked and I just stood there and said, "Pinch me." Getting the part was ... intimidating.

CHRIS COLUMBUS: Emma Watson embodies the soul and the essence of Hermione Granger. When we saw Daniel Radcliffe, Rupert Grint and Emma Watson together on screen, they had amazing chemistry. It was electric. We knew we had found the perfect team.

EMMA WATSON: When I got the part, I couldn't believe it, because I was expecting someone to get the part who had professional acting experience. I rang my best friend, just as I'd been told, and she said, "So, have you got it?" and I said, "Yes," and she screamed. She literally just went, "Arghhhh!" It was like five minutes. I had to hold the phone away from my ear not to be able to break my ear, and she was so excited she was almost more excited than me. They actually brought me to the studio and sat me down with Rupert and told me, "You got the part," and I just stood there going blank for, like, five minutes until it really sunk in. But it was really exciting and it's been a really good experience for me. And I truly love the character. She's got some really good lines in the first film. One of them is, "I'm going to bed before either of you come up with another clever idea to get us killed, or worse — expelled!" I like her, because she's really bossy and nerdy and all that kind of stuff. It makes her funny, even though she doesn't realize it.

A lot of people have asked if I am like her, but I don't think I was, really. She was a total bookworm and would do anything to get top marks. I enjoyed school, but I wasn't obsessed with school. I also hope that I had better fashion sense than she does. It was sort of hard being the only girl on the film for six months. Hermione had to be very "nose up." I think that was the whole of her charisma. If she didn't have that, she'd be normal and it's what created her, really; the fact that she was so, "Well, I'm right and you're wrong." I loved that in her.

Your hero isn't much of a hero if he doesn't have effective bad guys to deal with, and not only is Harry Potter dealing with various adult wizards and creatures, but he has to cope with tormentors his own age as well. On the home front, much of his childhood has been pretty miserable because of the aunt and uncle – the Dursleys – who are raising him. Particularly troublesome is his spoiled cousin, Dudley. The official Warner Bros. UK website describes the character this way: "Dudley Dursley is Harry Potter's cousin and son to Vernon and Petunia Dursley. Dudley loves all things material and edible and views happiness in direct correlation with the amount of presents he receives. He is soon to continue the Dursley tradition by attending the prestigious school of Smeltings. Dudley and Harry don't really get on, but Dudley is kind enough to give Harry his old, if somewhat big, clothes."

Dudley is played by 12-year-old actor Harry Melling, who began attending acting classes at the age of five. Four years later, he appeared in the Robert Hyman original musicals House *and* Y2K. *His grandfather, Patrick Troughton, was quite famous in England for being one of the actors to portray Doctor Who in the long-running science fiction series of the same name.*

In both the books and the films, it would seem that Harry has found true happiness when he reaches Hogwarts. Unfortunately, even there he has to deal with a bully, only in this case it's wizard-in-training Draco Malfoy, described as "the youngest member of the esteemed Malfoy family, following in his father Lucius' footsteps, who now holds the prestigious position of Standing Officer of the Ministry of Magic. Draco is a first year Slytherin student and he and his faithful sidekicks Crabbe and Goyle are always to be seen together, making their presence felt wherever they go. He is arch enemy to Harry Potter and all those who befriend him."

Not so mean is 13-year-old Tom Felton, who plays Draco Malfoy. He began acting at the ripe old age of six, appearing in the 1996 motion picture The Borrowers. *In that film he played the role of "Peagreen." In 1999, he co-starred in* Anna and the King *(a non-musical remake of* The King and I*), appearing as Louis, a son of the Jodie Foster character. In Britain, Felton appeared in a pair of top television series:* Bugs *(on which he played "James") and* Second Sight. *He loaned his vocal talents to the BBC Radio 4 dramas* The

Wizard of Earthsea *(on which he voiced the part of "Ioeth")* and Here's to Everyone *(playing "Hercule")*. Additionally, he gained attention for himself in 1995 when he appeared in a series of British television commercials and has also proven himself to be quite a good singer, serving as the member of four choirs at school and church. Additionally, then 14-year-old actor Joshua Herdman plays Draco flunkie Gregory Goyle.

TOM FELTON (actor, "Draco Malfoy"): Draco is very mean. To be honest, I am not that mean. I think he's jealous and he wants to be the coolest guy in school. Of course I prefer to play a bad character. It's more fun, because it's different.

JOSHUA HERDMAN (actor, "Gregory Goyle"): Goyle is a thug, basically. He's one of the cronies. Malfoy is the sneaky ringleader, but he's too weak to do anything himself. So he has to lug around these big cronies all the time. They are Harry's arch-enemies, and they're just meanies.

There are, of course, people who are very much on Harry's side. For instance, Ron Weasley doesn't get too far from his family, as his twin brothers, George and Fred, attend Hogwarts as well. The twins are portrayed by real-life twins Oliver and James Phelps. Also on Harry's side is the Hogwarts Quidditch captain, Oliver Wood, as portrayed by Sean Biggerstaff.

The Professors at Hogwarts frequently offer friendship beyond instructions, though that isn't necessarily true in every case. Academy Award nominee Richard Harris portrays Professor Dumbledore, the head of Hogwarts, in the first two Harry Potter films. Among his credits are Camelot, The Guns of Naverone, The Field, Unforgiven, Patriot Games, The Count of Monte Cristo *and* Gladiator.

Although Professor Snape doesn't turn out to be a bad guy, in actor Alan Rickman's hands one could be understandably confused. After all, Rickman re-defined the movie villain with his portrayal of terrorist Hans Gruber in the original Die Hard. *Since then the late actor appeared in such films as* Bob Roberts, Close My Eyes, The January Man, Galaxy Quest *and* Robin Hood: Prince of Thieves.

Warwick Davis, who plays Professor Flitwick, has spent a great deal of his career in Hollywood under a lot of makeup. He made his debut as the Ewok Wicket in George Lucas' Star Wars *adventure,* Return of the Jedi, *and reprised the role in two TV movies,* Caravan of Courage *and* Battle for Endor. *From there he appeared in the feature films* Labyrinth, Leprechaun *and* Gulliver's Travels. *One of his most popular roles was in the George Lucas-produced/Ron Howard-directed fantasy adventure,* Willow.

A good wizard needs a good wand, which is a lesson Harry learns when he visits the shop of Mr. Ollivander, portrayed by veteran actor John Hurt. His credits include I, Claudius; Crime and Punishment, Midnight Express, The Elephant Man, A Man for All Seasons, Love and Death on Long Island, Captain Corelli's Mandolin, *and* Contact.

*Harry Potter's nasty old aunt is portrayed by Fiona Shaw, who has scored as an actress on stage (*As You Like It, The Good Person of Sechuan, Electra, Hedda Gabler, The Prime of Miss Jean Brodie, The Way of the World, The Rivals, The Taming of the Shrew *and* The Widower's Houses*), and screen (*My Left Foot, Mountains of the Moon, London Kills Me, Jane Eyre, The Butcher Boy, The Last September *and* The Triumph of Love*).*

Famed actress Dame Maggie Smith was signed to play Professor McGonagall. Her credits include The Prime of Miss Jean Brodie, Travels with My Aunt, Death on the Nile, California Suite, A Private Function, Hook, Sister Act, The Secret Garden, Richard III, The First Wives' Club, Washington Square, Tea with Mussolini *and* The Last September.

If there is one person determined that Harry not become a wizard, it would have to be his uncle, Vernon Dursley, as played by Richard Griffiths. The actor, who brings a certain madness to the character's obsession, has a wide variety of credits, including Chariots of Fire, The French Lieutenant's Wife, Ghandi, Greystoke, Gorky Park, King Ralph, Blame It on the Bellboy, Naked Gun 2, Superman II *and* GoldenEye.

Zoe Wannamaker, who plays Madame Hooch, is comfortable moving back and forth between stage, screen and television. Her stages roles have included Electra, The Glass Menagerie, Dead Funny, The Last Yankee, The Crucible, Othello *and* Once in a Lifetime. *On film she can be seen in* Swept from the Sea, Wilde, Raggedy Rawney, The Hunger, *and* Inside the Third Reich: The Last 10 Days of Hitler. *TV appearances have included* Poor Little Rich Girl, Prime Suspect, My Family, David Copperfield, Gormanghast, The Widowing of Mrs. Holroyd, Countess Alice *and* Momento Mori.

OLIVER PHELPS (actor, "George Weasley"): He's very mischievous. He got me to do things I'd never done before, like being disrespectful to my elders. I try to be as respectful as I can.

JAMES PHELPS (actor, "Fred Weasley"): He's friendly and he likes to have a good laugh. That's something I enjoy, too. Like, if I could have a magic power, I'd like to be able to change things into something else. I think it would be funny. If you wanted some chocolate or you wanted fruit, you could just change it right there and then.

SEAN BIGGERSTAFF (actor, "Oliver Wood"): He's very sporty, slightly eccentric and very passionate about Quidditch. Wanting to win the Quidditch House Cup is like the Holy Grail for him. I can relate to the desire to win, but I'm not as competitive. Oliver's got more of a "winning is everything" attitude. And he's a bit more of an oddball than I am.

RICHARD HARRIS (actor, "Professor Albus Dumbledore): I was asked to play the part and I wasn't going to do it for various reasons. Then my eleven-year-old granddaughter Ellie telephoned me and said quite simply, "Papa, if you don't play Dumbledore, I will never speak to you again." So I didn't have much choice in the matter. Dumbledore's presence *is* felt right through the books, even though you don't see much of him. He's a very important figure in the stories and I needed to find a rhythm and a metre in this beautifully written dialogue in order to be able to play the part.

ALAN RICKMAN (actor, "Professor Snape"): I have lots of nephews and relationships with friends' children. They weren't so much excited as insistent that I do the part. I understand their enthusiasm. Harry Potter's like any great play or novel which obeys rules of storytelling. You're gripped from the first page and as you keep turning the pages, you get involved with the characters and want to see what happens next. It's a simple rule, but one which requires great talent.

DAME MAGGIE SMITH (actor, "Professor McGonagall"): I thought it was such a terrific book for kids and I was greatly interested to see how they were going to create this magic on film What people don't realize is that jobs like this don't come up very often — this story has captured everyone's imagination. And how often do you get to walk around as a wizard wearing great clothes?

FIONA SHAW (actor, "Aunt Petunia Dursley"): I wanted to play one of the magical characters, but I soon realized that the Dursleys' world is more exotic and more frightening than the one Harry experiences when he leaves them. In being ordinary, the Dursleys are a very eccentric pair. Their failure with their own son is all the more apart in the presence of Harry, a boy who is clearly gentle, very prestigious, civilized and a sort of natural knight, as opposed to Dudley, who is spoiled and hopeless. The Dursleys live on a knife edge of snobbery, aspiration and desperate disappointment that their son Dudley is *not* Harry.

RICHARD GRIFFITHS (actor, "Uncle Vernon Dursley"): Vernon distrusts Harry completely and is always concerned that he is going to do something strange at any moment. That is Vernon's biggest fear. He doesn't want anything strange happening that the neighbors might see. He is terrified that people will think there is something not right about him. The Dursleys want to be average and normal and the fact that they have Harry Potter in their care is dreadful, as he is anything but ordinary.

ROBBIE COLTRANE (actor, "Hagrid"): My son would have killed me if I hadn't [signed on], so there was no question about me *not* doing it. Hagrid is a bit lacking in social skills. I don't think he would ever be asked to join the golf club, but he's a good sort of fellow who likes dragons and things like that. He's actually pretty fearless and very fond of wild animals, which most people are afraid of. He's a giant and generally they aren't very nice, but he's got the good genes and takes the children under his wing. But he has to have an edge to him and they did it very cleverly. They said, "When he kicks the door in and then says, "Sorry," that's real Hagrid." He forgets how strong he is and that he could break your neck with a snap of his finger. But it's also quite clear in the writing when he's supposed to be funny. I mean, Hagrid's problem is that when he starts talking, he doesn't know when to stop. He actually gives away major plotlines, so that has to be an established part of his character. Otherwise, it just sounds like he's giving away plotlines. He has to sound very natural, and his statement, "I should *not* have said that," became a bit of a catch phrase in the shooting, because he keeps doing it. But this didn't change my approach to the character. It was quite clear to me how the character should be played in the movies. And, of course, Jo Rowling and I are great friends. We talked on the telephone for hours like a couple of adolescents about everything.

As the cast came together, production moved forward and everyone involved embraced all the inherent challenges — including working with the film's many visual effects.

CHRIS COLUMBUS: I initially didn't want to do a film like this *because* of the visual effects and I wasn't interested in working with them. But now they are at such a point where it's actually fun to work with them. My feeling has always been that you shouldn't let the effects overtake the story, and I've seen it happen in so many films where it's all about the effects. Our goal in *Harry Potter* was to make it just like the book, about the characters. The effects are icing on the cake.

That being said, the effects were nonetheless an important component of the first film, necessary to transport the viewer into Harry's magical world. And if you were to find one sequence in Harry Potter and the Sorcerer's Stone *that was more amazing than any other, it would undoubtedly have to be the Quidditch match during which Harry proves how phenomenal a wizard he will one day become.*

J.K. ROWLING: I loved the Quidditch match. It really looks the way I wanted it to look like. They asked me ages ago, "What is Quidditch? What does it look like?" I always said it was violent and scary, but I couldn't imagine how they were going to do it — but they have. And it looks *so* real. I was looking forward to it for the whole first half of the film, and it really lived up to my expectations. The creation of Quidditch came after I had a blazing row with an ex-boyfriend. I had been writing Harry Potter books for about a year and I had decided that one of the unifying characteristics of any given society is sport. Almost any society you can think of will have its own games and sports. Then we had this blazing row. I don't know whether it's cause and effect. I doubt it. But I walked out of the flat and booked in to a hotel for a night.

I invented it while spending the night in a very small room in the Bournville Hotel in Disbury, Manchester. I wanted a sport for wizards, and I'd always wanted to see a game where there was more than one ball in play at the same time. The idea amused me. The Muggle [non-magical] sport it most resembles is basketball, which is probably the sport I enjoy the most. I had a lot of fun making up the rules, and I've still got the notebook I did it in, complete with diagrams and all the names for the balls I tried before settling on Snitch, Bludgers and Quaffle.

JOHN RICHARDSON (special effects supervisor, *Harry Potter and the Sorcerer's Stone*): We created those sequences by combining footage taken of the actors on location with computer generated material. I suggested to Chris Columbus that we build a pole-arm attached to a bicycle seat, which, with the right equipment, could lift the actors on their broomsticks. Our main rig was a hydraulic pole attached horizontally to a broom, with a seat on at the end to support the actor. The attachment was adjustable, so the pole could swing in any direction. We then adapted that so the pole could be rigged from above or below the actor, for scenes where the kids were upside down or hanging from their brooms. The broomsticks were constructed from steel, which made them sturdy enough to handle the weight of the actors and the movements that were required. Seats were, in most cases, mounted rigidly to the broomsticks, but were adjustable to allow independent movement for shots of the riders pulling their broomsticks up toward them as a means of reining them in. To ensure safety at all times, actors were strapped to the seats with climbing harnesses attached across the groin and at the back.

ROB LEGATO (Quidditch visual effects supervisor, *Harry Potter and the Sorcerer's Stone*): This is not just one person flying. It's 15 kids flying. Everything is in flux. The camera is moving, the kids are moving, the balls are mid-air, eight or 10 kids are flying in the frame at any one time. Plus, you are inventing the vocabulary for a game that doesn't exist, figuring out a novel way of shooting it.

His view for the Quidditch sequence was to create a visual effects action scene in a live-action organic way.

ROB LEGATO: When you read the book, it's pretty wide open and we had 11 minutes of unscripted material to create. You have to imagine a game, what its rules might be, how you might play it. You have to picture Quidditch in motion; you can't picture it as a photograph or a still or even as a series of storyboard frames, because the game moves quickly. We designed the sequence as if it were a live game. How would one action affect the next one? How would this player attack? How would that player get out of a tight spot? The goal was to realistically portray a series of events. It was like a giant three-dimensional chess game trying to figure out how to meet all the constraints and maintain a degree of quality. Working the way we did, you have the opportunity to modify the effect as you go, just as you would in live action. In live action, you have a plan that can change when you go shoot it and all of a sudden, an actor does something that you really like, or you discover that the tone of the scene could change by adding a little music. All of a sudden, the scene gets better than what you planned.

ERIC ARMSTRONG (effects artist, *Harry Potter and the Sorcerer's Stone*): To test the digital model we made of Harry, we replaced Daniel Radcliffe's head with its 3D counterpart in a bluescreen composite for Chris Columbus. We didn't even mention that the head was digital. We waited to see if Chris would notice something weird about it. When we told him what we'd done, he was thrilled and that was when we knew we could give him a look that he could sell to the producers.

ROBBIE COLTRANE: I was very happy that the focus was on the characters instead of the effects. I actually got great enjoyment working with the young actors, which surprises people. The reason that actors don't like working with kids is because they don't have a very good emotional memory. If you say to them, "Imagine yourself at so and so, imagine when you were last really, really angry," and they have to be really, really angry fourteen times. It's bad enough when you're an adult. So what you do is that you always have fifteen takes with everything. It's the same with bloody animals and little Fluffy plops down and will only hit the mark once in forty takes. *And* it's three in the morning and you want to go home, and so they print the take that Fluffy hit the spot on, and you perhaps weren't very good in that take. That's what that's about. But the kids were great and I have to say, as much as it goes against the grain to be nice about the director, Columbus is wonderful with children. You can tell from seeing the film. He really knows how to get the best out of them, because they were doing a lot of really subtle stuff, weren't they? Normally, kids in movies are either being cute or they're just being ghastly. He managed to get all sorts of subtleties, the way their friendship develops and the way her mind is sort of likable to start with. You start to think, "Oh, she's really alright," just like in the book.

RICHARD HARRIS: They were full of confidence, these kids. After all, an eleven-year-old looked at me at one point and said, "That was quite a good reading. I think that you're really good in this part." I must say that Chris was like magic with them. He was like the Piped Piper. They actually worshipped him and he was very kind and totally patient. The rumor has it that he never once lost his cool.

DAME MAGGIE SMITH: I was thrilled when Daniel got the part of Harry. He has such special qualities. All the kids in the cast have amazing stamina. This film has brought out the child in practically everyone involved in the production, but particularly Chris Columbus, who is terrific and has such patience and enthusiasm.

While common for filmmaking in general, a production like Harry Potter and the Sorcerer's Stone *in particular depends on the connection between all the different departments working together to bring the overall vision to life. Among the people doing so were production designer Stuart Craig, director of photography John Seale and costume designer Judianna Makovsky.*

CHRIS COLUMBUS: This film was incredibly collaborative and it was the highlight of my career for several reasons, mostly because I've worked with such talented people. My cinematographer, John Seale, and production designer, Stuart Craig, in particular understood the richness and complexity of Harry Potter's world. In Hogwarts, we strived to create a realistic, magical place. A school that the viewer would believe actually existed.

DAVID HEYMAN: Stuart Craig is one of the finest production designers living. There is no one who designs with such taste and elegance. We wanted Harry's world to feel like it really exists. Stuart made Hogwarts, with all its splendor, seem like a place that truly feels real. We had loved John Seale's work in a variety of films, from *Witness* to *Dead Poets Society* and we knew he would give *Harry Potter* a fantastic look. For instance, Chris wanted low light in the interiors, as there is no artificial light in Hogwarts. John was particularly attentive to this and lit the set with torches and candles. He has this incredible energy and works at a remarkably fast pace, and yet he's able to retain tremendous depth and richness at all times.

JUDIANNA MAKOVSKY (costume designer, *Harry Potter and the Sorcerer's Stone*): It was a total fluke that I was hired to design *Harry Potter and the Sorcerer's Stone*. I went into the interview believing that they would never hire an American designer, because the Harry Potter books are so English. Director Chris Columbus and producer David Heyman had interviewed a lot of designers who were much better known, including Americans, but I believe Warner Bros. liked me because of my work on *A Little Princess* and they recommended me. "Well, I'll go and meet them so they know who I am, and that will be that," I thought. At the interview I was very open to many different ways to design the film and I was told I was the only designer who didn't scare Chris by having set-in-stone ideas. Still, I was shocked when they called my agent the next day and said, "We want her." (*from* **FilmCraft: Costume Design***)*

DAVID HEYMAN: Beyond the sets and the lighting, we wanted a bit of madness and eccentricity which Judianna created. For example, for Madame Hooch, the flying instructor, Judianna took classical professor's robes and added the black and white of a referee and then cut it in such a way it flows like the movement of a bird.

JUDIANNA MAKOVSKY: J.K. Rowling and I met only once, with Chris and David, and it wasn't a long meeting. Basically, I brought some research pictures and asked questions about the characters in the books. "You talk about robes on Dumbledore. Are these the kind of robes you're talking about?

And Madam Hooch, the flying instructor, to me she looks like the sort of gym teacher we all had that was a little mannish when we were in elementary school." And she said, "Yes, that's exactly right." J.K. didn't come around on a daily basis, she interfaced with Chris and the producers. Stuart Craig was the production designer and we worked very closely together. (*from* **FilmCraft: Costume Design***)*

During production, pretty much everyone involved knew that they were doing something special, and there was reassurance in the fact that Chris Columbus would be returning for the follow-up, Harry Potter and the Chamber of Secrets. *Particularly pleased were the young actors who had had such a great time with him.*

CHRIS COLUMBUS: I do remember that in the first conversation with Warner Bros., they did say, "Could you do two back-to-back?" and I said, "I think so, as long as I get the editing worked out with the pre-production on the first and I'm editing along." We were basically editing the first film while we were shooting, so I felt that under those circumstances, I could do that. So, it was already in my mind anyway. I think that they probably felt that, "Well, if he doesn't turn out to be a complete loss, we'll let him do two." I said to my cinematographer and production designer, "I want you guys to push this film visually beyond anything that I've ever done. It has to be visually stunning; that's more important than anything." Then I told the actors, "Your performances have to be incredibly real, naturalistic, it's got to be real." My feeling with Hogwarts and that whole world is that it would have been easy to take this into some fantastical places that exists only in the imagination, but I felt that when I read the books that Jo Rowling spoke to every eleven-year-old and said, "You know, *you* could potentially get a letter from Hogwarts School of Witchcraft and Wizardry." That gave these kids some hope in their lives and I thought, "*That's* what I want the two films to be like," that you could actually, potentially, get this letter. You want to make them believe in magic in a weird way. I know that sounds corny, but it's really how I felt. You want kids to believe in the magic of it all.

RUPERT GRINT: *I* believed. When I walked into the Great Hall at Hogwarts for the first time, it was absolutely incredible. There were all these effects, with all the candles floating, food on the table, all the flambeaus were lit — it was one of the most amazing things I've seen in my life.

EMMA WATSON: Chris Columbus is such a cool director. I hadn't worked with any others, but I was sure he was one of the best. He would say the scene himself and say, "How do you want to do it?" He wasn't really bossy and he wasn't telling us what to do or say or how to act. He is a fantastic director.

RUPERT GRINT: One of my favorite scenes was the giant chess board near the end where I was a piece being moved across the board. It was pretty difficult. There was loads of dust everywhere. But all the way through the film, Harry's been doing all the brave stuff. So Ron was really happy, because that's his fave thing — chess. I did one stunt in the Devil's Snare scene. They attached me to a harness and safety rope, pulled me up about 50 feet in the air and then dropped me down. I landed on the Devil's Snare. I was afraid of heights at the time, but after I did that, I wasn't scared. I was on a wire and I was dropped from really, really high up into the Devil's Snare. It was fun, so I liked it when we had to do more takes.

EMMA WATSON: We did a lot of pranks. Once, Daniel Radcliffe brought in a remote-controlled whoopee cushion. He tried it on me, but it didn't quite work. Then he tried it on someone else who was going to sit down on a massive sofa. When it went off, Chris Columbus said, "What is that thing?"

and everyone burst into laughter. Dan pulled other pranks, too — like making little labels that said, "Kick me" or "Punch me." He would stick them on the backs of everyone who came into sight. It was really good.

Radcliffe believes that the reason Harry Potter, in both book and film form, appeals to the audience is because the character is so relatable.

DANIEL RADCLIFFE: Everyone can relate to Harry in one way or another. I can relate to him, too. He's a boy who has had a very tough life, because he's never learned about his parents and he has come to Hogwarts and found it to be a place where he really belongs. He's very loyal and he's very determined and curious. He has a fantastic bond with his friends. He doesn't let people put him down. When someone puts him down, he only gets stronger, because it gives him a reason to want to do that thing that they say he couldn't do.

IAN HART (actor, "Professor Quirrel"): The ingredients are all there for any great myth. You have good and evil and avenging the death of your family. These themes are timeless, but in this story they're woven together in such a way as to be really funny. Although the film has a very serious side to it, there is also a lot of humor, too.

EMMA WATSON: I reckon it's so successful, because it's for all ages. I've seen just as many adults reading Harry Potter books as I have seen children. It's kind of got a mix of everything — comedy, adventure and it can make people cry. J.K. Rowling describes everything really well, because you kind of feel like you know the characters.

DANIEL RADCLIFFE: I was really pleased with the movie. I hate watching myself, but I was kind of able to enjoy the film thanks to the direction and, obviously, the story and the script. And especially the cast. They kind of allowed me to sit back as if I wasn't in it. And I was excited about the second film, because the second book is my favorite.

EMMA WATSON: The first time I saw the film, I was, like, "Oh my God," and I literally felt weird for a few seconds, because it's weird seeing yourself on screen. And then the second time I watched it, I enjoyed it a little. The third time I watched it, I actually picked up on how they had done it and I *really* enjoyed it.

CHRIS COLUMBUS: The most difficult part of making *Harry Potter* was excising elements of the book that I wanted to put into the film. If I had the opportunity, I would have made a seven or eight-hour picture. My strongest desire was to make a satisfying film for every single one of the fans, a movie that truly captures the heart and the spirit of the book, without sacrificing any of its darkness, edge or character.

Harry Potter and the Sorcerer's Stone *was released in the UK on November 10, 2001 and in the United States on November 16, 2001. The film's budget was $125 million and it grossed $1.017 billion.*

Scrapbook Memories of the Potterverse

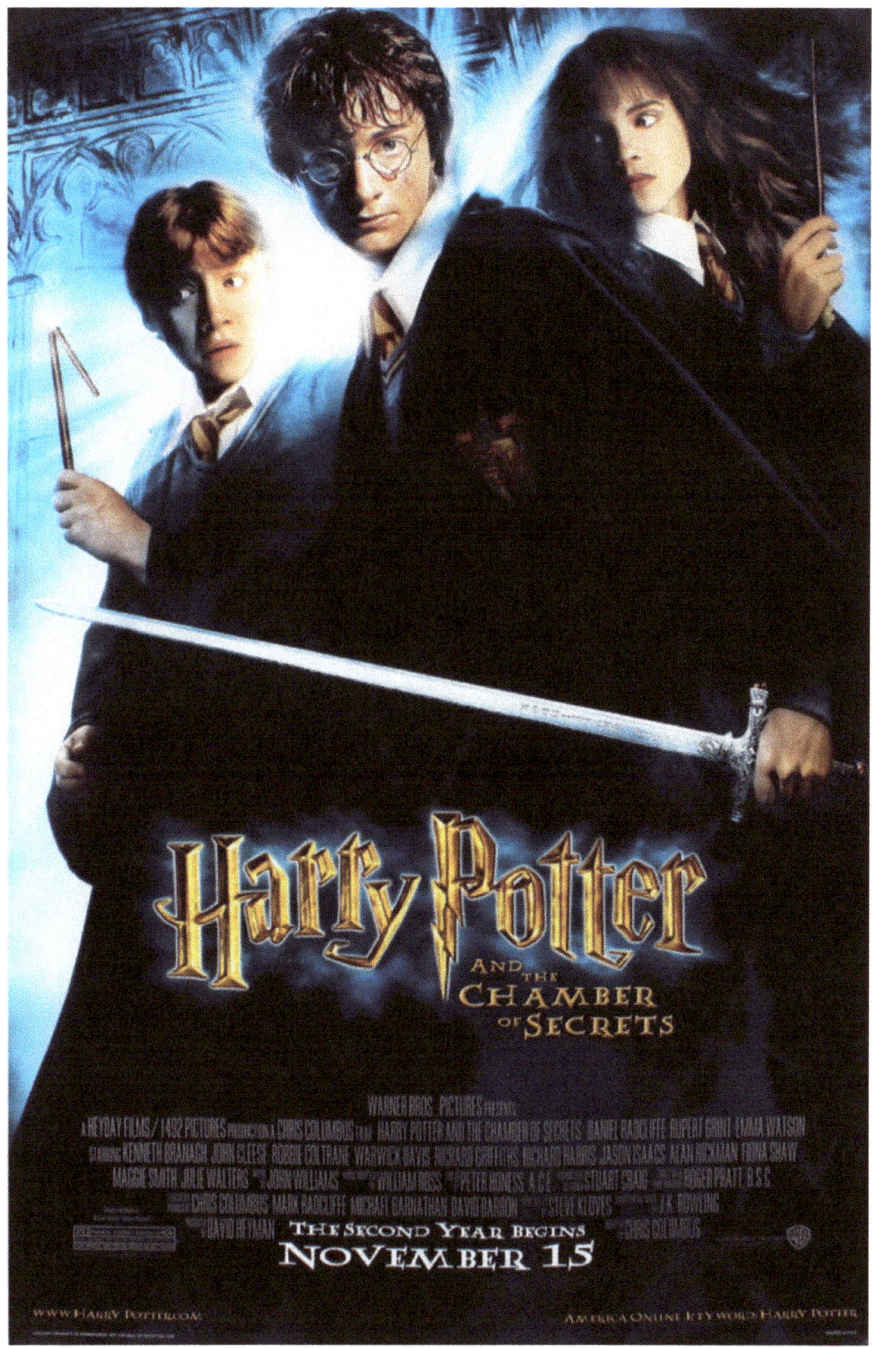

Harry Potter and the Chamber of Secrets
Copyright and Trademark Warner Bros. Discovery

CHAPTER 2: *HARRY POTTER AND THE CHAMBER OF SECRETS (2002)*

After spending an unhappy summer at the Dursley's house without so much as a letter from Ron, Hermione or anyone else he met at Hogwarts – particularly on his 12th birthday – Harry meets spindly little house elf, Dobby, who tells him it is too dangerous for him to return to Hogwarts. Harry also learns that it was Dobby who kept his mail from him. To make sure the Dursleys punish Harry enough to keep him home, Dobby uses magic to ruin a Dursley dinner party by dropping a cake on an important guest. Trying to stop Dobby, Harry attempts to stop the cake, but he's spotted by his guardians and it looks very much like Harry floated, then dropped the cake.

The result is that Uncle Dursley installs bars on Harry's window and multiple locks on his door so that Harry cannot get out. But Ron Weasley and his twin brothers, trouble makers Fred and George, "borrow" their dad's flying Ford Anglia and rescue Harry from his imprisonment. He is taken to the Weasley home from where they go to Diagon Alley to get their books and other items for the new school year. At the bookstore there is a book signing honoring Hogwarts' newest Defence Against the Dark Arts teacher, the famous Gilderoy Lockhart. Lockhart is a bit of a buffoon and uses Harry to improve his own image in the press. Harry's nemesis Draco Malfoy rears his slicked back head. After meeting Draco's father Harry is certain he sees Lucius, slip an extra book into the cauldron of Ron's little sister, Ginny, as he is talking to the kids before they make it outside.

Reunited with his friends and heading back to Hogwarts, things aren't getting any easier for Harry; he and Ron somehow are locked out of the wizard platform behind the wall at platform 9 3/4 and smash headlong into it. The express leaves without them, but Ron comes up with a plan. Ron "borrows" his dad's Ford Anglia again and with Ron behind the wheel, fly over the countryside, even passing the Hogwarts Express below. Not knowing they are actually ahead of the train, they are nearly hit by it as it comes up behind them. Ron nearly drops Harry when Harry's door comes open due to the rolling Ron accidentally made the car do getting out of the way of the train. They make it to Hogwarts, but instead of a proper landing, the car develops problems and is going down on its own accord. They are headed for the whomping willow and Ron breaks his wand trying to get the car to stop, failing miserably as the car comes to rest in the whomping willow. It is a very aggressive tree that smashes at the car and the boys. After much smashing they are dumped onto Hogwarts grounds, where they are summarily put in detention.

Harry starts hearing a strange voice talking of killing. Soon after this starts, Harry discovers caretaker Argus Filch's cat, Mrs. Norris, petrified and a message written in blood: "The Chamber of Secrets has been opened, enemies of the heir...beware." With the Chamber opened, a monster begins stalking Hogwarts, petrifying Nearly Headless Nick and a few students as well. This chamber, it seems was built by one of the school's founders, Salazar Slytherin, to contain this strange creature and ultimately to get rid of all muggle-born students, thereby cleansing the magical world of what he considered to be lesser beings. Most believe Harry is the heir after he talks to a snake in its own language but he, Ron and Hermione believe Malfoy is the heir and intend to talk to him by changing themselves into Draco's brutish companions, Crabbe and Goyle.

They mix a potion in a disused bathroom as the ghost, Moaning Myrtle, watches. Ron and Harry successfully transform themselves using Crabbe and Goyle's hair, but Hermione accidentally adds a cat hair and becomes a cat human hybrid and will need a while to recover. The boys learn that Malfoy is not the heir, but discover that the chamber had been opened before, and a young girl had been killed

Harry is injured during a Quidditch match, but that doesn't stop him from continuing his investigation into the chamber's history. He and Ron find water on the floor in the hallway outside the girls unused restroom and find that someone had thrown a book at Myrtle. After she leaves Harry finds the wet diary of a student named Tom Marvolo Riddle. Tom is a "memory" in the book and he takes Harry into the diary to half a century before, when the chamber had previously been opened. In this vision Tom accused Hagrid of opening the Chamber and got him expelled from Hogwarts. Now Harry believes that Hagrid is the one that caused the problems previously. After several students are found petrified, Hagrid is sent to Azkaban, the wizard prison, because of his "history" of opening it the first time. The diary is stolen from Harry and Hermione is petrified shortly after near the library. She did manage to keep a page of book in the library that describes the monster in the Chamber as a Basilisk, a gigantic serpent that kills with a look, or petrifies its victims if they don't look at it directly, such as in a reflection.

There is another message written on a corridor wall saying one of the students is in the chamber and will lie there forever. Ron and Harry overhear Professor McGonacall saying the student taken into the chamber is Ron's sister, Ginny. The boys guess that Moaning Myrtle was the girl killed all those years ago and go to tell Lockhart. When they get to his office, they find him rapidly packing to leave, from there they force him to go with them to see Myrtle to find out how she died. After talking with her they find the entrance to the chamber in the array of sinks. Once the chamber entrance is opened Harry and Ron, tell Lockhart to go first. When he is reluctant to do so they give him a push to get him started. Once at the bottom, Harry takes the lead while Ron brings up the rear making sure Lockhart doesn't turn around. As they are looking at the shed skin of the basilisk, Lockhart pretends to faint and then grabs Ron's wand. Not remembering that it is broken, Lockhart casts the spell to wipe Harry's memory only to have it backfire and wipe his own. The backfire causes a rock slide and Harry is cut off from the other two. He continues on and finds Ginny being watched by Riddle, who tells Harry that he used the girl to open the Chamber of Secrets to let the Basilisk out and to write the messages in blood on the walls. But Dumbledore is ready; he sends his pet phoenix Fawkes with the sorting hat into the Chamber. There, Fawkes blinds the Basilisk and, after running from the blinded Basilisk, the Sorting Hat brings forth the sword of Gryffindor. This enables Harry to kill the creature, but *not before being poisoned by a fang sticking in his arm when he stabbed and killed the Basilisk. With the venom surging through him, Harry finds the strength to crawl to the comatose Ginny. Riddle's enchanted diary is beside Ginny. Harry stabs the book three times with the venom filled fang that stuck in Harry's arm. This obliterates Riddle and brings Ginny out of her spell. Fawkes' tears heal Harry's arm. The students that were petrified as well as Mrs. Norris and Sir Nicholas, are treated by Professor Sprite and Madam Pomfrey, and returned to their original state.*

The new evidence frees Hagrid and exonerates him for the first opening of the Chamber, but leaves house-elf Dobby, whose been trying to sabotage Harry the whole time to keep him safe, under the control of the evil Malfoy family. That is, until Harry tricks Lucius into freeing the elf by hiding a sock in Riddles diary, which Malfoy then gave to Dobby. Thus giving the elf his freedom.

Like the Lord of the Rings *trilogy, the first two Harry Potter films were virtually shot back-to-back, with cast and crew returning to continue the magic. One sad bit of news during production was the announcement that this would be Chris Columbus' last directorial effort for the series; that he would be stepping back into the role of producer for the third film,* Harry Potter and the Prisoner of Azkaban. *Nonetheless,* Harry Potter and the Chamber of Secrets *proved to be not only a worthwhile successor to* Sorcerer's Stone, *but in many ways superior as well.*

The studio's confidence was pretty much there from the beginning, which is why production on the second actually began on the Monday following Sorcerer Stone's *release. What this meant was that the second film was gearing up for filming while the first was in the final stages of production. Despite the fact that things were so crazy production-wise, the filmmakers were determined that the new film would differ from the original in terms of structure, character and tone. Its story of mysterious happenings and cryptic messages at Hogwarts certainly captured their desire.*

J.K. ROWLING (author, *Harry Potter and the Chamber of Secrets*): The burst of publicity after the American publication of *Harry Potter and the Sorcerer's Stone* terrified me. I was teaching part-time by then and trying to write *Harry Potter and the Chamber of Secrets*. I felt frozen by all the attention. I found the book incredibly hard to finish, because I was worried that it wouldn't live up to readers' expectations. I'd heard that your second novel is the hardest to write. In the end, I delivered the manuscript on time, but took it back for six weeks until I was satisfied with it. When it was published, it went straight to number one on the bestseller lists, which I thought was incredible. You have to remember that these things were taking me hugely by surprise. But what mattered was that I had written a book I could be proud of.

CHRIS COLUMBUS (director, *Harry Potter and the Chamber of Secrets*): It was an intense time, but we'd learned so much on *Sorcerer's Stone* and I was very excited about taking all this knowledge into the second film. And none of us had the chance to sit back and think about the success of the first film, which I think was good for everyone, particularly the kids. By that point, the cast and crew had become like one big family. It was great that we could all share that sense of excitement without losing our momentum, and carry it into *Chamber of Secrets*.

DAVID HEYMAN (producer, *Harry Potter and the Chamber of Secrets*): We devoted a good part of *Sorcerer's Stone* to setting up the world of Harry Potter. There was so much to introduce in terms of the magic, the settings and the characters. With *Chamber of Secrets*, we jump directly into the narrative and into the adventure.

CHRIS COLUMBUS: *Chamber of Secrets* is darker in tone. And it's a little scarier, a little edgier. Jo Rowling, for instance, said that that's the book from which she got the most heat from a lot of parents because it was scarier. So we were aware of all that when we were making the film. But I didn't want to pull back because, to be faithful, I wanted the readers to have the same experience they had when they read the book.

DANIEL RADCLIFFE (actor, "Harry Potter"): If you take away the darkness in the film, you haven't done the book justice. And so, if you've read the book, then I don't think you'll be scared at all. Also, I think everyone has a dark side, really. However, much you like showing it or are afraid of showing it, everybody has it. So I think it was great to be able to show Harry's dark side, and it was great to be able to show that he's not flawless and he's not the perfect person.

CHRIS COLUMBUS: This film is darker and funnier, and it takes Harry's character to a new place. The first film was about Harry realizing that he's actually a wizard. In contrast to the colorful and larger-than-life characters that surrounded him, Harry was somewhat passive and didn't come into his own until the third act of the film. In *Chamber of Secrets*, Harry exudes a lot more confidence and strength right from the start.

DANIEL RADCLIFFE: I was excited about the chance to play a more active role in the adventure. The last line of the first film is like the beginning of the second film. Harry says, "I'm not going home, not really," because he's discovered his home is at Hogwarts and that is where he belongs. But when he returns to Hogwarts at the beginning of *Chamber of Secrets*, he discovers there's a real threat to his school and home and he's determined to protect it.

CHRIS COLUMBUS: Daniel didn't change personally between films, but I would say he was becoming more of a leading man. He had more confidence as an actor, which I think was pretty obvious from the film. As a person he was still thanking me after a take. You're not going to get Julia Roberts thanking me after a take.

DANIEL RADCLIFFE: As a character, I think Harry changed between movies. He developed so much as a character. I had to develop myself, too, and I found I had two instincts, Harry's and my own. So when we were filming each scene, I asked myself, "How would Harry react to this?" and I tried to get that feeling across on screen. We *are* similar in a way, because Harry's friends are very important to him, and my friends are very important to me. We're also very curious and sometimes our curiosity gets us into trouble. Also, like Harry I'm not afraid to stand up for myself and do what I believe in, and that's one of Harry's most important traits. I do think I'm going to have to have therapy one day. When I read the books, I actually found out more about *myself* that Harry has in his personality, too: like I said, curiosity, loyalty and getting in trouble. We don't break the rules, we just kind of bend them.

Changes in the young cast is not surprising, considering that it had been over two years since Radcliffe and his co-stars, Rupert Grint and Emma Watson, were signed for the original adaptation.

DANIEL RADCLIFFE: My own life hadn't really changed following the first film. People come up to me on the street and they see my face on, like, 50-foot-high billboards. I know that sounds like big changes, but it's really not as big as what could have happened. When people come up to me on the street now, I actually don't mind it at all, because they always seem to be really enthusiastic about the films. They just wanted to know about them — and it was so great speaking to them. Family life didn't change much between the first two films; I don't think Mom and Dad would let me change. We did the same things we always did. We'd go on holidays, I would see my friends, ride my bike, watched TV. What was exciting, was the premiere of the first film. Both premieres, in

London and New York. And the whole publicity tour; I really like interviews. I'm not just saying that. I do really enjoy being interviewed I just liked the premieres — there was such energy about it. And I got to meet Ben Stiller at the English premiere.

RUPERT GRINT: The three of us are friends. We got on really well on the set, but we lived far away from each other, so it was hard to get together between the first two films.

EMMA WATSON: I think most of the changes in my life happened after the first film, when I occasionally got recognized. On the second one, the public's reaction kind of became a bit more noticeable. It became a bit more frequent, but apart from that, it's been basically the same. My friends hadn't been treating me differently, and most other people were really nice about it. You get the odd kid who's a bit annoying, who'll go past you in the hallways and go, "Oooooh, it's Hermione." But that was kind of what you would expect really.

DANIEL RADCLIFFE: I think Rupert, Emma and myself all kind of matured between films, just as our characters matured. And I think we were still just really good friends. We didn't really get together between the films to hang out. We kept working a lot of the time, but we didn't actually see each other outside of premieres and working. But we saw so much of each other then, that I don't think that Rupert or Emma really *wanted* to see me anymore [*laughs*].

DAVID HEYMAN: One of the wonders of this process for me has been to witness the maturation of Dan, Rupert and Emma. The children seemed more confident and able to draw upon a wealth of new experience for their characters. Yet, at the same time, they maintained their enthusiasm, sense of wonder and their youthfulness.

CHRIS COLUMBUS: Both Daniel and Rupert, and to a lesser degree Emma, had obviously become more comfortable in front of the camera. We knew we weren't going to get fired on the second film, so it was a good experience. The first time around, honestly, I got on the set every day and thought I was going to be fired. The kids were terrified, because Rupert and Emma had never been on a set before. Rupert couldn't stop looking in the camera the first couple of days of shooting *Sorcerer's Stone*. Suddenly, after 150 days of what was almost this acting workshop, they got confidence, they felt better about themselves, they became accustomed to 250 people on the set. By the time we started shooting the second movie, there was a whole level of confidence and ease, and the ability to even do some improvisation, which we had never done before. That all made for a very easy shoot in one sense, but time-consuming and intense energy-wise. By the end of the shoot, I couldn't get Rupert to get through a take without smiling or laughing. He was having such a great time. I said to his dad, "Is everything funny to him?" He's amused by everything. His dad said, "He's just very happy. He loves it." So I think that comfort and relaxation showed in the second movie.

EMMA WATSON: I'd never done any professional acting before the first film. I was extremely nervous and didn't know anyone. Then I knew the people and my surroundings and I knew what I was doing, so I felt a lot more relaxed and could have a really good time. I definitely improved as an actress and felt happier with what I'm doing on screen. Hermione had changed, too. She became more friendly with Harry and Ron and she was definitely more easygoing. She was less obsessed with books and schoolwork and settled down a bit. And even though she softened, Hermione was still as fiercely loyal to her friends as ever.

RUPERT GRINT: Like Harry, Ron found himself in the center of much of the *Chamber of Secrets* action. I got to do a lot more fun things in this film, particularly with the flying car. The scenes in Spider's Hollow were particularly scary as I have a big fear of spiders. When I saw Aragog [an enormous ancient spider who lives in the Dark Forest] for the first time, I wasn't acting — I was genuinely scared.

EMMA WATSON: We just played our age. It's like we were growing up with the books, because we were the same age as the characters.

DANIEL RADCLIFFE: I think I was certainly a lot more confident with Chris [Columbus], and if I had an idea or something, I was more comfortable talking to him about it. Whereas on the first one I wouldn't have been able to do that.

RUPERT GRINT: I was a bit more comfortable, because unlike the first one, we knew what everything was, we knew the scheduling.

EMMA WATSON: I think everyone was a lot more confident and a lot more comfortable, because we knew the crew and the director. We knew what we were *doing* for starts, which was good. I just think everyone came back a lot more confident. I'd never done any professional acting before the first film. I was extremely nervous and didn't know anyone. Now I know the people and my surroundings and I know what I'm doing, so I feel a lot more relaxed and can have a good time. I've definitely improved as an actress and feel happier with what I'm doing on screen.

Reprising their roles from Harry Potter and the Sorcerer's Stone *are actors John Cleese as Nearly Headless Nick, Robbie Coltrane as the gentle giant, Hagrid; Warwick Davis as Professor Flitwick, Richard Harris as Hogwarts Headmaster Albus Dumbledore, Alan Rickman as Professor Snape, and Dame Maggie Smith as Professor*

McGonagall, among others. New cast members joining the Hogwarts family included Mariam Margolyes as Professor Sprout, Shirley Henderson as Moaning Myrtle, Gemma Jones as Madam Pomfrey, Sally Mortemore as Madam Pince, Christian Coulson as Tom Riddle, and Robert Hardy as Minister of Magic Cornelius Fudge. New children actors include Hugh Mitchell as Colin Creevey and Edward Randell as Justin Finch Fletchley.

And then, of course, there is Kenneth Branagh as Gilderoy Lockhart, the new Defense Against the Dark Arts Professor; and Jason Isaacs as Lucius Malfoy, the father of Harry's perpetual enemy, Draco.

CHRIS COLUMBUS: Ken is one of the great stage and screen actors of our time, and a great filmmaker. He's a perfect fit for our all-British ensemble, and he's one of the few younger actors who can hold his own against the likes of Richard Harris, Maggie Smith and Alan Rickman. I couldn't conceive of anyone else playing Gilderoy Lockhart.

DAVID HEYMAN: We needed someone who could be both annoying and charming, who would embrace Lockhart's narcissism, be hysterically funny and still keep him grounded in reality. Ken did all we asked of him and more. He's fantastic.

KENNETH BRANAGH (actor, "Gilderoy Lockhart"): I have to admit that I was nervous joining the cast. It was nerve-wracking, because I was aware that *Chamber of Secrets* is a major film with huge audience expectations and that fans already had a very established idea of who Lockhart is. He's very flamboyant, rather vain and terribly narcissistic. So he's a delicious character to play, ferociously irritating and charming, but we had to convince audiences that he could have done all the things he claims. We had to make him *plausible*. I trusted Chris Columbus and his comic timing implicitly.

DANIEL RADCLIFFE: In a way, it was quite intimidating when we first had to meet Kenneth Branagh, because he is an unbelievable Shakespearean actor. But then you actually meet him and he is one of the nicest guys I have ever met. It is an honor to work with him.

RUPERT GRINT: I was a bit nervous to start with, working with him, but once I got talking to him, he was just so easy to talk to and down to earth and really funny.

EMMA WATSON: When I first met him, I felt like I would be really intimidated, since he is such an amazing person. But he is really, really down to earth and he is a really nice guy. I think he portrayed his character of Lockhart perfectly — really cheesy, really funny. There's such a presence about him, which really goes with Gilderoy Lockhart. You can always tell when he walked into a room by the way he sort of shrugs his shoulders. He's actually hilarious. There's one scene I have with him — half of it I'm looking dreamily in love and the rest of it I'm fighting pixies off, which is really fun.

JASON ISAACS (actor, "Lucius Malfoy"): Lucius is a very dark character and a thoroughly unpleasant man. He's the most confident person I've ever stepped inside and completely supreme in his arrogance and ruthlessness. He is pure evil. This is also my first film about wizards, and I don't get to wear waist-length blond hair and walk around with a snake-headed cane very often. For me, the fun and challenge of playing this character was making Lucius as grotesque as I could, but somehow keep him real.

There was a weight of such expectation on the film The fans are rabid all over the world. I was thinking of not doing it, because I was offered Captain Hook in P.J. Hogan's *Peter Pan* at the same time, but my friends' children called up, livid; just spitting blood, because they'd heard I was thinking of not doing it. Only because they wanted to go the premiere and visit the set, *not* because they cared about my career [*laughs*]. But it was an absolute joy. The kids were fantastic, very skilled and seasoned. Plus, I got to sit in the green room with the cream of British theatrical royalty. Just to sit in the dressing room with people like Richard Harris and Maggie Smith and watch them being made up — just a thrill.

CHRISTIAN COULSON (actor, "Tom Riddle"): There are bits of me in Tom Riddle, but I don't behave like that all the time. It's such a serious part in many ways. And cold. He doesn't seem to enjoy anything, so a lot of it came from the way I behave when I'm miserable or angry or whatever. I guess that's kind of where I started from in order to put the character together. To get me in the proper frame of mind, I also listened to quite a lot of serious heavy music — a lot of trash metal and rap — around the time of filming.

An intention of everyone involved was to stay as true to the source material as possible, respecting the work of J.K. Rowling.

EMMA WATSON: I think it is amazing how much they *have* squeezed in. It is two hours and 40 minutes and they have put so much in; it is really amazing. Literally, I can't think of anything which wasn't put in that was in the book.

RUPERT GRINT: I can't say anything that was missed out. I think they have been really faithful to the book. It was wicked.

DANIEL RADCLIFFE: I don't think that you can be that critical of the books. I think the books are absolutely fantastic. I love the films. I think that they are really great, special films, but I don't think that in an adaptation you can really get absolutely everything into a film.

One thing that the filmmakers knew had to be part of Chamber of Secrets *was the house elf Dobby. And the challenge was not just in creating him via computer, but in having Daniel Radcliffe act by himself without someone else to play off of him.*

CHRIS COLUMBUS: Dan basically had to focus on a green ball at the end of a stick. The first day was a little difficult, and then he got into it. Even in the dailies, where you saw him interacting with this green ball, you realized, "God, it feels like there's someone else there," even though Dobby wasn't in the frame yet. The animators said they'd never seen any actor do it as well as Dan. They said they've had actors twice his age who haven't been able to focus. But he makes those scenes work really well.

DANIEL RADCLIFFE: It was kind of hard knowing what kind of facial expression an orange ball on a stick is making, so it was quite hard. But I think that most of the credit goes to Chris and everybody else who worked on the film for making it so easy for me.

The search for someone to bring Dobby and the film's other effects to life eventually led to Industrial Light and Magic (ILM) and visual effects supervisors Jim Mitchell and Nick Davis (whose collective credits include Jurassic Park III, Sleepy Hollow, Mighty Joe Young, Pluto Nash *and the original* Harry Potter and the Sorcerer's Stone*).*

CHRIS COLUMBUS: With Jim and Nick we found a team that really understands what I call the reality of visual effects. They understand our desire to transport people to a place they've never been before, but at the same time, make certain that they absolutely believe what they are seeing.

NICK DAVIS (Industrial Light and Magic): From the very beginning, Chris was quite keen *not* to use a puppet and to create Dobby through CGI.

JIM MITCHELL (Indutrial Light and Magic): Dobby is a major character in this story, and Chris wanted to be able to direct him just like any other actor in a scene, which is more thoroughly achieved through CGI.

CHRIS COLUMBUS: I wanted Dobby to be a character that felt very real and one that the audience would fall in love with. Jim and Nick created an adorable character who feels like he genuinely inhabits this special world.

JIM MITCHELL: With Dobby, as was the case with Gollum in *Lord of the Rings*, we were trying to embody some human aspects into a House Elf. That was quite unique. And it all being CG, it was a chore to hit the mannerisms and idiosyncrasies of what we thought a House Elf would be.

As would be the case with all eight entries in the film series, there were highlights during the making of each film, with Daniel, Emma, Rupert, David Heyman and Chris Columbus reflecting on some of their favorite bits of Chamber of Secrets.

DANIEL RADCLIFFE: The action scenes, for me, are so cool. When I'm hanging out of the car window, that's actually me! I was hanging like 30 feet up in the air and it was just really cool. I do as many of the stunts as possible, but then, of course, there are those that I can't do. But I do quite a lot of the stuff, so it is a lot of fun for me.

RUPERT GRINT: I got to do a lot more fun things in this film, particularly with the flying car. The scenes in Spider's Hollow were particularly scary. I also liked the Whomping Willow, which was really fun because it was like a theme park ride and I got to drive a flying car.

STUART CRAIG (production designer, *Harry Potter and the Chamber of Secrets*): In some ways, Spider's Hollow was the most difficult set, because it's like a big sculpture. To design something with no obvious structure was a huge challenge. I fashioned the set like a big amphitheater where the children walk in and are ambushed by spiders coming out of every crevice. We filled the set with tree roots and implied a subterranean world beneath which the spiders inhabit.

A fun moment of the film is the sequence in which Harry is locked in his room in his aunt and uncle's home, and Ron with his siblings mount a rescue using the Weasley family's flying blue Ford Anglia. They end up in the Whomping Willow, the enchanted tree with attitude that attacks Harry, Ron and the flying car when they have the misfortune of landing in its branches.

STUART CRAIG: The idea that this flying car lands in a tree, falls through its branches and then is beaten up by it is such a magical sequence, I always imagined it would be computer generated. But in the end, we resolved this practically by building the tree in several parts, which, when put together, stands 85 feet tall. This sequence involved a great deal of collaboration between the art department, visual effects and special effects teams.

JOHN RICHARDSON (special effects supervisor, *Harry Potter and the Chamber of Secrets*): We needed a total of 14 cars that we could dress in various stages, from mint condition when the boys first steal it and rescue Harry, until it lands in the trees and finally ends up going wild in the forest. Most of the cars we found for the sequences were not roadworthy and many were headed for the scrap heap, so we didn't destroy any vintage cars.

DANIEL RADCLIFFE: Filming in the flying car was like being on a fun fair ride, especially when one of the tree branches shot straight through the window between Rupert and I. It was amazing. I don't think we ever stopped laughing.

An additional visual effects highlight was an all-new Quidditch match that was actually even more amazing than the one that appeared in The Sorcerer's Stone.

BILL GEORGE (Industrial Light and Magic): For the second film, they wanted to take it to another level, so there were a number of creative changes we made. One of them was moving Hogwarts and the surrounding hills closer to the Quidditch area. This was done for two reasons: to make it seem like the Quidditch pitch was part of the school and to get a little more dynamic flying around up there. With the hills closer, you would see more movement.

A true standout set in the film was the Chamber of Secrets itself, which stood as the core setting of film's story. At 250' x 120', the set was the largest made for a Harry Potter film, actually dwarfing the Great Hall.

STUART CRAIG: J.K. Rowling states very clearly in her book that the Chamber is an enormously high and very cavernous place. But because the studio was originally an old aircraft factory, the tallest soundstage is only 28' high. We could have achieved a greater height with visual effects, but instead we built downward to create the illusion of depth. The result is a Chamber that appears to be hundreds of feet tall and flooded. In reality, the water is only a foot deep and dyed black to give it that sense of tremendous depth.

DANIEL RADCLIFFE: I like the Chamber of Secrets scene a lot. I think the dialogue between myself and Tom Riddle was awesome. It was really very intense, but I also like the dueling scene because there's a lot of action, plus it's a very cool scene. I thought that was really, really brilliant, because you have got the confrontation between Snape and Gilderoy Lockhart, who are completely different characters. I just love seeing them in the whole dueling scene. We basically learned fencing from the other actors, like them. They went up first and they were doing it. There's a certain salute before you start the duel apparently, so that was quite fun to learn. It was challenging, too, because there was so much dialogue. We had to keep it going and we had to keep it very intense in order to keep the audience's attention.

RUPERT GRINT: I also remember the Great Hall scene. Dan's really funny, and one time he got up on the table and he and Robbie Coltrane did this dance ... the Macarena.

EMMA WATSON: Imagine 300 extras in the same room for the whole week. The food is stinking, it's boiling and everyone is dying of boredom, okay? So imagine that, and we need to get them all to laugh, and we did so many takes. It got so bad that Dan and Robbie Coltrane had to stand up on the tables and dance. And they did the Macarena, they did the Can-Can — everything — and it worked. It was the highlight of the whole filming, I think. I never laughed so much in my life.

RUPERT GRINT: My favorite scene was the slug scene. I loved doing that scene, because I had all this different-flavored slug slime. There was chocolate, peppermint, orange, lemon and it made them taste really nice. Coughing *up* slugs was quite hard. I had these giant slugs in my mouth loaded with slime and I spat them out. I think it was plastic or something — at least I *hope* it was plastic.

DAVID HEYMAN: I really loved the mandrakes. They made me laugh and I think they're funny, so I really respond to that. I like the spider sequence because it's scary and I think it's really well done. And I like it, but I always get a little nervous, when Harry's in real danger with the basilisk. I want Harry to be okay, and so there's a moment when I'm watching the basilisk when I go, "Is he going to be okay?" I, of course, know he will, but once in a while I'm still not sure.

EMMA WATSON: I really love animals and I really enjoy working with them, like I have on these films. It can be quite hard work; it's pretty hard to tell a dog, you know, "Do it again, you weren't sitting in the right position" or something. You have to be quite patient with them, because Fang drools everywhere and it takes ages to get it off your robes. And Hedwig [the owl] flies in the wrong direction. But they're gorgeous; they're really cute. You don't expect an animal to do that kind of stuff, so it's amazing when they do it. But most of the time they get it right, which is absolutely amazing. Their trainers must have the hardest jobs ever.

GARY GERO (animal trainer, the *Harry Potter* films): Each of the animal behaviors has a different and distinctive cue. All the animals are individuals, each one is different and require a different level of attention, if you will. Some of them really have a little lack of attention and you have to have everything stepped up a beat just to keep their attention up. Other animals are 100% with you all of the time and everything is toned down a bit for them. The easiest animal to train is one that you like and one that you're interested in. That really is the truth. The training is basically the same with all of the species. It's all positive reinforcements and the steps that you take, approximations you take with each creature, with each species, differs a little bit. It also has to do with how much intelligence they have, so you operate on a different level of understanding. Just like the differences between working with a college freshman and a second grader — that sort of difference.

Offering different kinds of challenges are two animals that are probably the most prominent in the film series: owls (especially), rats (think Scabbers) and cats.

GARY GERO: Owls are about halfway through second grade. They're not the brightest. Contrary to the stereotype, they're not necessarily intelligent. For something it would take a raven or a parrot ten trials to learn, it would take them a thousand. So it's lots and lots of hours of repetition with the owls. They're wonderful creatures, and they're the most interesting things, and they get very dedicated to you and they really want to work with you, but it just takes a while to get the idea across. There's an owl that crashes into everything. He's a silly character and he runs into everything. He flies and crashes into bowls of potato chips. We had to teach him not only to fly and carry letters and normal things, but we also had to teach him how to lie on his back and get up from lying on his back. There really is just one Hedwig. He has a couple of helpers that help him out with the different things. We have a lighting stand-in so he doesn't have to do all of the lighting. And we have a couple of owls that will help him with his flying shots so he doesn't have to do all of the flying shots himself. In case they ask for more than he can do.

There's three Scabbers, depending on how animated they want Scabbers to be. Rats are very intelligent little guys. They learn simple things really quickly, like, "Go and stay on a mark," is one thing. We've trained the rats to retrieve, we haven't used that yet, but they come to a buzzer, they can do pretty nearly everything they're physically capable of doing. They have lots more to do in the next show, so we're developing all of their skills now.

We have to very carefully select cats. That's one of the keys — you get a cat who enjoys work and enjoys the environment and enjoys new people and new situations. And then, it's all about dinnertime with cats, isn't it? We take their dinner and we divide it up into training sessions, and they're pretty much working for their dinner and then they get a bowl of food at night as well. But their food is all regulated and they're fairly intelligent. Their training method is a little less direct than, let's say, a dog. You make smaller steps. And again, once you understand exactly how a cat learns and what progress they make, it's not difficult; they're trying, you just have to be careful that you don't expect too much of a single training session.

DANIEL RADCLIFFE: I think probably one of the most challenging scenes in *Chamber of Secrets* was the parse Tongue [snake language] scene. It was kind of hard to get hold of at first, but I got kind of used to it in the end.

CHRIS COLUMBUS: I think the hardest part to direct for Dan and myself was Dan's interaction with [CG elf] Dobby, because he didn't have anyone in the room. He was basically acting with a little green ball at the end of a stick. We also wanted to make sure that Dobby was lovable and existed within that frame. So when you see the frame, you believe that Dobby's in the room with Dan. Part of what makes that work is that ILM did a really wonderful job with Dobby's skin texture and the lighting and making it feel like he was in the room. The other thing that makes it work is Dan, because Dan really focused and even when we saw the early dailies and we saw a little green ball on the end of a stick, and we saw Dan talking to that ball, you believe that he is talking to someone.

DANIEL RADCLIFFE: The green ball on a stick helped, because the actual creature is so animated and jumps all over the place, it's hard to actually get a fix on where it is at any one time. But it was made so easy by everybody around us that we just got used to it.

Effects wise, there was also the climactic scene involving Harry and Gilderoy Lockhart, where it's revealed that the back of his head is actually Voldemort's face.

CHRISTIAN COULSON: We spent seven weeks doing a 15-minute scene. The scene was so long and the effects so heavy in the second half of it — to spend two months doing it was extraordinary. And we didn't have to imagine the environment we were in. In reacting to the creature there, the Basilisk, they had a mock-up of it; the head existed as an animatronic model. In terms of watching things fly around the set, it's a bit like being on stage and imagining where the walls are if they are not there. And you know the special effects people are going to provide the things that could have created that reaction.

One element of sadness that greeted the cast as things were winding down was the fact that, as noted, Chamber of Secrets *would be Chris Columbus' final film in the series as director. Alfonso Cuaron would be stepping in for film number three,* Harry Potter and the Prisoner of Azkaban.

CHRIS COLUMBUS: I knew that after *Chamber of Secrets* I would be stepping down as director and become a producer. My original intention was to do all seven movies as a director, but obviously that doesn't fit in with my life. I chose not to direct in order to spend time with my kids while they were young. Once they are older, they won't want to hang out with me nearly as much as I want to hang out with them. I just felt that it was an important time for me to be there. I was also mentally burnt out. At the same time, I felt I should stick around for *Prisoner of Azkaban* to make sure that there is a good transition for the actors in the film and that the quality of the films remained the same. I wanted to make sure that the comfort level was still there for the viewers, because of the familiar worlds and characters.

DANIEL RADCLIFFE: Chris would never let anything bad happen to us. I trust him. It's Chris Columbus' legacy and I think he found someone who would carry it on.

CHRIS COLUMBUS: I was putting everything — blood, sweat and tears — into the thing. I was performing with the kids. It was insane. I thought, physically, that I didn't think I could do a third. It's not like sitting on a set with Susan Sarandon, Julia Roberts or even Robin Williams and Ed Harris, and say, "Okay, can you bring it down a little?" as I sit back in the director's chair. This is not like that. This is completely interactive directing. I thought, "I'll die of a heart attack if I do the third film." It's just too intense. Directing Dan's sword fighting one day, I thought, "This is not a way for a 43-year-old man to make a living," but I had such fun and it kept me energetic and excited and going. But I did need about a year to just sort of recharge. I couldn't give back to the kids in a third movie what I gave them in the first two movies.

DAVID HEYMAN: Chris, just as I was, was really excited about Alfonso Cuaron coming in. Alfonso had already met with the kids and gotten along incredibly well with them. But Chris was here for support and for guidance and for us all to benefit from his great wealth of experience, having directed the first two. The third film grew out of what had already been created. The third book is slightly more mature. The film would be a little darker, more mature and more adult, as the book is. Also, Alfonso is a different filmmaker from Chris and I think he necessarily reflected that, because film is a director's medium.

Harry Potter and the Chamber of Secrets *was released in the UK on November 3, 2002 and in the US on November 15, 2002. The budget was $100 million and the film enjoyed a worldwide gross of $879.6 million.*

HARRY POTTER AND THE CHAMBER OF SECRETS BEHIND THE SCENES INTERVIEW

Jason Isaacs reflects on playing movie villains, in both a recent version of *Peter Pan* and *Harry Potter and the Chamber of Secrets*

Despite the fact that actor Jason Isaacs has appeared in over 20 films and offered filmgoers with a wide range of characterizations, it is undoubtedly his portrayals of Lucius Malfoy in Harry Potter and the Chamber of Secrets *and the live-action version of* Peter Pan *that he has made the biggest impressions on young viewers.*

In the following interview, the actor, who hails from Liverpool, England, reflects on his big-screen villainy.

So how did a guy like you end up playing someone like Captain Hook?

JASON ISAACS: It's an absolutely unique, amazing show business story. My agent called me, I had an audition and I got the job [*laughs*]. Actually, I went to meet with the director thinking, "I don't know the point of this, because, clearly, they're not going to cast someone like me in this part in a giant film like this." But it was such a magnificent script, I thought I would face the ritual humiliation of early rejection. A film like this had only to go to a big star. Sure enough, I went to the hotel room for the audition and there was a big star leaving the room. I came out and there was a big star going into the room. But then for some odd reason — maybe everyone at the studio had an aneurysm at the same time — they gave me the job and I did my best.

Was it a role you really wanted?

JASON ISAACS: Yes, mostly due to the fact that P.J. Hogan had written such a beautiful script and seemed to be channeling J.M. Barrie, because I can't see the joints between where he started to make things up and where Barrie's book ends. When I read it, I thought, "Well, this is Barrie's book verbatim," and then when I went back to the book and read it, I realized P.J. had made up whole chunks, but you just can't tell the difference. Truthfully, it's no surprise that *Peter Pan* has been enchanting children for 100 years. I'm very lucky to be in the Harry Potter films, which are modern day classics, but this has stood the test of time. It's been a hundred years and it hasn't lost any of its magic at all.

Did previous interpretations of the character impact on you at all and how did you view the character?

JASON ISAACS: The first thing that hits you when you start reading Barrie's book is that there is nothing comical about Captain Hook at all. He's a very disturbed, twisted, dangerous, neurotic mess. Peter says to Wendy, John and Michael, "Leave Hook to me." It's not because he wants the fun of it, it's because Hook *kills*. He's a dangerous man and people die on his hook. In this film, the hook is *not* a disability, it's an extra-savage weapon that he carries around that he's happy to use to gut people. That's not an aspect of the character that anyone has shown you before. That being said, the question of tone was something ever present in shooting the film and will be in the editing and post production: how to make sure it's okay for small children, but also okay for big children and even bigger people.

You also played Lucius Malfoy in Harry Potter and the Chamber of Secrets, *and will apparently be returning in* Goblet of Fire. *What was that experience like?*

JASON ISAACS: There was a weight of such expectation on the film. The fans are rabid all over the world. I was thinking of *not* doing it, because I was offered Captain Hook at the same time, and my friends' children called up, livid; just spitting blood, because they'd heard I was thinking of not doing it. Only because they wanted to go to the premiere and visit the set, not because they cared about my career [*laughs*]. But it was an absolute joy. The kids were fantastic, very skilled and seasoned. Plus, I got to sit in the green room with the cream of British theatrical royalty. Just to sit in the dressing room with people like Richard Harris and Maggie Smith and watch them being made up — just a thrill.

It's very, very rare for an actor to have done things like this back-to-back, where they can ham it up and chew the scenery in both *Peter Pan* and the Harry Potter films. Most of the time you're aiming for subtle understatement. That goes out the window in these things, which are looking for operatic magic. You just don't get to play for the gallery like that very often as an actor, so I can't wait to get back and start camping it up with my cane again.

Needless to say, Malfoy was a character you enjoyed playing.

JASON ISAACS: Oh yeah. He was a joy. I'm always looking for three dimensions, but every now and again you can revel in the fact that you don't have them. This guy is an unreconstructed, racist, genocidal maniac and I just love that. What would the movie world be like without them?

Harry Potter and the Prisoner of Azkaban
Copyright and Trademark Warner Bros. Discovery

CHAPTER 3: *HARRY POTTER AND THE PRISONER OF AZKABAN* (2004)

The past summer hasn't been any better for Harry at the Dursleys and reaches a head when Aunt Marge Dursley is rude to the boy and outright insults Harry's parents. Out of pure anger and without even realizing he's doing it he turns Marge into a balloon that floats screaming into the sky. Harry has had it at the Dursleys, grabs his trunk and runs out into the night, knowing there is nowhere for him to go. It is at that moment that he realizes a very large black dog is watching him from the bushes. Harry escapes using the bizarre Night Bus for stranded wizards and witches and makes it to the Leaky Caldron, to be forgiven for using magic by the Minister of Magic himself, Cornelius Fudge. He drops the charges with the defense, "the Ministry doesn't send students to Azkaban for blowing up their aunts."

Harry meets up with Ron and Hermione to find out that Sirius Black, sent to the wizard prison Azkaban for being an avid supporter of Lord Voldemort, and killing Peter Pettigrew, has escaped. He is coming for Harry to finish the job Voldemort couldn't do — killing the boy. Ron's father pulls Harry aside to warn him of the danger Sirius Black represents, as Black believes Harry is the only person standing in the way of Voldemort regaining his power over the wizarding community.

Harry, Ron and Hermione board the Hogwarts Express to get back to school, finding the new Defence Against the Black Arts teacher, Remus Lupin, asleep in the only car with room. The train comes to a stop and everything becomes extremely cold as the dreaded Dementors, spirit-like beings from Azkaban on the hunt for Black board the train. They search the train, and when one comes near Harry, it tries to take the boy's life force. The Dementor is driven back by Lupin, who finally wakes up. At Hogwarts, the students learn that the dark spirits are guarding all entrances to the school and the grounds searching for Black, and are to be avoided at all costs. The trio, though, is happy to find out that Hagrid is now the new Care of Magical Creatures teacher. His first class crashes around him when Draco Malfoy approaches Hagrid's pet hippogriff, Buckbeak. The creature lashes out, mildly injuring Malfoy, who plays his injury up for all its worth. At a hearing about the incident, his father, Lucius, demands Buckbeak be put to death for "attacking" his son.

This year there are changes at Hogwarts aside from Lupin and Hagrid. It seems as though Hermione, not willing to wait to learn class by class, has decided to take numerous other classes, some of which are taught at the same time. And the Fat Lady's portrait, which watches over Gryffindor, is found destroyed, with her hiding in another painting, terrified because Sirius Black has made it into the school. Security is heightened, but during a Quidditch match, Dementors attack Harry, causing him to lose control and fall from his broom. The broom falls into the Whomping Willow, which destroys it.

From here, things move quickly; Harry learns that Sirius is more than he's been painted to be; not only was he his father's best friend and, Harry's godfather. Lupin teaches Harry how to ward off a Dementor attack through the Patronus Charm. With Black apparently destroying parts of the castle as well as being after Harry, the students are forced to sleep in the Great Hall for safety. With Lupin unable to teach all of his classes, Snape has stepped in as a substitute for the Defence Against the Dark Arts teacher, and he begins instructing the students on how to handle werewolves. This seems opportune, since the teacher of the Divination Class, Miss Trelawney, sees Harry's death by a grim his tea leaves.

Lucius Malfoy makes good on his threat and gets Buckbeak sentenced to death. Ron's pet rat, Scabbers, bites him and when the rodent leads them to the base of the Whomping Willow, a large dog springs out and drags Ron and Scabbers down a hole below the tree and to the Shrieking Shack. The black dog is shape-shifting Animagus Sirius Black and when his old friend Lupin arrives, he explains that Sirius had been framed for the crimes that locked him in Azkaban, killing their friend Peter Pettigrew, who is not dead and is actually Scabbers. Severus Snape tries to take Black in, but Harry *knocks him down with an Expelliarmus spell so he can get answers from Black and Lupin. They transform Pettigrew back to human form from being Scabbers the rat.*

Once outside, a full moon turns Lupin into a werewolf and Sirius becomes the big black dog to do battle to protect Harry, Ron and Hermione. Pettigrew, who they were going to turn over to the Dementors as the true traitor of Harry's parents, turns back into Scabbers and runs away. Sirius stumbles down to the lake after fighting with Werewolf Lupin and Harry goes to find him. The Dementors find Sirius and Harry and start applying the Dementor's Kiss but they are stopped by someone across the lake performing the Patronus charm. This disperses the spirits and saves Harry and Sirius. From there Sirius is confined in the top of one of the towers awaiting return to prison. With help from Dumbledore, Harry and Hermione travel back in time to relive the night's events. They save Buckbeak from execution and Sirius from the wrath of the Dementors. Unfortunately, Lupin is revealed to be a werewolf, a creature that practically no one, including the well-to-do parents of Hogwarts students, wants around. He quits his teaching position.

Lupin gives Harry back the Marauder's Map, which shows every passage, regular and hidden, in the school and who is wandering where, knowing full well that the boy will have plenty of use for it some other time.

With Sirius gone, Harry is in a funk until he gets a package that includes the famous Firebolt flying broom. It comes with a gray feather which gets fastened to the broom (a gift from Sirius), which the boy takes up for a glorious first ride.

Behind the scenes on Harry Potter and the Prisoner of Azkaban, change was in the air. New cast members include Gary Oldman as Sirius Black, Emma Thompson as Professor Sybil Trelawney, Timothy Spall as Peter Pettigrew and Michael Gambon replacing the late Richard Harris as Professor Albus Dumbledore. Even bigger news, as noted, was that Alfonso Cuaron (Y Tu Mama Tambien,

Gravity) *was brought on as director, which he was actually reluctant to do.*

ALFONSO CUARON (director, *Harry Potter and the Prisoner of Azkaban*): I thought it would be really hard to make my own film and that was a reason for a little hesitation in taking this job. I talked to my friend, Gullermo del Toro, and he was championing me to do this. He said, "If you do it, serve the material. Don't try to do an Alfonso Cuaron movie, just serve the material and by serving the material you may be doing your best movie ever." Starting at *that* point, it then became very interesting, because then it was actually a pleasure trying to go into the transition from Chris. It then became a sweet challenge, not a difficult one. As long as it was serving the material that meant, above all else, first serving the book and then the position of this film in the franchise of Harry Potter.

CHRIS COLUMBUS (producer, *Harry Potter and the Prisoner of Azkaban*): As a director, you usually come in and the first thing you have to worry about are designing the sets and casting the movies. Our directors no longer have to worry about that. This is a great playground for directors and there's a sense of freedom and fun, coming in and directing a *Harry Potter* film. And I love what Alfonso did with the material and what he did with the kids, who themselves have become professional working actors. So I feel very proud.

ALFONSO CUARON: In the beginning it's a pleasure, because you don't have to put together a film, it's already moving and I was part of the machinery. But the thing about this machinery is that once it starts running, it doesn't stop and you have to catch up to it. After a smooth beginning you find you have to speed up, then you're running and soon you realize that your scarf got attached to the machinery and if you don't run at the same pace, you're going to get strangled.

So after a while it becomes kind of tough, because you're shooting long hours as you're editing and doing visual effects at the same time. *That* was the toughest thing.

DAVID HEYMAN (producer, *Harry Potter and the Prisoner of Azkaban*): There's a lot of hard work, but a lot of the foundations have been built by Chris and Alfonso embraced that, yet I think we as a franchise have to continue to allow directors to make their own films. It's really important that each director is able to put his or her own stamp on a film. Chris made his stamp, Alfonso made his. But the foundations are there and as long as you are true to those foundations and to the spirit of the books, I think we're in good shape.

CHRIS COLUMBUS: Originally, in a naïve way, I planned to be there all of the films. Once the studio was happy with the first one, about halfway through production they said, "We'd like you to stay and do all of them," and at the time I said, "Yeah! Sounds like a great idea." David Heyman and I sat down with Steve Kloves and Jo Rowling and the four of us talked about how these movies would progress. Remember, at the time we only had four books — we had just been given the manuscript of *Goblet of Fire* from Jo Rowling — so that was all we knew, and she would give us clues about what would happen in subsequent books.

One thing we *did* know is that we wanted to start the series with an almost golden, romantic, old-fashioned storybook quality, and as the films progressed, they would get darker and darker. And as Harry's age progressed, the films would get edgier and more mature and deal with more adult themes. So we knew this was going to happen, and that's why I stayed on with *Azkaban* as a producer, because I wanted to make sure we were moving in that direction. And by the time we'd finished *Azkaban*, I said, "We are at a point where I know that subsequent films will follow everything we'd set into motion."

I was extremely happy to see the films unfold in a way I absolutely hoped that they would.

ALFONSO CUARON: The challenge is that you didn't want people to feel like they were going into this movie and were suddenly in an alien world. You want them to feel as though they're in the same universe. It has to be recognizable enough, but at the same time I wanted to have fun. I was blessed to have great source material and to be surrounded by a universe that was very eloquently created by Chris Columbus and production designer Stuart Craig.

DANIEL RADCLIFFE (actor, "Harry Potter"): Basically, I think everything that we learned from Chris, we were now able to put into practice with a different director. I think the reason Alfonso was able to do longer takes and was able to do more complicated shots was because with Chris we just didn't have the experience or the focus to do that kind of stuff. And so, with Alfonso we were just getting the shot. And it is harder, it's more challenging — which is good, because if we're getting older and we're not being challenged, then there's no point in doing it, really. But I think it's just that we learn more with each director. With the fourth film with Mike Newell directing, I think we learned even more there as well.

EMMA WATSON (actor, "Hermione Granger"): Especially for me, as someone who hasn't acted in anything else before, it was great working with a new director and doing something different, seeing different techniques, different ideas. I think there's definitely a difference in style just looking at the two directors. Alfonso's done some amazing things with camera angles and camera shots, and this one is much more flowy — you can just tell the difference. Especially with the director, a lot of himself goes into what he's doing and you can definitely tell the difference.

RUPERT GRINT (actor, "Ron Weasley"): He was a bit different, but it was really sad to see Chris go. But, yes, Alfonso is really good, he's really funny and we got on really well.

ROBBIE COLTRANE (actor, "Hagrid"): Chris was always very hands-on. One of the many things I liked about Chris is that he wasn't one of those directors who sits by those monitors and goes, "Again, no, again." Between takes he runs to the set and tells everybody what was wrong, so everyone knows what was wrong and you have a chance at doing it right next time. You would have thought that was an obvious thing, but it's something a lot of directors miss. So he's very hands-on and very good with the kids, too. He knows exactly how protected they needed to be, but he also knew that they were up for a little bit of semi-adult situations. Alfonso has got a different style of shooting. I know he was very keen to get it out of the studio, because it had been very studio-bound. That's the trouble with anything which essentially has lots of bits which are physically impossible. You're stuck in a studio and that had to change. He was very keen to do that.

DANIEL RADCLIFFE: Chris always had this fantastically energetic approach to doing the scenes, which suited the first two films absolutely perfectly. He made two absolutely fantastic films. With the third one, Alfonso had a much more kind of laid-back, emotional, intense way of directing.

ALFONSO CUARON: These kids were a little older and in that moment of life where that little older means a lot older, while they're still carrying a lot of vulnerabilities of earlier years. It was not that *I* was trying to do something with their emotions, but it's implicit in the material. The age of 13 is archetypical in every civilization on this planet. It is the rite of passage; the moment of awareness and awakening or it is the moment of disappearance, if you like, if you think of Jesus when he was 13. We know his life from 0 to 13, and then he disappears until he is 33. Thirteen is the age of bat mitzvahs, first communions and so on. Because of that, it is not that the film is darker, it's just more internal.

A film I did called *A Little Princess* was a great experience in terms of working with a great group of girls. One thing I learned was the amazing emotional understanding that kids have when they are into acting or into make believe. It's not like they're just making pretty faces or faking it; they go into real places and they're willing. They have the understanding that it can be a game in that you can make believe your character is in a lot of pain, but that you have control of the make believe. With *Harry Potter*, I was so lucky that these three kids had done a couple of movies already, so they've got the whole technical experience. And they wanted to take themselves seriously as actors, so pretty much they put themselves in your hands. They were very eager and willing and courageous. They delivered really interesting performances. It's a natural evolution in terms of what these characters were becoming.

DANIEL RADCLIFFE: Harry, being a teenager, has the same feelings as every other teenager. But because of his past, I think he feels these feelings of anger or loneliness. That was hard for me, but because I obviously am feeling the same things as him, I just took what I was feeling and basically just exaggerated it and listened to music or anything to get me into the right state of mind for the filming. And then just hoped for the best once I was in there, really.

ALFONSO CUARON: I think it's a natural progression. I think the young teens found it cool, because they could relate to it. It's not dark for the sake of going dark. I don't even know if anger is the right word, but I will say there *is* a constant state of anger at that age. In *Prisoner of Azkaban*,

Harry comes to terms with his male energy, his father and what his father is. He knows that even though the man is dead, his fatherly energy is inside him. He knows how to work it out. The fifth book — *The Order of the Phoenix* — is about disappointment with the father figure. In that sense, I think the third and fifth are *very* connected.

DANIEL RADCLIFFE: The thing about this one is not only is Harry so angry, but he also has to deal with some truly horrific things. He actually hears his mother screaming as she is murdered, and it doesn't really get much worse than that, so there was a lot of preparing for that to be done. That was the main thing I had to prepare for. My dad grew up in Northern Ireland and he grew up when all the troubles there were really going on. There was a man across the street from him who was murdered by the UDA. And my dad, actually as an eight-year-old boy, heard the wife of that man screaming from across the street. So I just had a really, really long discussion with my dad about it. He helped me so much with all the stuff with the Dementors, particularly.

In many ways, Azkaban *is a more complex film from an emotional level, which presents a series of new challenges compared to the first two films, being misled about Sirius Black, discovering truths about his father and much more.*

DANIEL RADCLIFFE: This was a more emotionally intense journey in terms of Harry's character. So I think that's what separates it from the first two books in a very major way and what I love about this book in particular, because it does go into such great detail about emotion. I think Sirius is such an interesting character because of his relationship with Harry's father — and the same is true with Lupin. They knew Harry's dad very well; they were best friends. Now they've just met his son for the first time, really, and that's what I think makes it interesting. Harry is treating them as kind of new fathers in a way.

One thing that's interesting about the third book is that when we first see Harry, he thinks that he knew everything that there was to know about the past and his father. Basically, in this book, that's all completely turned upside down. That's where all Harry's self-doubt comes in. He thinks if he doesn't know certain things about his dad, what else doesn't he know? And if he's finding these things out, maybe there are other things as well. So I think that's what really makes it an interesting book, because it does deal so much with self-consciousness and worry and self-doubt. That kind of soul-searching everybody does, really. Everybody at some point or another in their life will want to find out about their past, or who they are. I think normally that happens slightly later on in life, but because Harry has grown up when he has, without parents, and is finding out new things about his father, I think that's why it happens this early in the book.

EMMA WATSON: One of the first things that Alfonso did when we first met him was he asked us to write an essay about our characters. Not just to help us, but also to help him to see the character through our eyes. It made me think about how Hermione uses her books and schoolwork as a comfort blanket. It's like a mask, so she doesn't have to deal with emotions or get homesick. She can just cover it all up by being clever. He gave us a lot of freedom with that as well, which was really good.

DANIEL RADCLIFFE: I think it's quite important to mention that when we did the essay, we basically did exactly what our characters would have done in the same situation. So I wrote a page and it was fine. It was OK, it wasn't great, which is what Harry does. The essays were basically the state of our characters at the beginning, when we first meet them at the beginning of the third film. It definitely helped. And every time there was a huge scene, I had it in the front of my script, so every time there's a big scene, I try to read over it a couple of times.

ALFONSO CUARON: I asked them to write a first-person bio of the character they were playing, but immersing them in their own experiences and their own emotions. They delivered these amazing essays, really beautiful, very honest, very bare and very courageous. That became an amazing tool and an amazing key to work with them. I also think it allowed them to have a better emotional understanding of the characters. Sometimes it was a shortcut to be able to say, "This is the Hermione side of your mind." Emma would get it immediately without having to go into big conversations or example, because it's honestly coming from something that she wrote, that she experienced. When it comes to their emotions, this is not something that I was trying to do, but I think it was implicit in the material.

DANIEL RADCLIFFE: Both Rupert and me were put to shame by Emma's 16-page essay. But it was fantastic. It was really fantastic.

RUPERT GRINT: I don't think I ever actually handed mine in.

DANIEL RADCLIFFE: I wrote one on four sheets of paper, which I was so proud of, and then we see Emma's written a three-volume novel! We were all slightly put to shame by that.

EMMA WATSON: Just for the record, I would like to say that I have big handwriting.

DANIEL RADCLIFFE: And mine is incredibly small. Mine would have been a huge book, but it just wasn't.

EMMA WATSON: Alfonso wanted a lot of our input in the characters. He often said, "Well, how would you do it, what would you do it like? No, I'm not going to tell you how to do it — it has to come from what you think and from your own experiences."

DANIEL RADCLIFFE: That wasn't a big change from Chris, I just really believe that it's an adaptation of a book, so it can't be the director who says what kind of film it's going to be — it's the book that says how the film should be made.

ALFONSO CUARON: What I also really wanted to do was to make Hogwarts more contemporary and a little more naturalistic. For instance, I studied English schools and watched the way the kids wore their uniforms. No two were alike. Each teenager's individuality was reflected in the way they wore their uniforms as they would if their parents weren't around.

DANIEL RADCLIFFE: Obviously, in the first two films, the story dictated that we were just in uniform a lot of the time, because a lot of the story takes place during the school year. In this one, a lot of it takes place during the holidays. So I think it makes it slightly more relaxed, I suppose.

EMMA WATSON: I definitely felt that. In uniform, everyone looks the same, so I think it's good, because it got all sorts of different people's personalities out.

RUPERT GRINT: I ended up with my tie totally messed up and my shirt half pulled out. It was fun, but it also had a serious purpose in helping us establish individual identities.

DANIEL RADCLIFFE: I thought it would have been too much of a leap for Harry to become very image conscious. He wouldn't wear badges or chains. But he was becoming more self-aware, and although his clothes aren't exactly cool, they are less formal and less childish.

EMMA WATSON: Hermione was out of tweed skirts and knitted grandma-type jumpers and, if I dare say it, wearing jeans! She's not trendy, but she was more stylish than she used to be. Hermione still wore her uniform with the top button done up, but she was trying.

JANY TEMIME (costume designer, *Harry Potter and the Prisoner of Azkaban*): We darkened the colors of the Hogwarts uniforms and included a hood with the house colors inside, so you immediately knew which house each student belongs to. To encourage individuality, we gave everyone a choice of singlets, jumpers, cardigans and other variations of the uniform.

Another significant change was moving things off of the sets with more on location shooting, which really served to shake things up.

EMMA WATSON: We did a bit of location for about a month in Scotland and the scenery was just breathtaking. It was amazing — massive mountains and proper fresh air and it was really good.

DANIEL RADCLIFFE: It was rainy.

EMMA WATSON: Understatement of the century.

DANIEL RADCLIFFE: And it's not normal rain, it's horizontal rain! Umbrellas are rendered useless. But it was really good to get out of the studio for a while.

STUART CRAIG: Hogwarts can be claustrophobic. The stories are often interior-based. We're dealing with classrooms and dormitories and the Great Hall and various corridors.

That's the way the books are, so that's the way the movie is. So obviously we try always to bring the changes in and to be impressive, certainly. But the opportunity to get outside into the huge Scottish Highlands in *Goblet of Fire* was a great new chance.

Working with animals was a part of the Harry Potter film series from the very beginning and certainly true of Prisoner of Azkaban, *which Radcliffe, Watson and Grint were quick to point out.*

DANIEL RADCLIFFE: A bat landed on my head! It was actually very funny. I actually really love the animals, especially the lizards. The lizards are so cool. And the mice are fighting — the mice are fantastic. We were taking bets on them. It's between who was going to win or who was going to escape first.

RUPERT GRINT: Spiders I hate, but when we were in there with the bat, I didn't know I was scared of bats as well. And there's a massive rat. Absolutely huge.

EMMA WATSON: I love my cat who played Crookshanks. They are *so* rude to my cat.

RUPERT GRINT: It's the ugliest cat.

DANIEL RADCLIFFE: It looks like it's been thrown against the wall at birth.

EMMA WATSON: Okay, so it's got a flat nose.

DANIEL RADCLIFFE: It doesn't *have* a nose. It's just 2D! It's like a cartoon cat.

EMMA WATSON: It's beautiful in its own ugly way.

DANIEL RADCLIFFE: Notice the word ugly.

Cuaron's dedication to character became apparent through every aspect of production, including the film's visual effects — an area that was, admittedly, new to him.

ALFONSO CUARON: My approach to the visual effects was that I wanted to do a character-driven piece with visual effects rather than a visual effects movie with some characters running around. I thought the first thing we should do was subordinate the visual effects totally to the story and to the universe, and part of the rule was to make it look as real as possible and as organic as everything else. Originally, I was suspicious about CG, so I went to use the more old-fashioned things like split screens and puppets. The Dementors were designed first, so we made puppets of them and used a puppeteer named Basil Twist, who is based in San Francisco. He does puppets underwater, so he has these beautiful fabrics for underwater. He came to supervise some tests for how the Dementors should work or move, but we knew we had to go CG. The wise men at ILM took our Dementor underwater test for motion reference, and those tests showed the fabrics floating and moving very eerily, and that was incorporated into the movement of the Dementors.

In the beginning I was a little frustrated, because with all the creatures — including the hippogriff, which is half-horse and half-bird — I wanted to start working on the design, but they kept working on bones and stuff. What they were trying to do was understanding the logistics of a creature that is impossible, because the way that a bird works is absolutely not compatible with the way that a horse works. So it was a whole anatomic thing and for a while we were immersed in that and *then* we started to create the design. It was amazing how the designers then started to have such an organic motion. My whole concern about visual effects was that they look good, and fundamental to that is the lighting. It's amazing to have a cinematographer like Michael Seresin involved in the visual effects aspect of finishing the film. So when we're doing the creatures like a hippogriff, a werewolf or Dementors, the light of the effects are dictated by the light on the set. We have Michael working with the light and every single shot has to have an eloquence of light. That's one of the keys to things looking good, just paying attention to the light.

As with each of the films, there were key moments in Prisoner of Azkaban *that the cast particularly enjoyed shooting.*

RUPERT GRINT: There were a lot of good scenes. The one I like is where I did my dragging thing. That was really good. A dog drags me into the tree. I had to have this harness on my leg and was dragged across the ground. It was really fun. It was quite a quick drag, because we go really fast, so it didn't take that long. I was all padded up, so it didn't really hurt. That was quite difficult, I suppose, because I swallowed a lot of grass. Oh, and I crashed into the camera and kicked the lens off.

EMMA WATSON: I had such a good time working with Emma Thompson. I had really good fun with the scene that we did, because she was very creative and she was very involving with me. She would say, "Oh, why don't we try this? Why don't we do it this way? Wouldn't it be good if we said this line here?" It was really flattering for her to involve me like that. It was really great and I had a really good time with her on it.

DANIEL RADCLIFFE: For me, the most interesting scene is probably the Shrieking Shack. I'm in the scene with Gary Oldman, Alan Rickman, Timothy Spall and David Thewlis all at the same time. It's like, "Oh my God, fantastic!" You know, you're surrounded by absolutely some of the most amazing actors, so that's probably the most interesting. As far as the most challenging — it could have been the same scene, actually. Obviously, you're putting in effort all the time, but particularly when you're with those actors you're going to really, really go for it. The other thing was that the walls actually leaned and creaked, so we couldn't hear what each other was saying. Also, all the stuff that went on with having my soul sucked out, that's also slightly harder.

EMMA WATSON: I also thought the Shrieking Shack was challenging. It's such a complex scene and a lot is happening in it, and so a lot of it kept changing and that was hard. It's all quite emotional, really. Well, not emotional, but you do feel drained.

DANIEL RADCLIFFE: There are two particular scenes that involved a lot of stunt work in *The Prisoner of Azkaban* — flying Buckbeak and, of course, Quidditch. With Buckbeak, I had to combine very precise physical movements with the visual effects, which was very demanding. Quidditch this time is in the rain and was probably the most exciting Quidditch sequence yet. Amongst other things, they had me spinning out of control and falling off my broomstick when I see the Dementors. I free fell from the broom, from quite a height, onto mats below. I always love this sort of stunt. I trained every day with a member of the stunt department who had trained me for the films, and as these films got more and more physically demanding. I'd have to be extremely fit to get through them.

EMMA WATSON: There is a moment where Hermione slaps Draco Malfoy and that felt good! It was great fun. We did a couple of takes and I was saying, "Come on, come on, let's do it again." I loved every second of it. Girl Power! It was great. I would have done it for a whole week, but, you know, we got it in a couple of takes. And I was, like, "*Well, I want to do it again. Let me do it again!*"

DANIEL RADCLIFFE: One thing that's interesting about the third book is that when we first see Harry, he thinks that he knew everything that there was to know about the past and his father. Basically in the book that's all completely turned upside-down. That's where all Harry's self-doubt comes in. He thinks if he doesn't know certain things about his dad, what else doesn't he know? That's what really makes it an interesting book, because it does deal so much with self-consciousness and worry and self-doubt.

ALFONSO CUARON: I was not trying to do anything unique. The funny thing is, I'm trying to serve the story, but at the same time, I'm a different mind than Michael Newell, who would direct *Goblet of Fire*, or Chris Columbus. I operate in a different ways and respond to different things and have different flows and different urges than the two of them. I made some decisions in this film that were not just to stand out, but because I felt they were the right things in my understanding of how to serve the story. You have to see the film to see what I contributed to it. The whole thing was an interesting lesson for one's ego, where you just surrender yourself to the material. And you find out that by restraining yourself, you're doing some of your best work.

EMMA WATSON: With *Prisoner of Azkaban*, I think J.K. Rowling's writing was so imaginative and completely takes you into another world. It just lets your imagination run wild. It describes something so specifically that you know isn't there, but it's written so brilliantly that you almost believe that it really *is* there.

ALFONSO CUARON: As familiar as millions of readers are with how the story unfolds in the book, I think that emotionally it's so charged that, even if you know the truth, you enjoy the moments in which the big information is revealed. And also because you're going along with the characters. Even if you know the twist — everyone knows the *Titanic* is going to sink — you still want to see how we carry on until that moment. So that creates a whole new dynamic and relationship to the material.

DANIEL RADCLIFFE: I think there is this really, really dark side to Harry that you don't see that much of in the third film. He actually has murderous thoughts. He would literally kill Sirius Black if he got the chance. The first two movies focus on Harry overcoming physical challenges like the Basilisk and things like that, and the Devil's Snare in the first one. *Azkaban* is focused a lot more on the emotional contents. It's a more emotionally intense journey in terms of Harry's character. So that's what separates it from the first two books in a very major way. Also, that's what I love about this book in particular, because it does go into such great detail about emotion and self-doubt, while still being able to speak to all kinds of different age groups.

EMMA WATSON: In *Azkaban*, Hermione really comes into her own, and I think you saw a different side to her than you had in the first two. I think it was much more personal and the film really tested and challenged me and I definitely enjoyed it the best out of the first three because of that.

DANIEL RADCLIFFE: By *Azkaban*, Harry's become slightly more used to things like seeing a giant squid in a lake and all this magical stuff around him. Whereas at first it was completely amazing, it's now becoming more commonplace. He's becoming slightly relaxed in terms of how he deals with the school, but he's a lot more paranoid about how he interacts with people.

Harry Potter and the Prisoner of Azkaban *was released on May 23, 2004 in the UK and June 4, 2004 in the US. The budget was $130 million and had a global box office take of $797.4 million.*

Harry Potter and the Goblet of Fire
Copyright and Trademark Warner Bros. Discovery

CHAPTER 4: *HARRY POTTER AND THE GOBLET OF FIRE* (2005)

Harry Potter's new adventure begins in a nightmare; a Muggle-born caretaker named Frank Bryce overhears Lord Voldemort, Peter Pettigrew and another man as yet unseen making plans for the Dark Lord's take-over of the magical world. Found out, Bryce is murdered. Harry and Ron are wakened at Ron's house by Hermione who tells them to not go back to sleep because breakfast is ready, and it's really early.

Harry, Ron and Hermione, with Mr. Weasley and the Diggorys, went to the 422nd Quidditch World Cup. All goes well until Death Eaters, loyalists to Voldemort, attack the camp after the end of the match. At school, the students learn that Dumbledore has found yet another teacher for Dark Arts Defense, the odd Alastor "Mad Eye" Moody, a strange eccentric with an eye that seems to look wherever it wants and former Auror. This year, Hogwarts has been chosen for the famous Triwizard Tournament, in which one wizard from three competing schools, including Hogwarts, will face three very dangerous competitions. Aside from Hogwarts, the schools are the Durmstrang Institute of Eastern Europe and the Beauxbatons Academy of Magic from France. A magic cup called the Goblet of Fire chooses a champion from each school, Cedric Diggory of Hufflepuff, Viktor Krum from Durmstrang, and Fleur Delacour from Beauxbatons. But something strange happens, the Goblet brings out a fourth name, Harry Potter. This has never happened before. Harry, being underage for the tournament, promises he never entered. Dumbledore tries to have Harry disqualified, but Ministry Official Barty Crouch Sr. states that the rules state that any name that comes out of the Goblet is a Triwizard Champion. This creates a problem for Ron, who insists Harry had secretly entered to show off. Harry denies this and the two friends argue — going so far as to swear at each other. Other students believe as Ron does, that Harry had cheated to get into the tournament. Sensing something odd,

Dumbledore asks Mad Eye to keep a surreptitious eye on Harry, just in case.

For the first task, each competitor must get an egg away from a dragon. The others succeed, but Harry's dragon breaks its chain and goes after Harry, who barely manages to avoid the creature until it crashes into a bridge and is not seen again. When Harry opens his egg to find the clue for the next task, all that comes out is a horrible, screech.

The champions and the schools take a break with the Yule Ball, but jealousy from Ron rears its ugly head when Hermione, resplendent and beautiful in her gown, goes with Victor Krum. The misguided boy verbally accosts Hermione and makes her cry. Cedric Diggory, the other Hogwarts champion, tells Harry that in order to understand the clue, he must open the egg underwater. Harry does this and learns that the Merpeople have taken someone valuable to each player and they must go into the Black Lake to retrieve them, but they need a way to breath underwater for an hour. Neville Longbottom has found just the thing in a magical text for Harry — gillyweed. It provides webbed hands and feet as well as gills to easily breath underwater. Harry eats some and goes into the lake. There he finds Ron, Hermione, Cho Chang and Fleur's sister, Gabrielle, tied in the lake. Cedric rescues Cho Chang, with Krum saving Hermione. It's up to Harry to get Ron. He also frees Fleur's sister, since Fleur could not finish this task. Due to his show of morality in rescuing Gabrielle as well as Ron, Harry is given second place in the second task.

Harry later discovers Barty Crouch's dead body in the forest and goes to Dumbledore. While waiting in the wizard's office, Harry bumps into a door and accidentally opens it. Behind is a Pensieve, a magic device that lets one view others memories. Harry takes a look and discovers one of Voldemort's Death Eaters at a tribunal naming names of the dark wizard's followers, including Severus Snape. Dumbledore defends Snape as a spy sent to keep an eye on Voldemort and his followers. But one last name catches Harry's attention, Barty Crouch, Jr, the very man the boy saw talking to Voldemort and Wormtail in his nightmare at the beginning of the movie. In the memory, a broken-hearted Crouch Sr. sends his son to Azkaban. Harry removes himself from the Pensieve, having heard and seen enough.

The final task is getting through a magical hedge maze to be the first to get the cup at the center. Viktor and Fleur are taken out of the competition, leaving Harry and Cedric to reach the cup together. The cup turns out to be a portkey that sends them to a graveyard where they find Pettigrew and Voldemort himself waiting for them. Pettigrew kills Cedric at the direction of Voldemort. He then begins a recipe of sorts using his hand, a bone from Voldemort's father, and a few drops of Harry's blood to restore Voldemort to his physical form. Voldemort tries to kill Harry but Harry holds his own. Then, with the help of his parents, the young wizard dives to Cedric's body and summons the port key, which returns them to the stadium area of the maze.

Harry tells Dumbledore that Voldemort is back. Mad Eye Moody gets Harry into his office and questions him about what happened. His questions start making Harry question things as the office door blasts open with Dumbledore, Snape and McGonagall rushing in. Dumbledore holds him down as Snape pours Veritaserum in Moody's mouth. They learn that it was he who put Harry's name in the Goblet of Fire and controlled the whole competition to make sure Harry won to get him into the graveyard to face the Dark Lord. As he is answering questions the Polyjuice Potion wears off revealing who he really is, Dumbledore, Snape and Minerva subdue him, rescue the real Moody and return Barty Crouch Jr to Azkaban. The Ministry of Magic declares that he-who-must-not-be-named is not back and refuses to believe anything else. Dumbledore disagrees and tells the students what has happened so they and their families can be ready for anything, setting the stage for the next adventure.

New cast members and characters include Robert Pattinson (he of Twilight Saga *fame) as Cedric Diggory, Katie Leung as Cho Chang, Stanislav Ianevski as Victor Krum, Miranda Richardson as Rita Skeeter, Ralph Fiennes as Voldemort, Frances de la Tour as Madame Maxime, Brendan Gleeson as Mad-Eye Moody, Clemence Poesy as Fleur Delacour and Predrag Bjelac as Igor Karkaroff.*

This one saw the departure of director Alfonso Cuaron with Mike Newell (Donnie Brasco, Four Weddings and a Funeral) taking the center seat.

DAVID HEYMAN (producer, *Harry Potter and the Goblet of Fire***):** This was, without a doubt, the most challenging of the films up to that point just from the scale of it. We have the Quidditch Worldcup and all that's involved in that. We have the "three tasks" and all that's involved with that. And the Yule Ball in between. From a logistical level, it was the most complicated film we'd made so far. In terms of the number of kids, the number of extras, Dan having to act underwater for six weeks of filming. Every time he would go underwater with an oxygen tank and oxygen mask, you'd remove the mask, he would act, get the thumbs up sign and get the oxygen back. That's quite challenging and it went brilliantly, but no question it was the most challenging of them all. But Mike Newell was up for what turned out to be a very different kind of film.

MIKE NEWELL (director, *Harry Potter and the Goblet of Fire***):** What Alfonso Cuaron did very remarkably in *Prisoner* is he evolved the films from a sunny vision of childhood into something that is much darker and blacker. And he's done that without taking away any of the romance of the thing. But he has transformed it into adolescence, and I had to go on from what he'd done. I couldn't go back. One thing I would say is that I didn't base this on anything. I watched all three films and I think there are brilliant things in all of them and things to be learned.

JIM MITCHELL (visual effects supervisor, *Harry Potter and the Goblet of Fire*): Chris Columbus worked on some big films, but Mike's background is more character-based films. So when a movie as big as *Goblet of Fire* comes along, it's just different. But he learned rather quickly and here we were, trying to be his right-hand man, which is a lot of what visual effects are all about. In a movie like this, where you've got over 1,000 visual effects shots — which is like a third of the movie — it's certainly a collaboration, and you're really involved in the day-to-day process with the director.

DAVID HEYMAN: Mike brought many things to this film. He obviously has a great sense of humor as demonstrated in *Four Weddings and a Funeral*. He is a great director of actors, as you can see in all of his films. He works with great actors and it was good for the kids to be continually challenged, and in this film, they were more challenged than they had been before. Dan, Emma and Rupert rose to the challenge that Mike put to them. I also think he brought a very British flavor to Hogwarts, more than the previous films have had.

MIKE NEWELL: What I did was simply to make a film of the book that I had, which was appropriate to 14- and 15-year-old children. That's what makes the difference. It isn't that you say to yourself, "Well, there are visual rules here we have to follow and extend." You simply say, "What is the internal emotional life of a 14-year-old?" and what happens to him can be tougher, because he's tougher himself. Naturally the challenges grow harder. They were adolescents; adults in training.

EMMA WATSON (actor, "Hermione Granger"): I don't think Mike held us back in any way. He always really, really pushed us. He was able to make it real. He really went there. The other thing is that he treated us as adults. He was expecting us to be professional the whole time, more than before in some ways. So there were no excuses and he really pushed all of us, which was nice, because it made me feel like I was well challenged.

DANIEL RADCLIFFE (actor, "Harry Potter"): I suppose that sort of the main thing that I got out of Mike's directing was that we were old enough to appreciate scenes being analyzed and broken down. The fact is that there is such a rigorous process of drafting the script on a *Harry Potter* film — on all films, but on *Harry Potter* we must go through about seven before we get to the one that we start shooting on. So basically by that time, if it's in the script, it pushes the story forward and it advances things. It's there for a reason, and Mike was fantastic about going into detail about things. I remember sort of the first time we were rehearsing with Mike. It was just me and Matt Lewis, who plays Neville. We were doing the scene and on the page the scene was around an inch-and-a-half long, and we spent about an hour-and-a-quarter rehearsing it and going through different things. We were sort of going, "Right. If this is how long a scene that's an inch-and-a-half long takes, how long will it be when we get to the 12-page scene with Voldemort?" We were sort of slightly apprehensive about how we were going to be pushed, but it was very exciting. I mean, he realized that we were old enough to appreciate really going into detail with us about the scenes. That was probably the main thing that changed.

DAVID HEYMAN: All three kids, but in particular Dan, gave more nuance to their performances. They were more able to draw from their own experiences in acting the roles. Dan knows what it's like at moments to be isolated, he knows what it's like to have disagreements with his friends, he knows what it's like to have pressure put upon him and responsibility. Those are all things he lives with in his daily life — some of which is extraordinary, because he's playing Harry Potter; some of which because it's just the normal things that a 14- or 15-year-old goes through. It is the stuff that Harry's going through in this film, and Dan was able to draw on his own experiences to do that. I think that's the case with all three of them.

DANIEL RADCLIFFE: I love a good thriller and I think the darker side of Harry brings a very thrilling feeling to the film. There are so many dark bits — not only the magic, but just Harry's teenage life. Some of that is very dark in *Goblet*. For example, one of the characters — Cedric Diggory — is killed, which I think challenges audiences. That's what sets these films apart, especially if you think of Harry Potter as a "kids' story." Most kid films are fluffy and nice, and the world is a wonderful place where criminals only exist in books and evil doesn't exist at all. In our films, we don't do that. We confront people with these darker images, which I think is great.

EMMA WATSON: Finding the tone of this film was quite difficult. I mean, the book has such a huge audience, which are children, and so you get a lot of young kids who are into this, and so part of the people who are making this film feel like we shouldn't make it too scary, because they'll cut out this huge audience who are so passionate and love Harry Potter films. At the same time, they want to be faithful to the book, which is darker and I think that they did a really good balance. I do think that it was faithful, and that this one is darker and scarier, and I think that was the best way to go. From the very beginning they wanted to stay faithful to what this is about and not please everyone.

J.K. ROWLING (creator, Harry Potter): *Goblet of Fire* nearly caused me a nervous breakdown, because for the first time ever I lost my careful plot. I had a false sense of security, because all my other plans had held up so well. So I sailed straight into the writing of the book, having just finished *Azkaban*. I had written what I thought at the time was half the book — it turns out to have been about a *third* of the book — and I realized there was this big hole in the middle of the plot and I had to go back and redo. That's part of the reason it's longer than I thought it was going to be. (**Southwest News Service**)

STEVE KLOVES (screenwriter): With *Goblet of Fire*, we came close to splitting the book into two films. We thought we were doing two films for a while. David Heyman and I ended up having four months of phone conversations about the pros and cons of one versus two. I always liked the idea of two conceptually, but you wanted to make sure we could do it the right way. (*Baltimore Sun*)

MIKE NEWELL: I wouldn't have done them if it had been two movies, because there's enough detail and texture for two films, but there isn't enough *story* for two films. I think it would have been slightly embarrassing to do it in two. What you have is a story at the beginning of which the powers of evil have a plan, which is absolutely not revealed to your hero. The kid just wanders into another year at school, then this huge notion of the competition surprises him. But there is, of course, a malign intelligence which is manipulating things. And so he gets more and more suspicious until there is a shootout between him and the bad guy. That's a really good, strong thriller shape for a story. We were going to be true to the book. We wanted fans of the book to be thrilled with the movie. The story is also about the return of the being of evil, and Harry is the vital ingredient for the potion which will bring Voldemort back. *That's* a thriller; that's the backbone the story was hung on — which is what the book does anyway. It's just a question of how you let the story ramble about.

DANIEL RADCLIFFE: In addition to the thriller parts of the film, there was a lot of humor as well. Striking that balance wasn't as hard for us as for Steve Kloves, who wrote the script. I certainly wouldn't envy that task, because the fourth book was so massive. He did an amazing job on it. To me, the humor is actually essential to the darkness in a way, because if you have that darkness running through the entire film, by the end you would be tired and it would be completely ineffective. Whereas if you've got the humor, it's easier. What's quite nice is that Mike Newell lulled you in. You've got that quick dark opening with the snake and the caretaker being killed, but it then goes into this sort of feel that's like the first film again. It's all wide-eyed and full of wonder and everything, and that highlights the fact that suddenly they come out of the tent and everything is ablaze. As a result, you're sort of instantly taken in, and it's more of a shock when you go into that darker world. I think that the humor is essential to that.

EMMA WATSON: I had a four-month break before this started and it was really good to go back to school and see all my friends. But being back at the studio felt like I had never been away. However, we had a new director again and a lot of new cast, so it made it different for us every day and *great* fun. The funniest things for me that were really unexpected are the things that Mike Newell did. He's a big man and he's quite old. There was one scene where he wasn't quite getting what he wanted — it's where characters are fighting together — and, complete surprise, he took off his hat, took off his coat, ran from the monitor and went down and got on the floor. He said, "Like this," and he was rolling about on the floor and punching, and everybody on set ran and watched this guy rolling around showing us how we should be fighting, which was great fun. The other thing he did that was really funny was I didn't quite know how to dance with Viktor Krum during the ball when he wanted a freestyle-type thing, so he took me by the hand and we had a dance, which was really funny.

RUPERT GRINT: There was a four-month break between films and it was really good to go back to school and see all my friends. But once I was back at the studio, it felt like I had never been away. However, we had a new director and lots of new cast, so it made everything different for us every day and great fun.

A centerpiece of the film is the Triwizard Tournament, a competition that brings together wizards from around the world. Included are Cedric Diggory, played by Robert Pattinson, who would, of course, go on to play vampire Edward Cullen in The Twilight Saga *and Batman/Bruce Wayne in* The Batman, *and who is the Seeker of the Hufflepuff Quidditch team; Cho Chang, played by Katie Leung, as the Seeker of the Ravenclaw Quidditch team, who is a year above Harry who, in turn, has developed a major crush on her; Victor Krum, played by Stanislav Ianevski, the Seeker for the Bulgarian national Quidditch team, a pupil at the Durmstrang Institute, who is described as being "dark with a large curved nose and thick eyebrows, walks duck-footed and round-shouldered, but is in his element on a broomstick;" and Clemence Poesy as Fleur Delacour from the Beauxbatons Academy of Magic in France. Additionally, joining the cast is Bonnie Wright as the youngest Weasley, Ginny, who, down the road, will end up marrying Harry Potter.*

ROBERT PATTINSON (actor, "Cedric Diggory"): We did a workshop before the principal shooting started. It was kind of bonding-type thing. I was star struck when I first came. I sort of identify with Cedric in a couple of ways. Generally, I am quite pleasant. I think he is, too, and I think that is one of the basic similarities.

DAVID HEYMAN: Katie Leung is of Chinese heritage, but hails from Scotland. She speaks the most beautiful, softest Scottish accent — it's really lovely.

KATIE LEUNG (actress, "Cho Chang"): My dad was watching the telly one day and he saw a commercial about the audition for the film. It said you had to be 16, have an Oriental appearance and have a British passport. I fit all the requirements, so my dad suggested we go down to London to try out for the part. I hadn't any acting experience, so I was a bit reluctant, but he insisted. The first audition involved taking a photo. A few weeks later, I went down to London for a drama workshop and they had gone from about 4,000 to 100 girls. We did a lot of improvisation with the drama teacher. We acted out scenes and played a lot of games and then it went down to the final five. I got called back to a screen test. It was basically the part where Harry asked Cho to the ball. We did that and after that I got the part. I found out I got the part when I was sleeping in bed, so it was really funny — when my mom called and told me, I didn't take it in. I was just, like, "Yeah, whatever." And then I went back to bed. *Then* I woke up and I realized what she said. It was hard, because I couldn't tell anyone for a while. The first person I did tell was my best friend — she was just ecstatic!

STANISLAV IANEVSKI (actor, "Victor Krum"): I went to the first casting and then was asked to go to two workshops. The most qualified person would be chosen for the part. I managed not to go to both of them! I had an exam on one of the dates and something else on the other. I thought I had lost my chance, but I got a phone call and they wanted to meet me again. Then I met Mike Newell and he liked me and I got the part.

Viktor doesn't really talk much, he's more of a physical being as he's described in the book. As well as being sort of cold, he's also very warm, because he develops feelings for Hermione and then he's really friendly. He and I share a lot, actually. He's very sporty and so am I. He's very good with girls and maybe I am as well. But he's a magician and I can only do a few card tricks.

BONNIE WRIGHT (actress, "Ginny Weasley"): There is a lot more "class" because of the Tri-Tournament. Besides Hogwarts, there are two other schools that come in, so there are a lot more people and there are bigger scenes with more people in the shots. There are so many people, it was quite odd because there *are* so many people cheering and they're all around you and quite loud and energetic.

As Jim Mitchell points out, the nature of Goblet of Fire *is such that it involves significant effects sequences involved with the different challenges the participants face.*

JIM MITCHELL (Industrial Light and Magic): Obviously there are the three tasks for the Tri-Wizard Cup Tournament, which involves the horn-tailed dragon that Harry battles, the underwater rescue of his friends and his meeting with the mermaids, and the maze. Which doesn't sound as crazy as dragons and mermaids, but we sort of created another creature in the maze. It all finishes up with the big wand duel between Voldemort and Harry. You're looking at those as big scenes all sprinkled with small little vignettes of other magic and creatures throughout. So it's a pretty daunting task — also quite fun to start from scratch and bring things like the mermaids to life, and to see Harry battle and fly around on his broom, trying to escape the clutches of the horn-tail.

Although, as stated, there are three tasks involved in the tournament, the most visually exciting is the one that puts each participant against a different breed of dragon, from which a golden egg must be recovered. Harry, naturally, is given "The Hungarian Horntail," the most fearsome dragon of them all. The sequence begins in an arena carved into the rocky Scottish landscape and continues in a set built in two parts at Leavesden Studios. Extremely truncated from the novel was the Quidditch portion of the story.

STUART CRAIG (production designer, *Harry Potter and the Goblet of Fire*): It was one of the biggest sets we've ever built for any of the films, but when you're battling a dragon, you need space. Also, we didn't just confine the chase to the arena. We decided to make full use of the magnificent backdrop of the Scottish highland. Certainly, from a visual effects point of view, this was the most ambitious of the films at that point and kind of extended the scope. Hogwarts is a huge but fairly claustrophobic place and here's the opportunity to get outside of it in a big way, and the story concerns three tasks. One is fighting a dragon, another one is going underwater and rescuing a friend from being tethered there, and the final one is their working their way through this malevolent and huge maze. From Harry Potter's point of view, the maze leads him into the final confrontation with Voldemort. So it's big in scope, though not in the way that *Lord of the Rings* is, which is truly apocalyptic.

JIM MITCHELL: Dragons have been seen enough in movies where you're always challenged to try to make something new and different. And I think what we've done here is put it in the world of Harry Potter. And where it was sort of a small little bit in the books, the sequence was expanded for the film, and I think we made it a bit more exciting with a chase. We really show Harry's prowess on a broom as the Horntail chases him out of the arena and up through mountains, viaducts and rooftops and all across the school grounds. Stuart and I discussed the design of the Horntail at length. Because dragons are so closely associated with dinosaurs, we decided to give it a raptor-like physique with bat wings. Then we aged it and tore up its wings to make it look like a creature that had lived for a great number of years.

DANIEL RADCLIFFE: The dragon battle was very physical and even terrifying at times. When we were doing the stunt where Harry falls down the roof, I found myself literally dangled by my ankles, hanging upside down 40 feet in the air. Then I was dropped suddenly and hurtled head first toward the ground. I knew it was safe, because our stunt team is so brilliant, but I did feel my life flashing before my eyes for a second. I'm not even going to try to lie — it was frightening and I didn't enjoy it one bit. The redeeming feature is that you fall so fast, your brain doesn't have time to catch up with your body to be frightened. You're falling, but your brain takes a while to internalize it, "Oh, I'm falling."

DAVID HEYMAN: In the first three films, Quidditch played an important role. The match itself was not a big deal in the third — it was just a place where the Dementors attack Harry. In this fourth one, we don't spend too much time playing Quidditch, because what happens when you try to condense a book of this scale to a less than two-and-a-half-hour film, you nervously have to make some hard choices. So the directive we take is that it's about Harry, and things that affect Harry are really what governs what is and isn't in the film. So Quidditch Worldcup is interesting and has a purpose because of the Death Eaters and Voldemort, and it has relevance in particular in that it introduces Victor Krum, who is one of the students who competes in the Triwizard Tournament. But we do not spend that much time with Quidditch game play.

Then, of course, Harry uses his broom to take on the dragon in one of the three tasks. So, yes, playing Quidditch and flying on a broom is part of it, but, no, it's not the most important element of the film.

Another challenge required Harry and other characters to spend a considerable amount of time underwater, interacting with mermaids.

JIM MITCHELL: The underwater sequence was our *biggest* challenge, because you're looking at trying to create an environment of a 500- to 800-foot-deep Loch up in Scotland, and we obviously weren't going to go up there and do a lot of diving. So we made it more controlled. We built this huge 60 by 60-foot tank that was 20-feet deep in the studio. John Richardson, the special effects supervisor, was involved in getting that all set up so that we could shoot with camera cranes underwater. And we rigged it with this whole back-lit blue screen. It was a massive undertaking to get to the point where we could shoot and get the elements we needed to start the process of making it look like Dan was swimming underwater with all these creatures, as well as the other contestants. And a good portion was shot by the second unit, so we were bouncing back and forth, between Dan working with the first unit, and trying to build up this sequence of him diving in the water and rescuing his friends. The whole environment — even when he's above the water and they're on the big stands waiting to dive in — was all computer generated. Nothing existed. We never went up to Scotland with the kids, and we certainly didn't make them dive into the frigid waters of the lakes up there.

DANIEL RADCLIFFE: I spent a month in a tank filming the underwater task, and I did think I was really going to sprout gills. It's a spectacular sequence. It's hard not to have a good time when you're working with all these wonderful costumes and special effects. For the underwater sequence I had these webbed fingers and the way we achieved that was we had to create molds for our fingers, and fill the molds with plastic or latex. Once you had your arm inside the mold, you had to wear a woman's stocking over your arm to keep everything in place. When you put your arms in water, you only see the plastic bits, not the woman's stocking. Everyone got quite a laugh out of seeing me wearing women's stockings on my arms. Every day was such an adventure.

CLEMENCE POESY (actor, "Fleur Delacour"): All the underwater bits were difficult at first. It's a bit scary, because you are scuba diving, and all of a sudden you have to take your air thing off and your goggles off and you have to swim to a point. You don't know when people are going to give you more air. You have to trust the people who are doing that. So it was terrifying at first, and hard in a physical way. And then it becomes something so fun. I had so much fun doing it.

DAVID HEYMAN: The underwater scenes were tricky. Three divers were constantly swimming around Dan to provide him with oxygen. But as soon as the cameras were rolling, he had to hold his breath, sometimes for nearly two minutes.

DANIEL RADCLIFFE: It was one of the hardest things I've ever had to do, because there was so much going on. At one point, I'm diving in the water and the director said, "Say your line!" And I thought, "I can't say my line, I'm underwater."

JIM MITCHELL: One-hundred-percent of that sequence was computer generation, short of the shots where Dan and the other contestants were swimming against blue screen underwater. The whole background around them, the interaction of the water, swimming through the plant life, and seeing those huge cliffs underwater, and the ruins where the victims are tied up in, as in the book — it's totally fabricated. It's amazing to see this world that you couldn't have realized any other way.

The maze is probably the biggest maze anyone will see. There's familiar sort of landscapes around Hogwarts, including a huge valley that sort of surrounds it. With that, we basically went up there and shot the valley, but at the same time we fabricated this maze — which must be about a mile long — that ties in with a bit of a set maze that was built at Pinewood Studios.

STUART CRAIG: These hedges are massive. They're a minimum of 25-feet high and 6-feet wide, so when you're in those canyons between those hedges, it's pretty intimidating, as you can imagine. And then when they kind of move and squeeze you out, it's even more intimidating. We attempted some physical movement on the set, but the whole maze was then built in CG in its entirety and able to move. So it's a combination of physical set and CG set extension.

JIM MITCHELL: One place where we did a little departing from the book was that we made the maze a creature. Mazes are scary enough, but you make them foggy and dark and then it starts to come alive, and it's hopefully even scarier. Moving Picture Company in London has done a lot of work on that aspect of making the maze scarier than it actually originally was.

STUART CRAIG: There are creatures in the maze in the novel. One of the slight changes to the movie is that the hedges themselves become malevolent; *they* become the enemy. In the novel, it's more creatures within, or creatures created by the maze rather than the hedges themselves. It's a slight change of emphasis, but the spirit of the thing is the same.

JIM MITCHELL: These 30-foot hedges are basically inanimate objects. It's not like we turn them into faces or anything like that, but they're just as powerful as the dragon in attacking our characters. That's what's fun about the Harry Potter films — you can twist reality. It's not just a 30-foot maze that's a mile long, it's a maze that's going to eat you if you're not careful and you do it. And you do it within the context of the story and try to amp that up. It was quite a challenge, as you can imagine, that sort of trying to take an inanimate object and make it look like it has a mind of its own, while still keeping it true to being plant life.

The visiting champions from other schools coincides with Hogwarts annual Yule Ball, which gets into challenges of entirely different kinds as it deals with the regulars finding dates for the event. Harry develops feelings for fellow student Cho Chang, who is dating Cedric Diggory, Captain and Seeker of the Hufflepuff House Quidditch team.

DAVID HEYMAN: One of the wonderful aspects of this story is the burgeoning interest Harry and his friends have in the opposite sex and the innate awkwardness this brings. Mike Newell has a wonderful sense of humor and incredibly intuitive comic timing, so watching these teens attempt to communicate with each other is painfully funny.

EMMA WATSON: Much to her surprise, Hermione gets herself a boyfriend in Victor Krum. This proves to be a huge shock for Harry and Ron, particularly Ron, who has only just realized that Hermione is a girl!

RUPERT GRINT: I think Ron's always been after Hermione. Throughout the first four films it was always pretty plain that he's got a thing for her and we've always had the sense that there is something growing between them, although neither are really aware of it. In this film, both begin to admit it to themselves. When Hermione turns up at the Yule Ball with Viktor Krum, Ron *finally* realizes that he has feelings for her.

DANIEL RADCLIFFE: One of the things I've always liked about Harry is that he is absolutely pathetic when it comes to the whole romance thing. He's a fantastic hero and he's brave and strong and loyal and trustworthy, and he's the greatest friend, but he's just *bad* with girls. He has no clue how to behave around them. He's a character for anyone who has ever felt awkward around girls. He just can't think of the right things to say when he's with Cho. That aspect of him is what everyone can identify with, because I think it happens to everyone at least once. People can deny it and deny it, but they're lying. At least once, everybody has been a complete dork with the person he or she likes, and they have no idea what to say, and Harry is that in this film. The scenes are fun and they look very real — awkward and sweet, like two people just getting to know one another.

EMMA WATSON: I could relate so much to what Hermione was going through in *Goblet of Fire*, and I so know that frustration where guys can be insensitive. I can relate to a lot of things that she experiences and all of her awkward moments, and what that's all about. What's nice about the relationship that she and Victor have, and what Mike really wanted to show, was that Hermione is so insecure about herself and she's never really had any attention from any guys before. So when she sees that they're looking at her, it's one of those, "Is that guy really looking at me or am I crazy?" moments. I mean, he genuinely wanted to come across as she is quite literally being swept off her feet. She doesn't know what is happening to her, and she gets caught up in the whirlwind that is this incredibly famous Quidditch player and she can't quite believe that it's happening to her. Mike wanted her to be quite naïve. It's really sweet, she loves it, but then Ron gets a bit jealous and it gets a bit tense. So it's quite an emotional roller coaster for her.

For fans, one of the most breathtaking sequences of the film was indeed the Yule Ball itself, which was staged just before the 2004 Christmas holidays.

MIKE NEWELL: We wanted to create a tremendous change in the Great Hall for the Yule Ball so that the characters and the audience feel like they've never seen this place before.

STUART CRAIG: The description in the novel is that it's an ice palace with icicles hanging from the ceiling. We took it a step further and made the magic ceiling out of ice. The walls are covered in highly reflective silver and everything you see, from the doors, flambeaus, windows and even the fireplace, was given an icy or silver makeover.

EMMA WATSON: I loved the Ball. It was so exciting. You see the Great Hall differently for the first time. It looks like the whole thing has quite literally been frozen. There's a beautiful ice dance floor and icicles on everything, and everything's silver and gold. The whole thing looks stunning; really, really beautiful. Everyone has the most amazing costumes; the dresses are beautiful and all the guys are wearing their suits and there was dancing and music. We had so much of the cast involved in that scene that it was really fun.

BONNIE WRIGHT: I really enjoyed filming the Ball. That was really fun, because they let us practice ballroom dancing. It was nice learning something else and bringing that to filming.

JANY TEMIME (costume designer, *Harry Potter and the Goblet of Fire*): We prepared over 300 costumes for the Yule Ball alone. First, we designed the boys' evening attire. Each has white or black ties and fancy waistcoats. Harry wears a very classic black waistcoat. The Slytherins have white ties, because they regard themselves as posh.

RUPERT GRINT: My outfit is *horrible*, all pink lace and flowers. But it was actually quite fun wearing it. It was kind of like something out of the 1970s and so hideous I actually quite liked it.

JANY TEMIME: The girls were so excited about what they were going to wear, it was as if they were going to a real ball. Hermione's dress had to be really special. I wanted it to be a fairy-tale dress, something that would make all the children gasp when she entered the room.

EMMA WATSON: It's unlike anything Hermione has ever worn before. Our hair and makeup team spent hours transforming me for the scene. I knew that all eyes were on me when I entered the hall, which was very scary. Behind the scenes, the girls were really looking forward to the dance, and the boys, being typical boys, were very nervous about it. I love dancing and really enjoyed learning to waltz, but what was interesting was that Mike Newell didn't want us to be perfect dancers. He wanted the camera to pick up that we weren't exactly sure of what we were doing.

DANIEL RADCLIFFE: It was *terrifying*. My parents are both very good dancers, but it seems to have skipped a generation.

One notable element of the film is that Voldemort was given a true physical presence beginning in Goblet of Fire, *notably in the form of Ralph Fiennes in make-up. It did raise the question of whether or not this chapter might be too intense for kids.*

MIKE NEWELL: The film *is* PG-13 for a reason, though there are two things to be said about that. One is that there were two test screenings, one was for children who were as young as eight for an audience of eight-to-14-year-olds. And then one for 14-and-up to 60. The eight-year-olds had no problem understanding it, no problem sitting there, they were *not* terrified out of their wits, but they were satisfied with what they saw and wrote down their impressions just like everybody did. I read them very carefully and clearly they got it and were unfazed by it. Certainly they thought it was scary from time to time, as it should be. It would be a real disappointment if it wasn't. So I was very pleased by that. The other thing was that I tried to make a film in which the parents could find as much to interest them as the children did. I think when I look at it, that I'm satisfied that I did that.

With Voldemort, we talked a great deal, very seriously, about what his motivations were. What does he want? Why does he want to come back? What sort of person is it that wants to come back and wants to impose a reign of evil? Does someone who wants to impose a reign of evil see it as truly being evil or is it, in fact, for them something good?

RALPH FIENNES (actor, "Voldemort"): It's quite hard to play someone who is the essence of evil. In my discussions with Mike about the character, we talked about giving Voldemort human qualities, because to just play "evil" is really impossible. "Evil" is often conveyed through gnashing of teeth and a lot of spit. I wanted my portrayal of Voldemort to be deeply, truly evil. That comes from fear, frustration, unhappiness. Voldemort was a rejected child. He had a very unhappy childhood and that's where his anger, jealousy and hatred began to fester.

BONNIE WRIGHT: Ralph Fiennes was really good. Another scene that was really good was the graveyard — Ralph is really good there. I watched some of the filming and he was really amazing. His take on it is like the book character.

DANIEL RADCLIFFE: I enjoy that the films show the darker side of things. There are so many dark bits — not only the magic, but just Harry's teenage life, some of that is very dark. Most kids' films are fluffy and nice and the world is a wonderful place where criminals only exist in books and evil doesn't exist at all. In our films, we don't do that. We confront people with darker images, which I think is great.

MIKE NEWELL: When you're dealing with an "ultimate evil," you really do have to walk a fine line. A great deal of that has to do with the actor, because if what the actor is going to do is choose to chew scenery, then people are simply going to think of him as some sort of Victorian figure of fun, and he mustn't be that, of course. He's got to chill the blood. Ralph Fiennes is absolutely real and cold and chilling and absolutely dedicated to doing bad. As soon as you have that, you can do anything.

This is what I thought of the Wizard world: I thought that they were like sort of medieval knights who would defend the borders of the country, who are innocent of it all, but they are out there knowing that there is evil, knowing that there are all sorts of weird and threatening stuff out there, and unknown to us, they keep us safe. They are the heroes that way. It has to be real. People ask me what it was like dealing with such a fantastic story, but it wasn't a fantastic story to me at all. It was absolutely real. Okay, it's got wands and stuff like that, but you could say this is what it was like living in Europe in the '30s with the spread of Nazism. There was something really bad out there, and people were either going to do something about it or weren't going to do something about it, but that really bad stuff was creeping ever absolutely remorselessly forward and it was getting worse. There are all sorts of things you can do, really quite recent manifestations of this that you can point to and make a very real world out of it. What that means is you have to have the actor to do it, and Ralph Fiennes is that actor. He doesn't chew the scenery and he isn't a 19th century melodrama figure. He's absolutely real and cold and chilling *and* absolutely dedicated to doing bad. As soon as you have that, you can do *anything*.

Harry Potter and the Goblet of Fire *was released on November 18, 2005 in both the UK and the US. Its budget was $150 million and it had a global gross of $896.7 million.*

HARRY POTTER AND THE GOBLET OF FIRE: BEHIND THE SCENES

Daniel Radcliffe's *Fiery* Q & A

Harry is Sweet Sixteen and still looking for love, as Dan reveals from the set of Goblet of Fire

Daniel Radcliffe was only 11-years-old when he won the coveted role of Harry Potter — quite a feat for a young actor who, before that, was known only to TV audiences in Britain as young David in the BBC production of the Charles Dickens' classic, David Copperfield. *Of course, since then, Daniel has absolutely inhabited Harry — for five years, he's taken the powerful Mr. Potter through a slew of scary situations, amazing adventures, wizardly wonders and a few very wild Quidditch matches.*

Goblet of Fire *is your fourth Harry Potter film — which has been your favorite?*

DANIEL RADCLLIFFE: I will answer completely honestly — I loved making all of them. I could never pick one. Each one is its own experience, and I've met such wonderful people on each film. I could never say the people from one film were better than the people on another film, and it's all about the people you're surrounded by.

Is there any one person you've met who's been the most fun to work with?

DANIEL RADCLIFFE: Michael Gambon, who plays Dumbledore, was always fantastic to work with. He's mad, and I love him to pieces. He's a fantastic actor, but he's also always chatting and joking and laughing, right up to and including while we're doing our scenes. I think it's because he's Irish, and Irish people are often the best storytellers. I'm half-Irish too, so I'm quite good at that myself.

Are the films themselves fun to make?

DANIEL RADCLIFFE: Amazing fun. I know it's boring for me to say this, but they've all been great fun. It's hard not to have a good time when you're working with all these wonderful costumes and special effects.

Harry, of course, is very courageous. Do you have any fears or phobias?

DANIEL RADCLIFF: (*Laughs*) No. I'm not afraid of anything! That's absolutely not true! I know a lot of people are afraid of spiders, but I'm not really afraid of them — *if* they're there and I can see them. If I turn away, and they're gone, and I don't know where they've gone, that freaks me out a little. And I don't like cockroaches. But those are the only things I'm afraid of, because I'm tough and manly.

Harry suffers through terrible dreams and nightmares. Have you ever had a strange recurring dream?

DANIEL RADCLIFFE: Well, I've dreamed that I'm being operated on. That happened three times. And then there's the falling one — I'm always falling to the ground in my dreams, and most people wake up before they hit the ground, which is supposed to mean good luck in real life. Did you know that if you die in your dreams, it's supposed to be good luck in life? So that works out for me… *fantastic*.

Is it true that you have your first love scene in Goblet of Fire *with actress Katie Leung, who plays Cho Chang?*

DANIEL RADCLIFFE: Well, not seriously — there are no kissing scenes, unfortunately, although I think there will be in the next one and I'm looking forward to that.

There have been some nasty rumors on the Internet — apparently some Harry fans don't want Cho and Harry to become a couple.

DANIEL RADCLIFFE: That was started by some British paper. Some website featured comments from people — not nearly as horrible as everyone has made out — and the British newspapers turned it into a whole story, because they didn't have anything else to say. There were some made-up quotes, supposedly by Katie Leung's father, and the paper hadn't even spoken to him! I thought it was very nasty, and I think that newspapers should think about the effects their stories have on people.

Do any of the other characters find love? It seems like everyone wants Hermione and Ron to get together.

DANIEL RADCLIFFE: Oh I would love that, just to see Rupe and Emma kiss! I think that would be great. Although I do think I'll have to re-read the books, because I don't know how much of that relationship comes through in the books, and how much is invented. Those two, their behavior toward each other is always, "I hate you, I hate you, I hate you... But I love you!" I personally would be very amused to see them develop a relationship, but, again, I'll have to re-read the books — I don't think they'll create a romance for the characters in the movie if that romance wasn't first created in the book.

Are you, Emma and Rupert close friends off the set?

DANIEL RADCLIFFE: Well, we don't get sick of each other or anything like that, but we see each other so much when we're working. I do see Emma, because she's become like a sister to me. She really is one of my best friends. The thing about Rupert is, we've known each other for a long time, but we don't know each other particularly well. He's a cool guy and very funny, but I've never really become that close to him.

I think it's because he's actually a bit older than me, and when I'm off at school he's doing his own things, so I don't know that we have as much in common anymore.

Do the three of you ever fight while you're working together?

DANIEL RADCLIFFE: When you hang around with someone, work with someone, for 10 or 11 months, it's so intense, you're bound to occasionally become irritated with them. I'm not saying we throw plates at each other, but sometimes things do become a bit tense. But with Emma and I, when we have arguments, we end up being even better friends, because we have the kinds of arguments that actually improve a friendship.

Everyone is waiting for Goblet of Fire *to come out in theaters. What was the last movie you waited for?*

DANIEL RADCLIFFE: I was crazy to see *Charlie and The Chocolate Factory*, because I am the biggest Johnny Depp fan in the world. And I was very excited about *Hitchhiker's Guide to the Galaxy*, because I loved the books and couldn't wait to see it.

Has anyone ever come up to you thinking you actually were Harry Potter?

DANIEL RADCLIFFE: Younger fans think that, which is fine. But there was one kid — he was the son of one of the women who did make-up on the set. And of course he believed that, so every time he saw me, he started crying. But in the end, she told him he was stronger than Harry, so eventually he decided he wasn't scared of me anymore.

There are more Harry Potter stories to come. Do you see yourself appearing in more HP movies?

DANIEL RADCLIFFE: I'll do the films as long as I'm enjoying them, and as long as I think they're going to challenge me as an actor. And I want to be an actor. I want to do other films, and eventually I'd like to write and direct movies, because I'd like to think I'm quite versatile. I'd like to try loads of things, and some of them won't work — some of them will be rubbish — but someday I may make another movie that people will remember.

MEET ROBERT PATTINSON

Reluctant at first, Credric Diggory's real-life alter ego has embraced the acting life

Note: Interview conducted with the actor prior to his being cast as Edward Cullen in the film version of **Twilight**

Robert Pattinson grew up a typical British lad. He loved sports and hanging out with his pals. He's the first to admit that he never really considered acting as a career, until his dad encouraged him to try it. It seems that Robert's proud papa thought his son would make a great actor, and Robert agreed to try it only after he noticed that there were lots of pretty girls in the local drama club. He also found out that he actually liked acting, and since he first stepped onto a stage, he's made his mark. He's appeared in the British movie Sword of Xanten *and, of course,* Harry Potter and the Goblet of Fire. *He also was cast in Reese Witherspoon's* Vanity Fair, *but his role ended up on the cutting room floor. Don't fear: that could never happen to Robert's role of Cedric Diggory in* Goblet of Fire. *Credric is Captain and Seeker of the Hufflepuff House Quidditch team. Selected to represent Hogwarts in the Triwizard Tournament, he is killed on Voldemort's command. He was described by Professor Dumbledore as "a good and loyal friend, a hard worker, he valued fair play."*

If you hadn't become an actor, what career would you have followed?

ROBERT PATTINSON: I have no idea. I think I would have just gone to university and would have kind of just done the average thing.

Do you identify with Cedric?

ROBERT PATTINSON: I sort of identify with him in a couple of ways. Generally, I am quite pleasant. I think he is, too, and I think that is one of the basic similarities. I am relatively sporty, but I think he is a better person than me.

How is Harry Potter and the Goblet of Fire *different from the first three movies?*

ROBERT PATTINSON: I think basically the characters have been pretty fully developed in the first three, and it's just going to take another turn into being more of a thriller. It's more boom, boom, boom, to the climax. I think it's a much faster-paced, action-oriented film than the others. And they kill off key characters. There's always going to be a little bit of a twist — killing someone is always a bit of a shock.

Music is very important to you. What instruments do you play?

ROBERT PATTINSON: I have been playing the piano for my entire life — since I was three or four. And the guitar — I used to play classical guitar from when I was about five to 12 years of age. Then I didn't play guitar for years. About four or five years ago, I got out the guitar again and started playing blues and stuff. I am not very good at the guitar, but I am all right. I'm in a band in London as well.

What's the name of your band and what kind of music do you play?

ROBERT PATTINSON: Bad Girl. It's kind of like rocky Led Zeppelin-type stuff. We only have done a couple of gigs. We are still trying to figure out its style. It is just a couple of friends of mine and some other people that I have met fairly recently. We just wanted to start a band for something to do. A lot of my friends are actors and we have so little to do all the time, so instead of just being bored, we were, like, "Why not start a band?" So we did.

Harry Potter and the Order of the Phoenix
Copyright and Trademark Warner Bros. Discovery

CHAPTER 5: *HARRY POTTER AND THE ORDER OF THE PHOENIX* (2007)

The Dementors are getting braver, attacking Harry and Dudley Dursley in the Muggle World. Harry saves himself and Dudley with the Expecto Patronum spell and Harry has to help Dudley get home because of the effects of the Dementor attack. Dudley tells his dad that Harry did it to him. The Ministry of Magic expels Harry for using magic outside of school and in front of a muggle. Dumbledore talks the Ministry into suspending the expulsion and holding a trial for Harry. Thanks to Dumbledore and a witness that saw what happened he is cleared of all charges. Harry learns of the Order of the Phoenix, a secret organization working to defeat Voldemort. He learns that the Ministry of Magic refuses to acknowledge Voldemort's return and Cornelius Fudge, head of the Ministry, hires Delores Umbridge as the new Defense Against the Dark Arts Teacher, someone who vehemently denies Harry's claim that Voldemort is back. Because of his claims, most other students stay away from Harry. They don't believe him because there isn't any evidence as to what happened.

Harry reunites with Sirius Black, who says Voldemort appears to be after a magical object that he's been searching for over the years. Nobody seems to know what that is, but Harry believes it to be some kind of weapon that must be kept from the dark wizard no matter what it takes.

Umbridge wastes no time in undermining the students' studies by refusing to teach any valid magic that will help them to protect themselves. This leads to an argument with Harry, who is punished by having to write about not lying, but with each stroke of the quill, the words are etched into the back of Harry's hand. Harry won't go to Dumbledore, who's distanced himself from the young wizard, which causes Ron, Hermione and other students to form "Dumbledore's Army" to teach themselves the magic needed to stop

Voldemort and his Death Eaters from regaining control. Meanwhile, Umbridge gathers Slytherin students, including Draco Malfoy, to spy on students to keep an eye on what they're doing, and to take those breaking rules to Umbridge for punishment.

Harry has a vision of Ron's father, Arthur, being attacked at the Ministry by some mysterious form. Other wizards barely get to him in time to save him. Dumbledore has Snape teach Harry Occlumency, a way to keep Voldemort from the boy's thoughts. This psychic thread between the two further convinces students that Harry and Voldemort might in some way be working together, alienating the boy even more. To make matters even more dangerous, Sirius' insane cousin, Bellatrix Lestrange, and nearly a dozen other of Voldemort's Death Eaters escape from Azkaban, making the evil wizard's power base ever stronger. And Umbridge's personal Inquisitorial Squad learns of Dumbledore's army and attempts to have him arrested, but he escapes. Harry uses this event as proof that Cho betrayed them, destroying the growing romance between the two.

With a vision of Sirius being tortured, Harry, Ron and Hermione attempt to take the Floo Network — a chimney transportation system that they can access in Umbridge's office, where they are promptly caught and about to be punished when Hermione tells her that Dumbledore hid away a very powerful magic weapon in the forest. Convincing them to take her there, Umbridge is herself captured by centaurs who don't like people in their woods. Harry, Ron, Hermione, Luna Lovegood, Neville Longbottom and Ron's sister Ginny fly to the Ministry on winged creatures to save Sirius. It's here they learn that the weapon Voldemort has been searching for is a glove containing a prophecy with Harry's name on it. Lucius Malfoy demands that Harry give him the orb and when Harry refuses, a magical battle breaks out between Lucius, Bellatrix Lestrange and several other Death Eaters and Harry and his friends. To save everyone, Harry surrenders the bottle to Lucius seconds before Sirius, Remus Lupin, and Order of the Phoenix members Nymphadora Tonks, Kingsley Shacklebolt and Mad Eye Moody arrive to take on the fight. During the battle, Lucius drops the prophecy, destroying it and its contents. Bellatrix, though, saves Lucius from Sirius, killing Harry's godfather in the process.

But the fight isn't over. Voldemort shows up to finally kill Harry, but Dumbledore arrives and fights the evil wizard until the Dark Lord takes over Harry's body. However, Harry's greatest power, the love for his family and friends, drives the wizard from his body. As Voldemort leaves Harry's body, Ministry head Fudge and his aides arrive. Once Fudge sees Voldemort, he has no choice but to admit he is back. Umbridge is dismissed and investigated for her actions while at Hogwarts and Dumbledore is reinstated as headmaster of Hogwarts. Feeling it's something Harry must finally learn about; Dumbledore discusses the cryptic prophecy that the Dark Lord so desperately wanted. Part of the prophecy read, "Neither can live while the other survives."

DANIEL RADCLIFFE (actor, "Harry Potter"): Umbridge in *Order of the Phoenix* is a character that somebody compared to a cross between Margaret Thatcher and Freddy Krueger. She is a figure of pure sweetness and pure terror as well, sort of like licorice. I don't think people are disappointed. I don't think the accusation we've watered Umbridge's evil down will be leveled at us.

MICHAEL GOLDENBERG (screenwriter, *Harry Potter and the Order of the Phoenix*): When I think of this story, the first thing that comes to mind is that it's an emotional knockout punch. What Harry has to go through, purely in terms of his own emotions, his own demons, his own challenges, his own anger, confusion and sense of isolation is what propels the story. Harry's journey in this film is incredible. He goes from being somebody who's got some very tough choices to make and somebody who's an outsider from the beginning, and through the process of confronting Umbridge, through realizing he has a responsibility to help teach the other kids to defend themselves as he becomes the leader of Dumbledore's Army, by the end of the film he becomes a leader. He becomes a grown-up and he has embraced everything he was running away from in the beginning. That, to me, is an incredible story and a universal one. It's about going from the last gasp of childhood, when you're still seeing the world in very black and white terms, to realizing just how complicated the world is; how many shades of gray there are and how complicated you are, and coming out the other side of that and realizing you're going to be okay.

With the fifth film came the arrival of the series' fourth and, as it would turn out, final director in the form of David Yates. On British television, he directed the miniseries The Sins *(2000),* The Way We Live Now *(2001),* State of Play *(2003), and* Sex Traffic *(2004), and the TV movies* The Young Visitors *(2003) and* The Girl in the Café *(2004). Yates would not only direct films five through eight of Harry Potter, but the first three* Fantastic Beasts *as well.*

DAVID HEYMAN (producer, *Harry Potter and the Order of the Phoenix***):** One always looks to new challenges and I think David Yates is a great director who understands actors, has a great visual sense and a real sort of energy about his filmmaking. I think that's important to this film as Harry struggles with new issues both internal and external. He's one of the brightest directors around. For all that a producer does, ultimately the film is as good as the director. If the director is our leader, it makes all the difference. Chris Columbus left his imprint very strongly on the first two, and lingers on today in terms of the kids he cast. Alfonso made the third film very much his own and Mike Newell did, too. My role, obviously, is as a protector and guardian of the world and also to create an environment where the director can do the best job that he can do. You don't hire directors like Mike Newell, Chris Columbus or Alfonso Cuaron to make cookie-cutter films. You hire directors like that to bring their own take to the material. You saw how different the third film was to the first two, and that was because everybody encouraged Alfonso to make the film that he wanted to make.

RUPERT GRINT (actor, "Ron Weasley"): The changing of directors is sometimes a challenge, but it makes it different. I mean, the first time it happened, losing Chris Columbus, was quite a big thing, because he was my first ever director and it was my first ever film. It was quite different not having him in there. But we've had some really good ones with Alfonso Cuaron, Mike Newell and, then, David Yates. David is quite laid back and much more calm. He's calmer than the other ones we've had, so it's been good.

KATIE LEUNG (actress, "Cho Chang"): *Order of the Phoenix* was very different than *Goblet of Fire*. There was a different director to begin with. Mike Newell and David Yates are very different from each other, but I love them both. Mike was the one who cast me and I felt really close to him. If it wasn't for him, I wouldn't be where I was and I just loved him to bits. He always gave really good advice and he also told me not to be nervous, because he knew from the beginning when I went to the auditions that I was a nervous wreck. David was very different from Mike in that Mike is loud and he has a large personality. David is very quiet and very gentle with all of the actors. He would speak to me in the corner quietly and asked me what I thought of my character, and he would ask me for my opinion and then he would give me his advice. I just really enjoyed working with both of them.

DANIEL RADCLIFFE: I was looking forward to working with David Yates, because I'd had a couple of preliminary meetings with him. The instant you meet him, you're just struck by the fact that not only is he a lovely guy, but also that he knows *exactly* the film he wants to make.

DAVID HEYMAN: David came in with a great passion for the material and a great sense of the emotional journey of the characters. It was really rewarding how the kids embraced him and he them. Like their characters, they are growing up and David treated them as equals. He realized that they know their characters well and was always soliciting their ideas and getting them to bring more of themselves to their roles in ways they hadn't before. That was exciting for them.

DANIEL RADCLIFFE: I have never been pushed as hard as I was on this film, partly because of the nature of the story and partly because of his directing. He never settled for less; he always wanted me to go deeper, which was exactly what I felt I needed. I can only speak for myself when I say this, but if I'm not pushed sort of fairly regularly, there is always a danger that I will get complacent. Although to tell you the truth, I don't think that would happen with me, because I try to keep myself aware of what's going on and ready for any kind of scene. Otherwise, I think you get paranoid; if you just drift through smaller scenes, you start thinking, "Oh, goodness, will I be able to really hack it when I get back into the big scenes?" There's no danger of that happening when David's around.

RUPERT GRINT: David is wicked; we got on really well with him. He was quite a bit different from the other directors, because he has a more relaxed approach, but he always gave great suggestions.

EMMA WATSON (actor, "Hermione Granger"): It was really lovely, because David listened to what we had to say about our characters. He was respectful of the fact that we have been playing these people for five films at that point. He appreciated the history and the special relationship that Dan, Rupert and I share, because it adds truth to the friendship between Harry, Ron and Hermione. David really looks for truth in all of the characters.

KATIE LEUNG: David is so calm about *everything*. It's such a big, big film and he's just so gentle. I just love that. Also, I think he always had a certain image in his mind of how he wanted the scenes to be, and he wouldn't be happy unless we did it the way he wanted it. I think that's great; even though it was going to take 50 or 60 takes, he didn't care, he was just so determined to get it right. And there's so much pressure on him because it *is* Harry Potter, but at the same time, he's just so cool and calm about it.

MICHAEL GOLDENBERG: Obviously it was very important to stay true to the spirit of the book. This story, in particular, is so much about Harry's journey. It's about Harry coming of age and realizing that things aren't as black and white as they initially appeared and the adults he idealized are perhaps more flawed and human than he thought. All of the kids are dealing with a more complex world than when they first entered Hogwarts.

DAVID YATES (director, *Harry Potter and the Order of the Phoenix*): It's classical. Anyone who's ever been through those very turbulent, difficult teenage years where you find yourself growing angry and frustrated, identify with it. Those years are truly formative; they're the years that can sometimes define you as a person. Some people can take that and develop in a positive way, and some people start on a route that ultimately leads them to difficult years. This film looks at the very emotional and turbulent time when you're growing up and suddenly questioning everything about the world. You're also discovering the world is quite a complex and complicated place, and all the adults around you don't necessarily have all the answers.

DANIEL RADCLIFFE: The books for me are not about magic or good or evil. To me, the story is about a loss of innocence. That's what Harry's evolution is — he goes from being this young boy awestruck by the magical world, to a young man very much aware of the awful things that people can do to each other, even in the magical world, which at first he views as utopia. At first, he thinks it's paradise, but he wakes up to the fact that actually really horrible things happen there.

DAVID YATES: When Harry comes back to Hogwarts, it doesn't feel as familiar and safe as it always has in the past. He feels like an outsider and he has to make a choice whether he is going to be defined by that or if he is going to hold onto the friendships that have gotten him through so much during his school years. There are moments where you see he could go either way, and that is the emotional center of the story, for Harry in particular. It was also a really interesting journey for Dan as an actor, because it was a complex piece of acting work.

For Harry, complexities come about when he discovers his parents had been among the original Order of the Phoenix, and counted among its current members are Molly and Arthur Weasley, Remus Lupin, Severus Snape and, to his surprise and delight, Sirius Black, who has opened the Black family home as the meeting place for the Order of the Phoenix. Harry sees the Order as a way to connect to his past ... and more.

DANIEL RADCLIFFE: Officially he's not in the Order, but he already thinks of himself as very much a part of it, because so many of his friends are in it. It means a lot to him, because, of course, his parents were in the original Order. So it has quite an emotional importance to Harry, as well as giving him a chance to fight Voldemort. I actually think there are parallels between Harry and Voldemort and Sherlock Holmes and Moriarty. Sherlock Holmes and Moriarty had to both perish in order for the villain to be vanquished. I think it will be something to do with the fact that maybe the only way Voldemort can be killed is if Harry is killed as well. My friend is the one who sort of compared it to Holmes and Moriarty dying at the same time, but obviously he hasn't read the sequel in which Holmes was revived.

MICHAEL GOLDENBERG: What Harry has to go through, purely in terms of his own emotions, his own demons, his own challenges, his own anger, confusion and sense of isolation is what propels the story. He goes from being somebody who's got some very tough choices to make and somebody who's an outsider at the beginning, and through the process of confronting Umbridge, through realizing he has a responsibility to help teach the other kids to defend themselves as he becomes the leader of Dumbledore's Army, by the end of the film he becomes a leader. He becomes a grown-up and he has embraced everything he was running away from in the beginning. That, to me, is an incredible story and a universal one. It's about going from the last gasp of childhood, when you're still seeing the world in very black and white terms, to realizing just how complicated the world is; how many shades of gray there are and how complicated *you* are, and coming out the other side of that and realizing you're going to be okay.

DANIEL RADCLIFFE: There is a line in the film "Hatred is easy, compassion is hard," and it's a lesson that Harry and a lot of the characters learn. It's a very simple statement, but it's actually true, because it's easy to dismiss someone you just dislike at first. It can be difficult, especially for someone like Harry, who's quite instinctual, and the lesson he's learned over these films is that you can't ever assume something about a person. Like I said, I think Harry's quite instinctual in his judgments of people. That when he meets someone, it'll be pretty instant whether he likes them or not, yet I think that is an important lesson for Harry to learn, that you have to sort of give someone a bit along the time span before you decide about them.

DAVID YATES: This point was a really exciting time to be at Hogwarts, because the characters are older and dealing with rather complex things. The cast was more interested in pushing themselves and being pushed as actors. Even though the film franchise had been going on for four pictures at that point, the attitude of the producers was really kind of open to new ideas and new ways of pulling things in a slightly edgier, more emotional direction, which is a good reflection of where book five is anyway and what Jo Rowling created in the first place. It's about rebellion and about understanding the limits of adulthood; it's about discovering how difficult the world can become and how sometimes you have to make your own way in the world.

RUPERT GRINT: Ron certainly seems a bit older in *Order of the Phoenix* and is getting more mature than he was in *Goblet of Fire*. He's much more together and much more a part of things. When you look back at those early films, it does seem like a really long time ago. What comes to mind in one way he has changed, is his relationship with Hermione. They clashed a bit in the beginning and as time has gone on, they've become much closer — which I think is sort of parallel to us as well. As the books have gone on, the characters have grown up, and I think that we've been growing up with them. So you can definitely see just how much Ron has grown up and gained some maturity.

DANIEL RADCLIFFE: Any kid who was 11 when the films first came out would be 17 by the time they saw *Order of the*

Phoenix. So the audience had grown up with the films. Because of that, we had to grow up with it, and the film's appeal is more to teenagers who are going through some of the same confusion and anger that Harry is, and adults who have been through it already. While kids enjoy it for the action and magic, teenagers were able to connect with Harry more than they ever had before.

EMMA WATSON: David Yates would not settle for anything that looks like acting. What kept coming up a lot is his search for truth in the characters and the performances. He really wanted it to be real. The fourth film was sort of about all of the tasks, fighting dragons and all of that. This film is about Harry fighting his inner demons more than dragons. It's about the emotional journey. So I think David was the perfect director for that.

DAVID HEYMAN: Harry is definitely affected by Voldemort and the connection between them as he starts to actually see things through Voldemort's eyes. When Voldemort discovers this, he starts to manipulate Harry, and I think that messes with Harry's head, in a way. The brilliance of what both David Yates and Dan have done is that it's been made completely believable, real and emotional.

DAVID YATES: Dan as an actor is incredibly intuitive and sensitive. I use the word sensitive instead of emotional, because he's quite strategic about his empathy for people and things. All the kids are really bright and intuitive, so getting them to deal with some of these story issues wasn't difficult at all.

MICHAEL GOLDENBERG: Harry spending time in Voldemort's mind is terrifying, and then when that's reversed, it's incredibly frightening, intense and emotionally harrowing. So there's a weird kind of intimacy that begins to develop between the two of them because of that connection, and it somehow makes it even more scary.

DANIEL RADCLIFFE: One of the more interesting aspects in the film is the relationship between Harry and Dumbledore. Of course, Dumbledore thinks Voldemort might be using my eyes as a portal to my mind, as a way of seeing what I'm seeing, so when I look at Dumbledore, Dumbledore thinks he might be seeing Voldemort in me, which is a pretty heavy thing. As a result, Dumbledore is ignoring Harry at the time when Harry actually needs him most. That's one of the things I think is actually fascinating about the book and the film, and it's the reason that Dumbledore tells Hermione and Ron they can't contact Harry over the summer.

DAVID YATES: In our story, you see Voldemort try and influence him and try and shape him. It's part of how Harry's story evolves. I think it's a theme that's especially pertinent to that stage of life; the point in our life where you make choices. Subconsciously, you make choices when you're in your teenage years and you start to shape the person you will be for the rest of your life. That's what this film and this story partly looks at: this very emotional and turbulent time when you're growing up and suddenly questioning everything about the world. And you're also discovering that the world is quite a complex and complicated place, and all the adults around you don't have all the answers. And also you discover, ultimately, how complicated you are within your own self. What Jo Rowling is brilliant at doing is exposing that universal truth of the transition to adulthood in this magical universe.

One important element of the film is Harry coming to terms with his heritage – no matter how painful it might be, including the image he's held on to dearly of his father. Another is his dealing with death, in particularly the aftermath of the death of Cedric Diggory in

Goblet of Fire *and that of his godfather, Sirius Black, in* Order of the Phoenix.

MICHAEL GOLDENBERG: One of the scenes that's really powerful to me — and it was a technical problem and difficult to integrate into the film — is the scene where Harry sees his father as a young man and not at all the idealized figure that Harry had imagined. When I first sat down with Dan to talk to him about the story, he brought up that scene and I was really happy he did. That scene, to me, is the dramatic heart of the movie, because it's that moment where you go from seeing your parent as perfect or this God-like infallible person, to seeing them for what they are, which is just another kind of flawed, struggling human being. I think that Harry goes through that passage with his father and, at the end of the story, with Dumbledore. That's the universal epiphany that we all have at some point and this is the story where Harry has it. It's kind of a loss of innocence in one way, but it's also a gaining of something else.

DAVID YATES: Right at the beginning, you always have rehearsals with any actor you work with. With Dan, in particular, who had to go through this quite complex journey, we sat down several months before we started shooting and would meet every week to talk about what Harry was dealing with. One of the things we did, and it sounds quite intense for a family film, is we brought in a bereavement counselor to talk to us about how Harry Potter dealt with witnessing the death of Cedric. This woman came in to talk to both of us about how people deal with quite intensive emotional and disturbing experiences. She deals with people in the police and rescue services who, every day, witness trauma and death, and she kind of showed us how people process that and deal with that and what it does to them.

DANIEL RADCLIFFE: Harry's two main relationships in the story, first with his godfather Sirius Black and also Cho

Chang, are grounded in a mutual need to bond with another person after a great shared loss. Sirius is clinging on to James Potter, Harry's father and Sirius' best friend, through me, and I'm trying to know my father through him. The same thing happened with me and Cho. I was the last person there when her last boyfriend, Cedric, was killed.

KATIE LEUNG: Throughout this movie, Cho is very lonely, very solitary. She prefers to be alone, she doesn't want to have friends around and basically, she hasn't gotten over the death of her boyfriend. She is a very complex character. There's still that issue with Harry — she likes him, but at the same time, she's not over Cedric, so she just gets very, very complicated. As the story progresses, it's obvious that the relationship between her and Harry is ill-fated.

DANIEL RADCLIFFE: Their relationship is *so* complicated. Basically there's two instances in the film of Harry having a friendship or a relationship with someone, and sort of through that he reaches a dead person [*laughs*]. Harry and Cho both knew Cedric, and so through each other they feel guilty about it, but at the same time it's almost therapeutic, because they've both lost someone. It's a similar situation with Harry and Sirius, because Harry gets to know quite a lot about his father through knowing Sirius. And Sirius gets a sort of younger version of James in Harry, so they're both very complex relationships. Hopefully, that comes across in the scene with the kiss with Katie.

I was slightly nervous about that scene, because I knew Katie was so nervous. There was lots of courtesy chewing gum going in my mouth that day. But we did it a few times and then it wasn't a big deal, really. But it's odd. It's quite a clinical sort of thing, because you're there and you'll sort of be in the kissing position and someone will say, "Dan, move to your right." And you sort of do that. And it's just a very odd thing to do. I mean, it'd be a nightmare if you were actually kissing someone and someone said, "Move to your left." It'd be bizarre.

KATIE LEUNG: Cho's grief was tough to play, because I haven't known anybody who's died, so I wouldn't really know that feeling. But through friends whose family members have died, it's clear that it's very hard to see how you're supposed to go forward. And just before I did any scenes that involved any sort of emotion, David Yates would always speak to me about it and he would explain to me how Cho would feel, with his quiet and gentle voice. It was heartbreaking listening to Cho's story. He would tell me that she just lost her boyfriend, and she's all alone and people are blaming her for messing up Dumbledore's Army, she's got nobody on her side. When he told me that, I just felt like breaking into tears, because I just felt so sorry for her. That really helped; that really put me in the right mood.

DANIEL RADCLIFFE: It's a sort of slightly odd relationship between the two of them because it's a relationship forced by death. If Cedric hadn't died, he would still be with Cho, probably. That's why there's an overwhelming sense of guilt all the time, I think, but at the same time he can't sort of resist.

DAVID YATES: At the start of our story, and it kind of hangs over the entire story like a shadow, Harry is having to come to terms with what he witnessed, the tragedy he's seen and how it's affected him. Dan was able to glean quite a lot from what the grief counselor showed us and what she'd learned talking to people about death. That was useful and helpful in the development of Harry's journey in our film. Death is part of the subtext of the film and Sirius black is a hugely important figure to him, because he represents the only family he's got left after his mom and dad were killed.

MICHAEL GOLDENBERG: Both Dan and Gary Oldman have amazing chemistry; a real connection between them that you can see on screen. In a funny way, I think Sirius' death in the film may be more intense than in the book, because in the book you're spreading it out over a certain period. But because the film really has to focus and economize story wise, we really do get to see how much Harry depends on Sirius. And how in this story Sirius is kind of the one person who understands him and what he's going through, and who Harry can confide in. As much as Ron and Hermione love him, they don't really get what he's going through, and Sirius is the last living member of his family. His death represents, for Harry, another kind of loss of innocence, but by the end, the kind of experience that tempers a leader and gives them what they need to lead an army and ultimately face off against an antagonist as terrifying and powerful as Voldemort.

DANIEL RADCLIFFE: Harry's anger grows in this film and he worries he's becoming more like Voldemort. That's sort of always been the worry for Harry, because ever since the first film when the hat said, "You should be in Slytherin," he realized that he's got that potential for evil inside of him. That's what that must mean. And to a certain extent, I think he knows everything that has that same potential for darkness in them. But, at the same time, because there is such a connection with Voldemort, he thinks this sense of evil must be stronger in him than it is in other people. I think Sirius is the person who really helps him through that situation. He basically says our choices are what defines us as being good or bad in the world. I think that's a very true sort of statement, actually.

EMMA WATSON: The book and film deal, in part, with how the Ministry of Magic begins to restrict personal freedoms and civil liberties following a wave of attacks. I think this film was and is quite relevant to what we're all experiencing. Hermione, who is so clever and willing to learn, can't accept this and becomes the leader of the rebellion. Which is quite strange indeed, considering how she's always been against rule-breaking and everything. In this film she learns to see things from a different perspective. Somehow it talks about life after tragedy. The way people behave when they're scared; the way truth is often denied and all the things our society has to face. Facing the fact that the authority is corrupted means having a non-conformist approach to reality and power.

DAVID YATES: Instead of a constructive, strategic response to the threat of Voldemort, what they end up doing is closing down and ultimately stifling the wizarding community by taking quite conservative measures. An interesting theme in the fifth book and our film, consequently, is how fear can sometimes make people do terrible things to their own community and their own society. We're not in any way trying to parallel anything — we're trying to deal with what fear does to people and people with authority and the responsibility of leadership.

DANIEL RADCLIFFE: At first Harry is reluctant, but he is talked into it by Hermione, who, as usual, is irritating, but happens to be right on this occasion. So we go underground and form Dumbledore's Army. Harry becomes their teacher, using the knowledge he has gained to train the students and teach them how to fight. The way he looks at it, there is a war coming, and there is a sense of growing danger. If Umbridge isn't teaching us what we need to do, we won't stand a chance when we are called upon to fight.

EMMA WATSON: They know that if they are not learning spells, then they will be unable to defend themselves. And while the Ministry is in denial that Voldemort has returned, *they* are not. They believe Harry; they know there is something dark and scary out there. I think that's the reason that, for the first time in her life, Hermione feels the need to rebel. It's the first time she realizes that doing what you're told all the time doesn't quite work. You can't always trust.

RUPERT GRINT: One of my favorite scenes is the formation of Dumbledore's Army; that's very good. It's the students forming a sort of underground, secret sort of army, and we get to do some stunts and things like that. The forming of Dumbledore's Army is definitely where the heart of the film is, because it's all about friendship and loyalty and that sort of thing.

DANIEL RADCLIFFE: In the books, Dumbledore founded it about 15 or 16 years before our story. The Order means a lot to Harry, because, of course, his parents were in the Order of the Phoenix, as was Dumbledore as was Sirius and Lupin the first time around. I think it's got quite an emotional value to Harry as well, as just being a chance to fight Voldemort.

DAVID HEYMAN: To see Harry go from classmate to teacher represents a critical moment in his character arc. We see Harry start out being a bit of an outsider, feeling like people do not trust him, do not believe him, thinking he doesn't belong anymore. Then, ultimately, he finds out that he *does* belong. And not only does he belong, but he has people who are willing to follow him. That's a really powerful and moving thing, watching Harry go from feeling isolated, even within his group, to becoming a leader of that group. Moreover, he is a better teacher than some he has had.

The battle eventually comes as a half-dozen young wizards work together, casting spells that they've only just learned, though their opponents are Death Eaters. As those teens are on the verge of being vanquished, Sirius Black brings in the Order of the Phoenix.

MICHAEL GOLDENBERG: Trying to capture the essence of what was in the book and shape it for the screen was a real balancing act. We wanted to make sure there was a real sense of danger — that anything could happen and anyone could live or die. That's what keeps people on the edge of their seats.

PAUL HARRIS (fight choreographer): David Yates wanted me to set rules of engagement for fighting with the wands, which had not been established in the previous films. He wanted a range of movements and positions from which the spells could be delivered, but they had to be unique to the world of Harry Potter.

DAVID YATES: The battle between Voldemort and Dumbledore needed to be epic and visceral. I wanted audience to feel that they were inside the battle, experiencing it firsthand, so we tried to use a hand-held camera whenever possible.

TIM BURKE (visual effects supervisor): David Yates came up with the inspired idea to keep everything grounded in the elements — fire, water, sand. It's all very logical and, at the same time, astounding.

DAVID YATES: Ultimately when you are watching this great battle between Dumbledore and Voldemort, it is the climax of the first five stories thus far. We had a duty to make it the most spectacular battle between good and evil, with Harry at its center.

DAVID HEYMAN: What they are ultimately fighting for is Harry's soul. And in the midst of that, Harry, who had begun the story feeling completely isolated and alone, even among his friends, finally sees that he has been given a priceless and irreplaceable gift of the people in his life.

DANIEL RADCLIFFE: What Harry realizes is that Voldemort may have the followers and the power, but, ultimately, he will never have what Harry has, which is the true and unconditional loyalty of his friends. Unconditional is the important word, because Voldemort's followers stay with him because if they tried to leave, they would be killed or tortured. Whereas the people who surround Harry and the people who Harry looks up to don't care about what happens. No matter what, they will stand by each other and that's what Voldemort does *not* have.

DAVID HEYMAN: And Harry has been given something by his mother and by his friends that Voldemort will never have — the gift of love.

In many respects, the makers of Harry Potter and the Order of the Phoenix *feel that its storyline and what they had achieved resulted in the strongest entry of the series to that point.*

DAVID HEYMAN: I think the performances are astonishing. You see Dan Radcliffe exposed with nuances and depth that he hadn't shown before. That's largely because he's had the experience of working with Chris Columbus, Alfonso Cuaron and Mike Newell, and also where he is in life itself. I think you can see an incredible performance. I also think this film is incredibly tightly-structured and the direction has real dynamism. It's the most emotional of the first five films. There are themes of isolation that David Yates really captured, with Harry becoming something of an outsider and gradually being brought back into the fold by his friends. I think the very nature of Voldemort beginning to enter Harry's mind and mess with it, has necessitated a means for us to gain a better understanding of Harry and where Harry is.

DANIEL RADCLIFFE: Not only is this about politics — and that's one of my favorite things about the film — but it's dark and it's about Harry growing up and realizing that not all adults are friendly. It's something he sort of got a glimpse of before, but he really sees it in this film, because the dark remnants of society are sort of existing right at the top echelons of society as well as with the Ministry. And at the same time, it's a story about teenagers growing up and Harry falling in love for the first time. And the comedy is stronger and slightly more adult as well, I suppose, than it has been previously.

MICHAEL GOLDENBERG: While the effects are absolutely spectacular, especially the battle between Voldemort and Dumbledore, I think what we come away with from these movies is not how cool they are to look at, but how much we love and care about these characters. You've never seen characters grow up on film like this; you've never seen a story evolve this way. What I admire is that Jo has taken risks and never played it safe. The stories are darker, psychological, political; there is such integrity to them. They've grown in sophistication and complexity and depth; just as the characters have. I can't think of anything that compares with that.

DANIEL RADCLIFFE: We know that a war is coming and it's a real sense of a growing danger that you can't quite define. And things become scarier when you can't put a name to them. *That's* what it is in this film. We know it's Voldemort, but we don't know when it's going to happen or how it's going to happen or what form it will take. That's the sort of theme that really drives this film forward, the sense of mounting tension over a war that's imminent.

Harry Potter and the Order of the Phoenix *was released on July 11, 2007 in the US and July 12, 2007 in the UK. The budget was reported as being between $150 million and $200 million, and its global box office take was $942.2 million.*

Harry Potter and the Order of the Phoenix: Behind the Scenes Interview Section

ONE-ON-ONE WITH MEMBERS OF DUMBLEDORE'S ARMY

Looking at the making of the film with the actors who play Ginny Weasley, Neville Longbottom, Luna Lovegood and Fred and George Weasley

While most of the attention on the Harry Potter *films justifiably goes to Daniel Radcliffe, Emma Watson and Rupert Grint, there is a virtual army of actors who play supporting roles and add to the reality being created by the filmmakers. In the following Q&As, you'll meet Bonnie Wright, who plays Ginny Weasley; Matthew Lewis, so endearing as Neville Longbottom; Evanna Lynch, who makes her debut in the film as Luna Lovegood; and James and Oliver Phelps, who play Ron and Ginny's twin brothers, Fred and George Weasley.*

BONNIE WRIGHT ("GINNY WEASLEY")

How do you compare yourself to your character, Ginny?

BONNIE WRIGHT: I think in the first few films she is quite shy, but as the films go on, she's gotten more outgoing and feisty, especially in *Order of the Phoenix*. And I think that's more going towards me. I'm not a very shy kind of person, so I think as she's gotten older, she's gotten closer to who I am really.

How do you feel about getting more screen time in the past few movies?

BONNIE WRIGHT: It was really fun to film. The big scenes in the Ministry of Magic were really good. Concentrating on the six of us from Dumbledore's Army was really good. It's a few more characters to focus on.

This particular novel was very dark. Do you think this movie reflects that same sort of seriousness?

BONNIE WRIGHT: Yes, definitely. The few scenes I've seen are definitely more spooky than the last four — but spooky in a good way. Everything is serious and that's really reflected in the film.

Do you enjoy being a part of the stunts?

BONNIE WRIGHT: In the Ministry of Magic, there were quite a lot of different stunts. There's a scene where we fall thousands of feet, and that was really fun to film, because we were literally flying through the air.

How does David Yates compare to the other directors of the films?

BONNIE WRIGHT: He was a more personal director. He definitely added a more personal kind of relationship level. As a result of that, we all kind of have this strong bond and relationship together, especially the people in Dumbledore's Army. He really brought that through, and it definitely shows in the film.

In the next book, Ginny and Harry Potter get to kiss. Are you nervous about that?

BONNIE WRIGHT: Yes, it was quite weird when I did read it. It will be daunting and kissing on camera is always a bit scary.

Have you and Daniel talked about it at all?

BONNIE WRIGHT: Not much, just briefly. I suppose we'll see when we come to it.

What aspects of the darker storyline are you most intrigued by?

BONNIE WRIGHT: Well, in this film, it becomes really clear that Voldemort is back, and everyone becomes more aware of it, and that's sort of what Dumbledore's Army in *Order of the Phoenix* kind of brings through to the Ministry. And I think in this film and in the next film, the sixth one, it will be interesting to see how Voldemort comes through and what will happen.

What was your favorite scene to film?

BONNIE WRIGHT: Definitely all the Dumbledore's Army in the Room of Requirement scenes were really good. There was a lot of energy in the room. And then also, the Ministry of Magic scenes were definitely among my favorites because of the acting side of it; that was the most challenging to film.

Why do you think Harry Potter has become such a global phenomenon?

BONNIE WRIGHT: Although it's in a world of its own, it still touches on global issues that you face as a child, and I think that's why it's been so wildly effective on children. Also, because it's in a world of its own, you detach yourself from normal life and you relate to the story as it all comes through.

MATTHEW LEWIS ("NEVILLE LONGBOTTOM")

Before we get into some specifics about Order of the Phoenix, *it would be great to get a sense of what you enjoyed most about being on the set.*

MATTHEW LEWIS: I have always thought that the best part about reading a book or watching a film is that you forget everything else that's going on around you and you immerse yourself in this universe. That's what happens whenever I read a book, and as soon as that book is closed, you come right out of it. But on the set, I really do feel that you are able to forget about your life for a moment. It feels like I'm doing it for real and it's strange to get all dressed up. You know, you've got all your makeup on and you're around all of these props and you see the other characters — all of it is just very bizarre. But it's a great way to forget about everything and become somebody else for a while. It's good to do something else, because being myself gets a bit boring.

Would you say that Neville is different in Order of the Phoenix *from how we've seen him in previous Harry Potter films?*

MATTHEW LEWIS: If you look at him in the first four films, he's kind of soft. I don't think he's as soft in this one. He's shy, vulnerable and very nervous about all the things he has to do at Hogwarts, but then all these things around him start happening that he knows just isn't right. He totally believes Harry when it comes to Voldemort being back and he hates everything Voldemort stands for, because he took his parents away from him. So Neville has something to fight for when Harry starts this rebellion named Dumbledore's Army. He's terrified and has no idea how he's going to help, but he does know that he wants to help in some way. So you really get to see another side of him that's honorable and courageous.

How would you compare and contrast yourself to Neville?

MATTHEW LEWIS: I'd like to believe that I have a bit more courage than he does when he's at school, although, as I say, in the new film you'll see him be more courageous. So I guess I'm not too different in that respect now. I'm a little better at schoolwork when I do it; a bit more accomplished in that area. But like Neville, I'm very forgetful. I'm clumsy as well and knock things over all the time. My parents are always saying, "Oh, that was a Neville moment."

Do you have a favorite scene that you enjoyed filming in Order of the Phoenix?

MATTHEW LEWIS: I would say it's the final fight scenes in the Ministry of Magic when we're in the Prophecy Room. I've never really done anything like that before — the stunt guys were there training us, because there was a lot of running about and colliding into each other and jumping off high platforms and things like that. It was really active.

EVANNA LYNCH ("LUNA LOVEGOOD")

Would you say there are any similarities between you and Luna?

EVANNA LYNCH: Yes, quite a few. We both have kind of alternative taste and are not shy about expressing that. We're both creative and don't like everything to have a basis in fact. I think we're both open-minded and we both love animals. I would also say that our taste in clothes is very similar. I proudly and happily wore her clothes, and I think she would wear mine, too. I believe that almost anything is possible if you see the possibilities rather than the obstacles. Luna has some very unconventional beliefs that need no basis in fact. While I don't share them, I think it shows us that she won't believe things are untrue until you have some very firm evidence.

Order of the Phoenix *is your first film, and I'm just wondering how nerve-wracking an experience was it in the beginning?*

EVANNA LYNCH: Extremely. I was quite intimidated by all the actors, having worshipped them for a long time. They didn't try to be intimidating, but that just happened. I was also afraid of being the one who would mess up the scene and they would have to keep cutting because of me. But the nerves also went away quickly, because there is such a nice atmosphere on the set and it's easy to fit into the family quite quickly. It calmed me down to see that most of the time, no one gets the scene on the first take.

Does this happen to be your favorite Harry Potter book?

EVANNA LYNCH: It does. I love it because it is the book where Harry goes through such a transformation. He has a different, darker perspective of the world and he has to endure so much slander in this book. It makes him grow and become more independent. He is definitely more alone, less protected and he realizes that Dumbledore and many people he relied on make mistakes, too.

Did entering the world of Harry Potter the way you have live up to the expectations you had built up in your head?

EVANNA LYNCH: In a different way to what I was expecting. I thought I would be reliving the book of *Order of the Phoenix*, but it wasn't like that at all. I was a little bit heartbroken to find that all the sets were in separate parts of the studio or that some of them had been dismantled. Also, as I got to know the actors, I realized how different a lot of them are from their characters — extremely nice, but different. As a fan, that was tough to learn at first. But I made so many good friends and met so many interesting people and I didn't expect that at all. I didn't think I'd fit in as well as I did, but I had the best time with all those people and I looked forward to it every day. It didn't matter whether it was a Monday morning or a Saturday morning. I loved either.

Was there something special for you about being on set?

EVANNA LYNCH: I love being abler to relive certain parts of the books. It's fun when we are doing a particularly long scene and can really get into it and I can pretend I really am Luna. I'm so glad that I can portray Luna; I can add my personal touches to her, to a certain degree. I adore her, and I'm not sure I'd trust anyone else to accurately portray my vision of Luna.

JAMES & OLIVER PHELPS ("FRED & GEORGE WEASLEY")

Since you guys have been around from the beginning, has there been an opportunity for your characters to evolve over the course of the films?

JAMES PHELPS: I think they weren't as expressive in the first two films as they were in the novels in terms of their mischief. In the third and fourth films, they became more mischievous — especially now in the fifth one, where they're up to all sorts of mischief.

OLIVER PHELPS: The first time I ever went on the set I'd never been so scared in all my life. There were hundreds of crewmembers and everyone at work on the film, but now it's become much more of the norm to see so many people. At the same time, every time I went into work, I still thought how privileged I was to be doing the job I was doing.

Can you describe the working relationship with each of the directors?

OLIVER PHELPS: They were quite different in their styles. We obviously got used to filming with Chris to begin with, and then when Alfonso came on to it, he was very much into changing how the characters spoke in terms of cutting each other up a lot. He was quite keen to keep that in. And when Mike came in, he was very hands-on. I remember there was one scene where we had to have a fight, and we weren't fighting the way that Mike wanted us to fight, so he came marching over and said, "Who wants to fight me, then?" I said, "Yeah, okay," and Mike jumped on top of me and proceeded to show me how he wanted me to fight. And Dave is quite the opposite. He's quietly spoken and much more into what a character is going to be thinking at a particular moment. I think we seem to have learned quite a lot from the different directors and their styles.

Are you pleased he's coming back for Half-Blood Prince*?*

JAMES PHELPS: I think it's always nice to keep the train going, especially as we had a good time shooting the last film. We haven't seen the final product yet, but from what we *have* seen, it's absolutely superb. So I'm sure they know what they're doing when they appoint Dave to direct the next film.

On screen, we see you goofing around with Rupert and the others, but what is the behind-the-scenes relationship like and how has it changed?

OLIVER PHELPS: It hasn't really changed at all, especially with Rupert. If anything, we've gotten a lot closer. We like playing golf with each other, we go to rock concerts and everything, we hang around a lot and have become really good friends with Rupert, especially. More because he doesn't have to be tutored like the others as he's finished school.

JAMES PHELPS: Like Oliver was saying, while the other guys are in school, we're able to hang out and have a great time doing whatever catches our eye.

And it actually plays on camera that you guys have gotten a lot closer.

JAMES PHELPS: It really is kind of like brothers. All three of us know what to say, what not to say and what will push someone the wrong way. That's always fun to know.

So far, your movie credits are limited to the Harry Potter films. Are you planning on trying to go beyond that at some point to seek other roles?

JAMES PHELPS: I'd like to try and work behind the camera, to be honest with you, in an assistant director role eventually. I worked on the crew at the end of the fourth *Harry Potter* and on *The da Vinci Code*, because a lot of the crewmembers went on to shoot that. I really enjoyed that aspect of just being part of the team.

OLIVER PHELPS: I'd like to do a bit of both, really, in terms of acting and working behind the scenes. We didn't go into this thinking we were going to have a life in the movies, largely because there are not a great deal of movie people from our part of the world. So it will be nice to continue with the acting, but the competition is so fierce, which is why I think you obviously have to look behind the camera as well.

THE MINISTRY OF DESIGNERS

Harry Potter production designer Stuart Craig is entrusted with the task of giving each film a unique look

The word family is bandied about a lot on movie sets, but in the case of the Harry Potter films, that seems to have been the absolute truth, as the vast majority of the cast and crew have been working together for many years. One of those people is production designer Stuart Craig, whose job is to create the look of the numerous sets featured in the films.

What would you say was your biggest challenge with Order of the Phoenix?

STUART CRAIG: Remember, I've done all the films, which, in a freelance industry, is quite amazing. Normally, by going from project to project, it's a way to keep things fresh and keep a variety in your life. But with *Harry Potter*, amazingly with every novel J.K. Rowling finds some major new ingredient that has a huge visual impact on the films.

And what was that ingredient this time out?

STUART CRAIG: This time, it was the Ministry of Magic, away from Hogwarts, away from where we've placed Hogwarts — Scotland — and in London. We decided this time to make a parallel universe. We went to Whitehall, where all of the real government ministries are, and decided that this underground ministry, the Ministry of Magic, would literally be a parallel universe under Whitehall. That was a big challenge and it was a combination of a big set, or several big sets, and a lot of CG magic as well in terms of set extensions. And for the first time ever, we have made our first entirely digital set. I know that George Lucas has been doing that for a few years now, but it was the first time on the *Harry Potter* sets.

What is the digital set?

STUART CRAIG: Within the Ministry of Magic, there is a Department of Mysteries and the Hall of Prophecies is a big part of that, and a big part of the final showdown in the film, the denouement. There are a whole series of rooms that get more and more mysterious and threatening, but the Hall of Prophecies is entirely digital. I'm pleased to have done that, and I feel as though I've entered the 21st century at last.

Was this your first digital set?

STUART CRAIG: We've done lots of set extensions. There were a lot of visual elements in *Goblet of Fire*, including the World Cup stadium. A lot of that stadium was a CG set. So this is not the first, but it's the first one that's *entirely* CG.

Are there any differences from your point of view in creating a real-world set and a digital one?

STUART CRAIG: There isn't. Our department is made up of people drawing on computer and, in the same room, people whittling pencils and still drawing with pencil and mahogany and T-squares. The results are entirely the same, and even on these entirely computer-generated sets, we would sometimes still produce pencil drawings, which were then redrawn digitally and modeled. It's the same discipline.

Were there any sets in the film that were particularly challenging to you?

STUART CRAIG: Certainly it was challenging to conceive of this underground world and what it would be made of. In the end, as I often do, I just start with a simple bit of research and think it through logically. I said, "Underground spaces. What do you think of? The underground London train, of course." We went to some of the older stations and realized that they were entirely lined with ceramic tile, but — better than that — the ceramic tile was also very richly decorated.

Which served as an inspiration?

STUART CRAIG: A little piece of research like that may sound very obvious, but it gave the key and a way in to the whole thing. So we built this enormous world of highly reflective surfaces of ceramic tile and decorative, too. In terms of challenging, I must say that that gave the director of photography a *huge* challenge. He felt absolutely persecuted by me and the art department, because it seemed that that every surface he faced was mirrored in some way, which was very frustrating to him. But he rose to the challenge.

Last year in talking about Goblet of Fire, *I remember you said that the one thing you really wanted to do was get upstairs in Dumbledore's office to show it off. Did you get that chance this time out?*

STUART CRAIG [*laughs*]: No. It's still there, waiting to be seen. We did take a camera up there, but we looked out of there, away from it, so it remains an ambition.

As the director, did David Yates bring anything different to the table in terms of the look of these sets?

STUART CRAIG: The succession of different directors does make it, for me, fresh, and they all have slightly different priorities. David had a way of achieving, and insisted on, great clarity in the storytelling. So he wasn't looking for, as designers often enjoy, huge, elaborate establishing shots. I haven't seen the final film, but it's very pacey in a good way.

You get into the scene and the performances very quickly and immediately, so if the set has a message, it is delivered in one key wide shot, and we don't linger on things. It's good for the film and it's good for the design.

BRINGING ACTION TO THE POTTERVERSE

Stunt coordinator Greg Powell's mission is to thrill audiences while keeping his cast safe from harm

Another Harry Potter behind-the-scenes player is Greg Powell, who has served as stunt coordinator on the film, and who has worked with Daniel, Rupert and Emma from the very beginning. What follows — from Greg's point of view — is a look at his role in the making of one of filmdom's greatest sagas, particularly in terms of the challenges facing him on Harry Potter and the Order of the Phoenix.

As far as the kids are concerned, has there been an evolution in what they can or can't do between Sorcerer's Stone *and* Order of the Phoenix?

GREG POWELL: Oh, yeah, absolutely. When the kids started, as you can see in the film, the action things they did there are a lot different compared to what they're doing now. They're more physical now, they train more and are able to do so much. Like any film with young kids, you can only do so much before you have to get the doubles in, but we've always tried to do all the stuff that we can with Dan, Emma and Rupert.

Teenagers think they're indestructible anyway.

GREG POWELL: I must say that the three of them have always listened very well, taken our advice on how to do stuff. They've always said, "Oh, I want to do that," and when we've said, "Well you can't," they've all taken that well.

Now that you're on the fifth film, do you find that they're trying to push to be able to do more?

GREG POWELL: They definitely want to do more. As soon as the action stuff comes up, the kids are in there as quick as anything, really keen to do it.

Of the three leads — Daniel, Rupert and Emma — do you find any one of them takes more to the physical aspects of the film?

GREG POWELL: Dan has always led the way, because he's always been in the action, whereas Rupert, who has done bits and pieces of the action, has not. Emma is very game to do stuff as well, but because of the way the films are, it's always Dan who's been in the middle of things.

For you, what was the toughest or most challenging aspect of this film?

GREG POWELL: It's not just one thing, it's getting everything right, because each director's got a different view on how things are done, and they slightly change things each time. The fight in the Veil Room, for instance, that took quite a while to work out. It might not be much on film, but there are differing interpretations of things, so that's got to be worked out. But all the films are challenging, especially with the kids, because it's harder to do stunts with them than with grownups. But as I said, I think the Veil Room sequence is definitely the big one.

When you're coordinating a battle, such as the one in this film, do you try and create individual or specific group movements in combat?

GREG POWELL: You try to approach it as individually as you can. You try to find out what they feel, how they would like to fight, what they see, and we tend to do two or three different fights or movements in order to create something different. Everything's sort of been done before, but we definitely try and work on different styles for each individual performer. A lot of the fights in Potter films are done with wands, with people being blown back on their feet or lifted up in the air.

Even though it's an action sequence, when you're working on something like the death of Sirius Black, do you go for something more nuanced than him just getting blasted by a wand?

GREG POWELL: The fight with Sirius Black is fought with wands, but what we tried to do was approach it as though they were using swords, spinning around, doing a parry and that sort of thing, and at the end of the wand comes these spells. So it's like a swordfight, only from 10 or 12 feet apart.

Does any aspect of this film stick out in your mind?

GREG POWELL: All the films have been the same to me, to be honest with you. When we did the first one, we did the flying broomstick, then we had the flying car, we've had the hippogriff — to do stuff and see the finished product, how it turned out, and all the work that went into it, it's all satisfying. The whole *Harry Potter* thing has been a ride and a challenge with all of the different things they've thrown at us to do. They've employed me on each *Harry Potter* film, so I couldn't have done that bad a job. Hopefully I'm around for the next two.

HARRY POTTER TAKES FLIGHT

Visual effects may allow him to fly, but special effects supervisor John Richardson is the man who gets Harry off the ground

Right from the beginning, the Harry Potter *films have been filled with a variety of amazing sequences that have all been designed to allow the audience to believe in the magical setting of Hogwarts. Among the most impressive have been the sequences involving students climbing atop their broomsticks and taking flight, usually for games of Quidditch.*

When watching any of these scenes, from Harry Potter and the Sorcerer's Stone *to* Order of the Phoenix, *the genera; impression is that all aspects of flight have been handled by the visual effects department, but what few people may realize is that much of it starts with physical effects — a.k.a. elements that are done live on set, or "in camera." Veteran special effects supervisor John Richardson, whose credits include the first* Superman *movie in 1978 (yes, he's helped both the Man of Steel and the Boy Wizard to fly), has been there from the start of the film series.*

JOHN RICHARDSON: As always with Potter, the challenges are many and varied. Because there are now six of them — we've begun work on *Half-Blood Prince* — they all tend to blur into one. But starting at the beginning of *Order of the Phoenix*, one of the first conversations I had with director David Yates was that he wanted to get more out of the broomstick flying. In this film, there's not a vast amount of broomstick flying, as in a Quidditch game, but with the broomstick flying that there is, he wanted to have much more of a reality of movement. From there, we did a twofold thing. One was to try and come up with something that gave us a better flowing movement than we've had before. The other thing was to bear in mind that when we had originally designed these broomstick flying rigs, they were designed for kids weighing 120 pounds. Over the years, they upgraded a little bit for each subsequent film, but on *Order of the Phoenix*, we decided to rebuild them from the ground up, so to speak — while at the same time changing the method of doing it. Although we still use the same technology and we still use part of the original configuration of the rigs, we put it in a whole new rig environment, which gave us a lot more movement and it made the riders move better on the broomsticks.

As I say, it's only for a little bit of film here or there, but what I think it does is look and flow much better than it has in the past. And part of the jerkiness you do see on film comes from the fact that we build the rig, but we're still following the pre-vis we get from visual effects. Basically, what we do is feed their pre-vis movements into our system, and the system then movies the way it's being told to.

How would you describe this system?

JOHN RICHARDSON: It's a four-winch wire flying system that gives us the ability to move people, things or even the cameras themselves throughout any set of environments with a grid of wires. It was used in the Great Hall, which is a set that's approximately 200-feet by 60-feet, with a winch placed in every corner. And because the winches are computer-controlled, we could program any movement that was needed. In this film we used it for flying the camera in the sequences in the Great Hall where the Weasleys are throwing fireworks up into the air and chasing Umbridge down.

I do think *Order of the Phoenix* is a good example of how different departments on a film have to work together to create the final vision. What we tried to do was a little bit of backwards engineering. We said, "We can get this flow now, so how about changing this or that?" As with everything these days involving visual effects it is much more of a team effort in that we are all striving to get the best on film. So, between the visual effects guys, the programmers, the pre-vis guys and us, we are dove-tailing together much better than we did 10 years ago. I think that's due to a combination of things — it's knowledge for us, it's knowledge they've gained and technology they've gained. A perfect example is that on this film, we shot far more elements for visual effects that we have done in the past. I think they've grown to appreciate that if they have to do something digitally, if we can give them part of it for real, and they can then twist and maneuver that as they want, having a real piece of film allows them to put it all together more effectively.

HARRY POTTER AND THE WORLD OF VISUAL EFFECTS

Harry's big-screen magic is brought to life by the amazing people behind their unprecedented F/X

The way things are going, you simply cannot have a summer blockbuster without a team of visual effects artists who manage to bend reality and bring movies heroes' larger-than-life adventures to life. To provide an inside look at how some of the magic has been accomplished, we turn to Harry Potter *visual effects supervisor Tim Burke to discuss the climactic battle between Voldemort and Dumbledore in* Order of the Phoenix.

Visual effects are always making great strides, but considering you've been involved with the films since Chamber of Secrets, *are there things you can do now that you couldn't before?*

TIM BURKE: I think it all has changed since then, and I believe that the *Harry Potter* films have pushed the boundaries of what you can achieve in visual effects. When you think you've cracked something on one film, along comes the next one and you're really pushing the envelope again. We're employing new, cutting-edge techniques on this one that have some pretty spectacular results.

So, specifically, what could you do on this film that you couldn't on the others?

TIM BURKE: There are several aspects of *Order of the Phoenix*. We used a new software to create photo realistic elemental features, such as fire and water. In the final battle where Dumbledore and Voldemort fight, they are basically using the elements as magic. Dumbledore uses water against Voldemort, while Voldemort uses fire in the form of a serpent. We basically used very new cutting-edge technology that was developed by a company called Flowline. I truthfully don't think we could have achieved such results and such technically challenging work five years ago. Additionally, we employed new facial capture techniques for character animation that allows us to transfer the actors' faces to CG bodies. That, again, I don't think we could have done as well.

Obviously, the battle between them is a genuine highlight of the film, so how did that sequence come back from a visual effects point of view?

TIM BURKE: It's a massive, massive battle. Working with David Yates in the early conceptual stages, it was very important that the drama escalate in the third act, and we started in this very spooky, low-key environment and worked our way up to probably the most spectacular battle between the two greatest wizards, employing various techniques in that battle.

And the spells themselves are not just shooting energy blasts out of the wand — you're creating creatures and different manifestations of the magic they're conjuring, correct?

TIM BURKE: Exactly. They are using the elements and the environment around them. Stuart Craig made a fantastic set in what we call the atrium, and we used green screen at either end of the stage to extend it beyond and really open up the space. Within that, there were fountains with running water and the architecture had a lot of tiles. There were basically ceramic tiles everywhere. At the start, we harken back to the end of *Harry Potter IV*, because we wanted to link something familiar for the audience. At the end of that film, Voldemort and Harry duel in a graveyard, which was probably the biggest thing we'd seen so far in *Harry Potter*. We thought we would use that as a starting point for this battle, so we employed the same spells, which are very energetic, sort of plasma-like, molten metal-type spells between the two wands when they're fighting. That was the basis for the duel, and from that Voldemort conjures up fire, from which he makes this huge animated serpent, 60-feet high, which attacks Dumbledore, and Dumbledore deflects that spell and throws it back at Voldemort, so we've got fire everything. It's quite spectacular.

And he's deflecting the fire with water?

TIM BURKE: From the fountain, and he turns it into this fantastic concept, which is basically a water prison. It gathers up around Voldemort and basically lifts him up and holds him trapped in this vortex of spinning water. The idea is that Dumbledore is trying to capture Voldemort, whereas Voldemort is trying to kill Dumbledore, and eventually Voldemort escapes from that. We shot Ralph Fiennes on a blue screen and did a little dry for wet preshoot with him and put him into the water and gave him sort of a wet look. That worked quite well. But then he escapes from there and they're back into dueling, and then he basically explodes the environment and the whole set, which has all these thousands of glass windows in these offices, shatters and bursts and rains glass. Then he commands the glass to attack Dumbledore, which is quite a spectacular sequence where Dumbledore has to defend Harry and himself from shards of flying glass, which he turns into sand, breaking the glass down to its basic element. It's a very energetic, high-intensity scene which culminates with a little bit of peace and quiet before Voldemort decides to possess Harry, entering Harry's body, and we get into these sequences and images of Harry fighting against Voldemort in a mental way. It's a lot of fun.

DANIEL RADCLIFFE: HARRY POTTER AND BEYOND

While embracing his most famous role, the actor is looking to refine his craft in a variety of projects

(Originally written in Fall 2008)

Occasionally, an actor becomes so defined by a popular role that he's played that it's impossible for him to break away from it. Christopher Reeve, for all the positive reviews he received for other films, will always be associated with Superman; for most people, Mark Hamill will never be anything other than Luke Skywalker.

Daniel Radcliffe is well aware that he faces the same dilemma with the Harry Potter series. But while he maintains his association with the wizard proudly, he's also vigorously working to show that his range extends well beyond J.K. Rowling's bespectacled hero, via such recent projects as the theatrical drama *Equus* and the made-for-TV movie *My Boy Jack*, set during World War I.

"Right now, it's very tricky because of Potter," he says of seeking out other roles. "I don't have a spare moment to make something until at least 2010 somewhere. I do the sixth Harry Potter ... then I'm going to have a break, then I'm going to New York to do *Equus* on Broadway, which will be great. Then I'm going to do *Harry Potter 7*, and by the time that's over, I'll be 100 years old."

Still, undertakings like *Equus*, *My Boy Jack* and last fall's film *December Boys*, about a group of youngsters on the cusp of becoming men, have helped showcase the nearly 19-year-old's abilities to play distinctly un-Harry-ish characters. "Realistically, if another seven-film fantasy series came along tomorrow, I probably wouldn't do it," he says. "I don't think that would be the smartest career move in terms of separating myself and having people see me as an actor, as opposed to a character."

Equus has become Radcliffe's most famous non-Potter project. It's a complex, searing story about a horse-obsessed stable boy who tells his psychiatrist of one particularly harrowing, violent event in his past. Richard Griffiths (Vernon Dursley in the *Potter* films) will also reprise his role as Dr. Martin Dysart on Broadway, a part played by Richard Burton in the 1977 film version. Daniel received strong reviews for the London performances.

In *December Boys*, Daniel had a fumbling romantic scene with a girl, just as he did with Katie Leung as Cho in *Order of the Phoenix*. "Kissing someone on camera is just not sexy, no matter how attracted to them you are," he says. "No matter how beautiful they are, when you're surrounded by crew who are taking measurements on the focus and making sure you're in the right light, it becomes totally clinical. And clinical is not a word I would associate with any good sexual experience."

Although *December Boys* didn't make much of an impact at the box office, "It gave me confidence to think I can do other things, go off and do other movies," Radcliffe says. "That's really nice."

For *My Boy Jack*, Radcliffe took on the real-life role of Jack Kipling, the son of author Rudyard Kipling, who went missing in action at the battle of Loos, aged just 18. Also 18 at the time of filming, spent six days in trenches dug in Ireland to simulate the dirt and grime of the World War I fighting experience. "I felt a closeness to World War I and the people who fought in it," he says, "but I don't think I could ever have a real understanding of what they went through."

In the film, Jack goes off to war despite failing medical tests, due to his poor eyesight, after his patriotic British father uses his influence. "I hope people are moved by the story and it will stick with them," he offers. "To forget all the people who fought is terrible. I think we need to make the effort to remember them and realize how lucky we are to never have to endure those conditions again."

Nevertheless, he adds, he sees some parallels between World War I and the current wars going on in the Middle East. "There was a certain point during filming when it did suddenly occur to us that the film is so relevant, given the current situation. You couldn't help but feel there are parallels between them and when there are boys of Jack's age still going to war. It will certainly resonate with people; people possibly serving in Iraq or Afghanistan."

The only other non-Potter project currently on Radcliffe's horizon is *Journey*, based on the true story of Dan Eldon, a photojournalist who was stoned to death by a mob in Somalia in 1993. However, as noted above, the actor won't be able to begin work on that film until at least 2010 due to his Potter commitments.

"I am absolutely attached to it and it would be amazing to play that part," he says, before sounding a cautious tone. "But people are making assumptions about when it's going to happen and it won't happen — if indeed it does happen — for a while yet."

To prepare for the role, Radcliffe spoke at length with Eldon's family about his life. "They showed me some of his diaries, which the film will be based on mostly. They're incredible. There have got to be 20 books and they're all inches thick. He was someone who died very young, but seemed to live as full a life as much as anyone who lived to be a ripe old age. It will be incredible to play him."

In the meantime, it's full steam ahead for *Harry Potter*. Filming recently wrapped on the sixth film, *Harry Potter and the Half-Blood Prince*. "If we pull it off right, it should be the funniest of the films so far," Radcliffe says, a view backed up by director David Yates, who reminds that the story includes romantic scenes for several characters, including Harry, Ron, Ginny and Lavender.

Bonnie Wright, who plays Ginny, says that if some female fans objected to seeing Harry kiss his first love, Cho, in 2007's *Order of the Phoenix*, they'll really be seeing red after watching Ginny and Harry make out. "But remember," she laughs, "at the end of *Prince*, Harry and I can't be together. It'll be funny to do the make-out scenes, but it's just a film! Hopefully, people will just enjoy it and not get too jealous."

"I knew Bonnie when she was 10, so that's going to be very odd," Radcliffe grins. "It's going to be fine, but it's going to be funny."

Then there's the concluding *Harry Potter and the Deathly Hallows*, which will be made into two films. "It's a really positive thing," Radcliffe says. "And I think the fans will appreciate that more than had we tried to make it into one film. We'd have to cram so much in there and actually have to skip over things. And in the seventh book, there are a lot of things you can't afford to skip over. The challenge now is for David Yates and the writers to find where the breaking point is between the two films, because I don't think there is an obvious place to do so."

Having started this *Harry* journey seven years ago, Radcliffe says that he's gotten used to the enormous amounts of work involved. "*Potter*'s a marathon, not a sprint, as the saying goes," he notes, adding that he expects to spend nine-and-a-half hours a day on *Hallows*. We'll get a break at Christmas, and other than that, you're there," he says. "It's fun for me, because I'm there every day, so you get in a rhythm, a very regular rhythm with it so it's very easy to relax."

Off camera, Radcliffe tries to keep things normal — not so easy when you're listed as the UK's richest teen start, worth $46.5 million. He doats on his two border terriers, Binka and Nugget — the latter, coincidentally, the same name of the lead horse in *Equus*. "They're just great and I love them and miss them very much when I'm not with them,' he says.

Support from his family and friends also plays an important role in keeping him grounded. "They keep you level-headed, just because they're honest and they would never pander to me if I was being demanding or difficult or anything like that. I'm not naturally like that as a person at all. Even if I was, they would slap me down again. I don't understand why actors become arrogant and are completely unapproachable, because as an actor, the most valuable thing you can do is talk to people and hear their stories, because it'll all come in handy."

Asked if he plans to continue acting, Radcliffe grows philosophical. "There are plenty of fields I'm interested in, but acting is certainly the focus for me at the moment," he says. "Hopefully people will do as they've done so far and keep giving me the chance to do that."

Harry Potter and the Half-Blood Prince
Copyright and Trademark Warner Bros. Discovery

CHAPTER SIX: *HARRY POTTER AND THE HALF-BLOOD PRINCE* (2009)

After his near lethal adventure at the Ministry of Magic, Harry spends the summer riding the trains around London. Dumbledore finds him at a café and takes Harry with him. They apparate to another borough where Dumbledore is hoping to convince a reticent Horace Slughorn to return to the school to be the new Potions teacher and he's using Harry to get Slughorn to say yes. As they are leaving Slughorn agrees to return to Hogwarts. As Harry and Dumbledore are walking away, Dumbledore tells Harry that Slughorn will try to "collect" him.

Matters are getting grave not just in the wizarding world, but Muggles are also being targeted as Voldemort gains strength. London's Millennium Bridge is destroyed and wand maker Mr. Ollivander is kidnapped by the dark wizard's Death Eaters. Voldemort feels it is time to move in on Dumbledore, and since his right-hand man, Lucius Malfoy, is locked in Azkaban, he directs Draco to kill Dumbledore. Draco's Mother and Belatrix get Severus Snape to make the unbreakable vow to act as protector to the boy, and to finish the deed should Draco be unable to complete the task.

Things are getting more dangerous everywhere with Voldemort's return and the rise of his slavish and evil Death Eaters. Certain that Draco Malfoy is now a Death Eater, Harry uses instant darkness and the invisibility cloak left him by his father to sneak into the car, up on the luggage rack over the table where Draco is sitting to overhear any upcoming plans. But Malfoy sees a magazine move on the rack and guesses correctly that Harry is up there. Upon everyone leaving the train Draco stays behind and petrifies him, leaving him on the train to return to London. Fortunately, Luna Lovegood comes across the frozen Harry and frees him with a spell of her own.

Finally at school, Harry finds a Potions book lined with helpful notes and attributed to "The Half-Blood Prince," with very detailed and easy to follow margin notes. Harry uses the book to ace his Potions class and accidentally bring about the jealous chagrin of Hermione, usually top of the class, and greatly impressing Professor Slughorn, who gives Harry a vial of Good Luck Potion as a reward. Surprising everyone, Ron has won the keeper position for Gryffindor's Quidditch team. He also has caught the eye of Lavender Brown, which also upsets Hermione. Harry attempts to calm Hermione and sits with her on the stairs. After Ron and Lavender go past Harry talks to her and confirms his feelings for Ron's younger sister, Ginny, when Hermione asks how it feels when Harry sees Ginny with Dean Thomas. At the Burrow, the Weasley home, Belatrix and other Death Eaters attack, enticing Harry and others out in the open and burning it to the ground.

Attempts are made on Dumbledore's life; a possessed necklace that nearly kills Katie Bell, who tries to deliver the gift under the Imperious Curse; the second is a bottle of poisoned mead that Ron takes a drink from — the wine Slughorn intended for Dumbledore — and he nearly dies. Suffering in the hospital, with Ginny and Hermione at his bedside. When Lavender Brown finally arrives in to check on Ron, he whispers Hermione's name, sending the broken-hearted Miss Brown out of the room crying.

Later, Dumbledore asks Harry to get a memory from Slughorn because the one he, Dumbledore, has was altered. Dumbledore is sure the real memory is the key to beating Voldemort. After several attempts and failures, Harry has just the right plan, to use the Liquid Luck that he had won in Potions class. He headed to see Hagrid, and collected Professor Slughorn on his way. After having a small farewell ceremony for Hagrid's dearest spider friend, they go to Hagrid's house where he and Slughorn enjoy considerable mead, Hagrid falls to sleep which leaves Harry alone to convince Slughorn to give him the correct memory. When Harry and Dumbledore finally see the correct memory, they learn that Voldemort was asking about how to make Horcruxes, seven of them. A Horcrux is an object that a wizard can put a piece of his soul into for protection. Then if he is attacked and killed it will be just his body that dies. The piece of soul in the Horcrux will keep his soul alive and he can be brought back to life. Two of them are Riddle's diary and his mother's ring. Dumbledore finally discovers that one is Slytherin's locket. When he and Harry are at the cave where the locket is supposed to be, Dumbledore, makes a cut on his hand and wipes it across the wall of the cave to gain entrance. Now weak from the effects of cutting his hand, they follow the path down to the lake inside the tunnel. Once to the area where the Horcrux is they find a pedestal with liquid in it that must be drunk. Dumbledore insists that he will drink the liquid because Harry is too valuable. The liquid takes its tole and Harry must keep convincing Dumbledore to finish drinking it. Once they get to the bottom Harry tries to get Dumbledore some water, but he gets pulled underwater by the Inferi from which Dumbledore saves him and they make their way out of the cave so they can apparate back to Hogwarts' astronomy tower. Dumbledore sends Harry to get Snape but they hear a noise and Dumbledore tells Harry to hide himself below and not to be seen or talk to anyone without his permission. But Bellatrix and other Death Eaters are in the school thanks to the Vanishing Cabinet that Draco repaired in the Room of Requirement.

Draco is prepared to launch a killing spell on Dumbledore as Harry hides, but the young would-be Death Eater can't bring himself to do it. Severus Snape steps in and, in what seems like the ultimate betrayal to the Head Master, Snape kills Dumbledore, sending his body off the tower to the ground far below. Out of pure joy, Bellatrix destroys the great hall and burns Hagrid's hut to the ground. As Snape, Draco and the other Death Eaters escape, in parting words Snape tells the shocked young wizard that he, Snape, is the Half-Blood Prince.

Dumbledore is mourned by staff and students. Harry finds that the Horcrux they got is a fake, the real one having been snatched long ago. The fake, though, has a message from someone with the initials R.A.B. Harry says he's not coming back to Hogwarts next year and will instead go hunting this R.A.B. and whatever Horcruxes there are out there so he can finally destroy Voldemort. Ron and Hermione again have to insist on joining him in this most dangerous search.

New cast members this time out include Helena Bonham Carter as Bellatrix Lestrange, a Death Eater serving Voldemort; and Jim Broadbent as newly appointed Potion's master Horace Slughorn. Also, for the first time since Chris Columbus, a director returns to the franchise in the form of David Yates.

DAVID YATES: It just felt like a natural progression as the Harry Potter world is shifting a wee bit in that it's getting a little bit more mature, a bit more complex and now that we've kicked it off, it feels natural to see the next stage of it through. And also, I really fell in love with the whole world and became completely involved with the characters. I really liked how Daniel and Rupert and Emma were developing as actors. I wanted to be there to push them in *Order of the Phoenix* and push them more in the next film, because I thought they all could be really great. So it just felt like a natural progression. I had so much fun that it was really hard to walk away when they asked me to stay.

RUPERT GRINT: Actually, each time it's been sort of nerve-wracking meeting a new director, because you get used to the one that you had before. You become comfortable talking to them, and it's quite strange to have a new person each time. It's really good to have something more regular, so I was looking forward to working with David Yates on *Half-Blood Prince*.

DANIEL RADCLIFFE: The great point of a consistency of directors, especially with David Yates, is that we know each other very well professionally. We know how each other wants something to be done, and we're very good communicating with each other. In fact, the other directors were very good communicators, too, but with David, sometimes nothing needs to be said. I'll get to the end of a take and he'll say, "Cut," and I'll say, "That's crap, let's go again immediately," because I know what I will have done will not be what David is looking for.

BONNIE WRIGHT: I think everyone has to kind of create a new film, because it's obviously their film and they want to put a new energy into it. I think he's a real kind of actor/director; he likes to have your opinions gel, he wants you to be a part, I suppose, of what it will end up as. He's thinking about every character and we're thinking mainly about how we're reacting and what we're doing. He's not someone who says, "Right, this is how I want to do it and everyone this is what you're doing." He always kind of lets us know what's in his mind, and I think that's good for us. He's very direct in what he wanted and I think that created a bit more kind of energy and fluency.

EMMA WATSON: At first I was nervous working with David, just because I thought, "Well, I just don't know this guy. I'll go and watch some of his previous work." And just looking at the films he's done, I got into *The Girl in the Café* and *Sex Traffic*, and just the performances he got out of those people in those pieces of work was amazing. I wondered, "How am I ever going to live up to that sort of standard of acting quality?" I was amazed at how real everything was. I guess the thing that occurs to me most about David and the Harry Potter films he's directing is that he really made me feel something. It really makes the audience feel. I know that sounds weird, but I was really so eager and really earnest to live up to his expectations and for him really to get the best out of me that he possibly could. So I was nervous and really excited, because I thought, "Wow, I really think this guy can take me to a new level." Which I think he does with all of us. And it doesn't feel like I've learned all that I can from David. I still feel like there's so much more that I can learn and get out of him. So it's still a really exciting concept even though we're working with the same person again.

DAVID HEYMAN: David continued to push the actors in a good way. A perfect example of that is Tom Felton as Malfoy. I think Tom's always been wonderful, but he's always played it slightly more heightened. He's been the villain, as it were. But in this film, partly because it's in the book, partly because of what we've chosen to emphasize in the script and partly because of what David is bringing out as director, it's a much more complex role and Tom Felton is embracing that. He is the chosen one just like Harry is the chosen one; he's been chosen by Voldemort to kill Dumbledore just as Harry is the "chosen one" and Voldemort is his destiny. Draco is not altogether comfortable with the task he's been given. On the one hand, he's excited about making a name for himself and the import, but he struggles with his conscience and whether it's something he wants or should be doing. And those nuances that Tom is bringing to it is terrific. It feels like a deeper, richer character than we've been able to see to date. So I think David is continuing to deepen the characters. And the comedy is really very human; the awkwardness of romance, how people are brought apart and brought together is done in a very real but very funny way. Listen, I'm very excited about this film. We presented a 20-minute reel to the studio and they seemed very pleased. But let's not kid ourselves, what are they going to say? "We're in trouble here!"

DAVID YATES: *Half-Blood Prince* is very different from the fifth film. Michael Goldenberg did a brilliant, lovely job writing the fifth film, and Steve Kloves came back to write *Half-Blood Prince* and he delivered a really terrific and fun draft that felt different to all the earlier films in a very interesting way. And I thought this series itself was unique in that the audience was growing up with these characters and felt as though they truly knew them.

J.K. ROWLING: I always leave myself latitude to go on a little stroll off the path of my plot, but the path is what I'm essentially following. So much that happens in *Six* relates to what happens in *Seven*. And you really sort of ski off the end of *Six* straight into *Seven*. You know, it's not the discreet adventure that the others have all been, even though you have the underlying theme of Harry facing Voldemort. Whereas in *Six*, although there is an ending that could be seen as definitive in one sense, you very strongly feel the plot is not over this time and it will continue.

DAVID YATES: We took the first presentation of *Order of the Phoenix* to an audience to test it and it was a real revelation to me how much of a connection the audience feels with these characters. We wanted to let that fly in *Half-Blood Prince*, because it's extremely character-driven. It's a great coming-of-age story, ultimately. The romantic elements of it are really key to it — Harry's unrequited feelings for Ginny Weasley, and the relationship that develops between Hermione and Ron is delightful and funny and tender and true. There's a sort of universality to the kind of way those romantic engagements or unrequited moments play out. Anyone who has grown up with a crush on someone or fumbled with a first sort of relationship, will absolutely get what Jo has given us in that book.

DAVID HEYMAN: David Yates is able to bring a genuine reality to everything that he does, and that's very important. With *Half-Blood* Prince, he brought a comedic sense to the film, while at the same time grounding the comedy in reality. He was able to bring the kids to places they might otherwise have been unable to go with someone they hadn't worked with already. Also, the last one was a tightly-wound film, very intense and dark. This one, I think, has more colors, more variety in its palette. It's very emotional, very truthful, very funny and at the same time it has some of those adrenalized moments which are very exciting. What excites *me* — and it was true of each film — is that each one is different and that's what makes it so fresh each time.

DAVID BARRON (producer, *Harry Potter and the Half-Blood Prince*): Each of these films presented an enormous challenge, because even though it's another episode in the life and times of Harry Potter, you never stand still. We continually kick the tires of our operation and try very hard to make sure that we do everything we can in the best way we possibly can give the facilities at our disposal — and Jo with the source material. Because Harry and everyone is another year older in each book, it enables her to each time take a look at different themes and change the tone of each book. Each film feels very different, and we're confronted all the time with big set pieces, the possibility of achieving brilliant effects, huge sets, big crowds — they're all challenging and we never got bored with them. What was particularly new and exciting about this film is this core of wonderful adolescent romance; the entanglement that is sort of new and fresh. We touch upon it very briefly in *Goblet of Fire* and the Yule Ball.

EMMA WATSON: Hermione's part in *Half-Blood Prince* has very much to do with her relationship with Ron, and this kind of new girl who comes on the scene called Lavender, who has a bit of a crush on him. It kind of looks as though, in the beginning of the film, that Hermione and Ron are going to *finally* get it together, and then Lavender kind of steps in and Ron, as usual, is hugely insensitive and quite mean, really. So it's very much about how much she despises Lavender, who's played by Jessie Cave, not only because she's taken Ron away, but because she's kind of the opposite of Hermione. It's very comical and also quite sad for Hermione.

RUPERT GRINT: The romantic scene in this film was okay to shoot, because me and Jessie's relationship was quite funny and over the top and intense, which kind of scared Ron a bit.

That was easy to play. It was quite an awkward scene to do, though, because we'd only known each other for, like, two days and one of the first things we shot was the kissing scene. At first, we were quite self-conscious, because the set we shot in was filled with people, so that was embarrassing, but we got through it.

EMMA WATSON: I got along very well with Jessie Cave, who plays Lavender. There's a great scene where Hermione and Lavender are fighting over Ron, and we had good fun with that. What also sticks out for me are Ron's Quidditch scenes. They're so funny; I was in stitches. Rupert's comic timing is just brilliant and he's so funny.

RUPERT GRINT: I was happy to do the Quidditch scene, but we didn't film it for very long because in the film the Quidditch sequence isn't that long. There was one shot where I had to save a series of quaffles, and there was one shot where they were throwing about 350 of these rubber quaffles. They pelted me and I did actually fall off the broom and was hanging by a wire off the broom. That was a bit embarrassing. My trousers are sort of two pieces and they come apart, which is what happened — that was embarrassing, too. But it was really fun, actually, and it looks really cool as well.

Beyond the romantic and comedic aspects of Half-Blood Prince, *however, are darker elements having to do with Voldemort and, in an effort to do what he can to curb the dark lord's rise, Dumbledore ultimately being sacrificed for the cause.*

DAVID YATES: I think you need the light as well as the shade, and it's good to kind of bounce between the two. Basically the second half of *Half-Blood Prince* and the final third in particular get quite emotional and intense, but I was kind of desperate to pull everything into the light in the first two thirds after *Order of the Phoenix*. There's a balance and there's a balance in the books that Jo finds particularly easy between the wit and the entertainment and the fun, and some fairly dark stuff. We tried to follow her lead in the movies.

RUPERT GRINT: We've all grown up through the films. I suppose it was *Order of the Phoenix*, really, when Dumbledore's Army was starting to form and we had to stand up in this fight against Voldemort — I suppose that's where everything turned a bit nasty and Ron had to grow up. In *Half-Blood Prince*, Ron seems to grow up a lot, because he's got a girlfriend in this one and there's all that going on. I think in *Deathly Hallows* we will see him growing up a little more, because the Wizard world is becoming quite a scary place.

DANIEL RADCLIFFE: The core of *Half-Blood Prince* is paranoia. It's a very, very strong theme in this film, because it's all about Harry's increasing paranoia about Draco Malfoy becoming a member of the Death Eaters. That's part of it, and it's a theme that's part of all of the films, really. The image of Dumbledore knowing all of that is a very, very sad one, because he carries on anyway. He doesn't give up. He absolutely fights to the last minute to try and leave behind him everything that's necessary to eventually lead to Voldemort's undoing. Those are probably the two things at the heart of this film.

TOM FELTON: I had read the script and the book, and it seems like almost everything in the book made it to the movie. I think that fans who truly love the book will be pleased with the way this film plays through. And I was happy, of course, because in the past I would think my role was bigger, and then it would be cut and I would be disappointed. This time, I really have a substantial amount of work to do, and Draco is right in the middle of the battle with Harry and Voldemort.

DANIEL RADCLIFFE: I took the films very seriously when I was 11, and I've taken it more and more seriously as we've gone on. If you've been involved in something for so many years, you want to be able to talk about it articulately and explain why you love it, explain why you love being involved in it so much.

I think the script for *Half-Blood Prince* is great and I think it's a really great film, But I'm just one of those people that, in what I'm doing, I always lean toward the dark side and I really enjoy doing the dark stuff. I know Emma and Rupert really, really like the lighter stories and all that. And Rupert particularly had a field day on this, because he's got fantastic comic timing and he could use all of that to great effect on this film with his relationship with Lavender Brown. But I actually missed the morbid stuff.

DAVID YATES: It does become a dark story. There's the tremendous third act where Dumbledore is killed. There's a wonderful sequence where Harry and Dumbledore are trapped in this cave and this army of the dead kind of comes out of the water to get them. There are some pretty scary things in the story as well as the fun and romantic things.

That sequence comes towards the end of the film with Harry and Dumbledore searching for one of Voldemort's horcruxes that involve them battling the undead. Creating it all represents a showcase of a bit of movie magic.

DAVID BARRON: In visual effects terms, the cavern is the most challenging aspect of the film, which is fun. It's a tremendous sequence because in it we have the Inferi, who are the zombies of our world. Of course, to try and come up with something that is not a generic zombie and not something that immediately makes you think of George A. Romero, who directed *Night, Dawn* and *Day of the Dead*, is difficult, because the moment the words "living dead" are mentioned, those films spring to mind. Obviously, that's the last thing one wants to conjure up, so that was a challenge, but we came up with something quite special and scary.

STUART CRAIG (production designer, *Harry Potter and the Half-Blood Prince*): J.K. Rowling always writes a big scene in a big venue, and in *Half Blood Prince* Harry and Dumbledore go off into a mysterious cave, and that cave is a big challenge. We only physically built two tiny little parts of a huge-scale model and a small physical part of it. Those models are then scanned and the scans of those physical three-dimensional models become the blueprint or the structure on which the CG set is finally made and rendered. It's a challenge in that it needs to deliver dramatically and yet have this fantastic otherworldliness about it. It's another challenge when sets are almost entirely computer-generated. Hardware is comparatively easy and organic, rock forms less so. And it's a challenge for somebody of my generation, frankly, to catch up with 21st century movie technology.

We started by saying, "What's interesting about a cave?" Well, stalagmites and stalactites are probably the most familiar, almost clichéd, of limestone caves. So we started to examine crystal caves and looked to pictures of this incredible quartz crystal cave in Mexico. We did visit one in Switzerland and thought, "What other crystal caves are there?" It turned out to be a salt crystal cave outside Frankfurt in Germany, so we went there and it's part of a vast phosphate mining complex, but there's also rock salt down there. In this one area are salt crystals, which are completely transparent and glass-like. We took extensive photographs and used that as other inspiration. What it's done is given us this fantastic set and fantastic world, but with a bit of geological credibility at the same time.

As noted, Dumbledore and Harry travel to this island in the middle of a black lake and on the island, in the film, there is a crystal reservoir with a liquid in it that Dumbledore has to drink in order to discover the horcrux that lies beneath it.

STUART CRAIG: So we built that island, we built the boat that they travel in and part of the shoreline they leave to get to the island. But they are, like, one percent of the total that you see in the final film.

DAVID YATES: One of the things that Jo has done brilliantly in the books, and something we try to do in the films, is these gear changes between these very intense moments of drama or horror or excitement, with just very delicately drawn character stuff. When you spend this much money on a movie, you have to give the audience spectacle and the fun of a real roller coaster ride, but all of that means absolutely nothing unless at the heart and soul of it are these characters that you care about. That is absolutely foremost to balance the intimate with the epic; to have characters that you love and believe in and that matter to you, within the context of this epic, grand spectacle. If you can hit both levels, you've given the audience a really generous experience.

DAVID BARRON: We actually added a scene that wasn't in the novel. This was brought in because Jo was able throughout the quite lengthy book to keep dropping little snippets of what was happening in the outside world — there's been people reading newspapers and talking about how somebody's parents had been killed, or somebody had been withdrawn from school because their parents didn't think it was safe. We're made aware that the Muggle world is also experiencing these disasters, but thinks they are disasters rather than the world of Voldemort. The book is peppered with those moments, but we couldn't do that quite so easily in the film. So the extra scene comes in the middle of the film, and it just reminds us the world is no longer a safe place. Even in what would normally be considered the safe haven of the Burrow, nobody's safe.

DAVID HEYMAN: *Half-Blood Prince* is the final chapter in Harry's education, as it were, and Dumbledore's preparation for Harry. At the end of it, Dumbledore effectively passes the mantle on to Harry as being the one who can take on Voldemort. In a way, it's the completion of the education of Harry Potter that leads on to the final films. In *Half-Blood Prince*, Harry essentially says goodbye to Hogwarts, suggesting he will never return. I think that but for the fact that his battle with Voldemort leads him back, he would *not* have returned, because his education is complete and his final chapter has begun.

Harry Potter and the Half-Blood Prince *was released July 7, 2009 in the UK and July 15, 2009 in the US. The budget was $250 million and the global box office take was $934.5 million.*

HARRY POTTER & THE HALF-BLOOD PRINCE BEHIND THE SCENES INTERVIEWS

DANIEL RADCLIFFE: COMING TO TERMS WITH HARRY POTTER

While Daniel is enjoying the diversity of the roles he's been playing, he doesn't seem to be in a rush to put Harry Potter behind him

Originally written in 2009

Daniel Radcliffe has literally grown up before our eyes in his portrayal of Harry Potter through the first six films in the series, a truly historical and unprecedented experience for moviegoers. Audiences have seen him mature as he's moved a bit away from the sanctuary of Hogwarts to star on London's West End and New York's Broadway in productions of the controversial Equus, *and he's recently received critical raves for his roles in films like* December Boys *and* My Boy Jack, *proving that there is much more to his magic bag of tricks than just J.K. Rowling's Harry Potter. But as you'll discover from this interview with the actor, he embraces it all with the same amount of enthusiasm.*

Would you say you're still a big kid at heart?

DANIEL RADCLIFFE: Yes, I am. I still love doing normal kid stuff, like listening to music all day, having friends over to watch TV, eating pizza and playing videogames on my PlayStation.

With such devout, adoring fans, how do you manage to keep your feet on the ground?

DANIEL RADCLIFFE: I don't know; I just sort of do it. It's not a conscious thing; I don't sit myself down every night and talk to myself and stop myself from becoming arrogant. I think it's just probably down to my parents, because my parents are really good people and they're not going to let me become arrogant or big-headed, or anything like that. Also, I would never want to be that, because I deplore those values in anyone. I could never get used to this [the fans], though, because it's a bizarre experience, but it's just something you take in your stride.

So the fame and press coverage hasn't gotten to you?

DANIEL RADCLIFFE: You have to laugh against that, because it is bizarre, but it's funny, too. Obviously, there will always be certain things that some people will be able to do and we can't do, and that's fine. But I've also had loads of opportunities through this that have been extended to us, and that's amazing. So we're also very fortunate.

Can you live a normal life?

DANIEL RADCLIFFE: Yes, I can. My life really hasn't changed that much. I'm "famous" for maybe two days a year — at the premieres — but other than that, it doesn't actually come into my life. I know some people find it hard to believe that we can live normal lives — and I can see why some people refuse to believe we're telling the truth or think we're liars when we say that — but we are still able to go out and do things ... although it's often sensible to wear a hat! Not one that draws attention to you, though, like a cowboy hat, but maybe just a baseball cap pulled down.

Given your experience, what advice would you offer an 11-year-old about to embark on starring in a series of films like Harry Potter?

DANIEL RADCLIFFE: I suppose I'd just tell them to make sure that when you're starting out, to tell the people around you to be completely honest with you so that there's no room for sycophants to creep in. I think what makes the difference in terms of growing up in front of media and things like that is if you have people around you that are honest with you and don't just say what you want to hear. If you do have that, then you'll be well adjusted and you won't be arrogant. So, that's the one thing I would say: just be honest.

Speaking of honesty, what's the biggest lie that you've read about yourself?

DANIEL RADCLIFFE: Probably that I insist on a huge chariot to take me to work every morning and, when I'm there, a throne to be carried around in.

Do you think Harry Potter is going to have any lasting legacy?

DANIEL RADCLIFFE: Yes. I think one thing that Harry Potter has actually done is to make wearing glasses have a kind of coolness attached to them. So, I feel that by portraying him, I'm kind of sticking up for any kids who have ever been called four eyes or teased about wearing glasses. I think that is one of the cool things that Harry Potter has given to the world.

When did you know that Harry Potter was going to be with you for the rest of your life?

DANIEL RADCLIFFE: Never, really. I don't think of it in those terms, because for me I just want to be an actor rather than a character. But at the same time, I've loved playing Harry. Like I said, it's given me these amazing opportunities, and so I'd never try to shirk him. The funny thing is that people say to me a lot, "How do you feel about being thought of as Harry for a long time, playing him?" To be honest, I think that some people will always see me as Harry, but that's *their* problem rather than mine. As long as they're not the people that are casting me and directing me, it shouldn't really affect my career in too major a way.

Now that you're 18 and we know you're going to be appearing in all of the Potter films, you're going to be doing young adult roles. It will be a different kind of career. Do you think about that in terms of doing roles that are far away from Harry Potter so that people can see you in different ways? Equus *is a good example.*

DANIEL RADCLIFFE: *Equus* was never about shocking people. *Equus* is just a great play, and if people are shocked by that, again, that's their issue rather than something to do with the play. It's a difficult question. Personally, I just want to carry on doing things that are different and interesting, but it's not just that I want to do something that's different from Harry and different from other characters I've played. I think that any actor who really wants to do this never wants to repeat a performance under the guise of another character name. He wants to go on and do as many different things as he can, and that's actually for me. It's not that I want to distance myself just from Harry, it's that I want to prove to people that I can do as well with other roles. I like to think that I will be fairly versatile. I just need to keep working and keep showing people that.

Going back to when you were a kid, what was the real deal about getting cast as Harry Potter? You'd done David Copperfield *on television and* The Tailor of Panama. *You were a child actor, but I understand David Heyman saw you at a theater and said, "That's the kid we need," and then had to persuade you to do it.*

DANIEL RADCLIFFE: It's not quite as good a story as that. My dad was a literary agent and he'd been working with David Heyman and Norma Heyman on a film that my dad had worked on. Through that connection, David Heyman had asked, after seeing *David Copperfield,* if I would come audition.

At that point, the deal was to do, I think, six or possibly all seven films and they were going to be done in L.A. My parents felt that was too big of a disruption and, frankly, rightly so. I wasn't aware of this at the time, but then later on the theater comes into this. David Heyman spotted me at a theater when we went to see a show called *Stones in His Pockets*. He sat in the row in front of us with Steven Kloves, the writer, totally coincidentally. It was at that point that my parents thought, "Maybe." I personally believe in fate, but my parents thought, "Well, maybe this is a sign. Maybe we should actually listen to this." At that point, they found out that the deal had changed to doing two films and for them to be filmed in London or around London. So then I auditioned and it went from there, really.

Was there ever a point where you wanted to walk away from the Harry Potter films and just be a kid?

DANIEL RADCLIFFE: To be honest, I was quite happy to have acting take over my life. I love acting. It's what I want to do. It wasn't a thing that I had always aimed to do or aspired to do. It was something that as soon as I got to the third Harry Potter film, ^ started taking it more seriously and I just found that I had a real passion for it. You need to know that before you sign up for a film, because it's at least one year of your life, not including publicity and all the rest of it. It's a big commitment, so you think before you do each one. But I don't remember ever thinking, "Gosh, I really don't want to do this film." It was never like that. I was never in a situation where I thought, "If I do this next film, I will be unhappy at that point." It never came to that.

Where do you see your future in terms of schooling and your career as an actor?

DANIEL RADCLIFFE: University is not for me. I don't think so, anyway. I think the two main things that people discover and what university is good for is, you will have a clearer impression of what you want to do with your life. I've got a fairly clear impression of what I want to do with my life: I want to act. Also, you meet people from a lot of different backgrounds, which you do on a film set. So for me, the two things that I would achieve by going to university I've gotten from filming. I've not got a degree, but that's something that I'll have to live with.

What about Hollywood? Your career seems based in the U.K. Have there been offers or just nothing that's interested you?

DANIEL RADCLIFFE: There have been things that we've talked about, but for now I'm quite pleased that it's based in the U.K. or Australia and places like that, because there's a certain almost stigma that I think goes with Hollywood. Especially at such a young age, I want to prove that I can survive in the world outside of Hollywood, in the independent movie world, and that I don't have to be there. There is the stereotype of the movie industry as being very glamorous and it's not all red carpets and champagne. You do work, and though Hollywood isn't probably all glamour, that's the reputation that it has. I want to prove that I don't need to make films there to survive in the industry. I can survive quite happily.

At this stage, are you planning for a goodbye to the character of Harry Potter?

DANIEL RADCLIFFE: No, I'm sort of clinging on to every moment that there is now in a way, because this is the beginning of the end, but I'm not really thinking about that. I'm not thinking too far ahead. I'm just enjoying the moments and hanging on to them while I've got them.

EMMA WATSON RETURNS AS HERMIONE GRANGER

Balancing career and academics is the most important thing to Emma as she prepares for a life beyond Hermione
Originally written in 2009

As has been well documented, Emma Watson seemed somewhat reluctant to sign contracts that would have her reprising her role of Hermione Granger in Harry Potter and The Half-Blood Prince *and the two-part* Harry Potter and The Deathly Hallows. *Many people interpreted this to her becoming a diva and attempting to hold the studio ransom for a higher paycheck, but the truth is that she was more concerned with continuing her education than whether or not she completed the series. Essentially a balance had to be found, which is exactly what happened. In the following interview, Emma details her inner turmoil over this subject, discusses her hopes for the future and reflects on a career filled with magic.*

You seemed hesitant to sign for the last two, now three, Harry Potter films. Why was that?

EMMA WATSON: I didn't immediately sign the contract, because I knew there was some time to just figure out the logistics, if you can imagine, of combining making the Harry Potter films with a school timetable, and I really want to go to university. I really want to continue what I was doing. I didn't want to have to give up either one, so I was in this really difficult position. It just took a bit of time to work out how I was going to make that work and Warner Brothers have been extremely supportive of helping me figure out ways to do that. For instance, they've given me Monday mornings off so I can go into school and I can see my teachers and pick up my work. They've provided all the teachers I need to get my work done. Even though I'm over the age of sixteen, they're still supporting me, giving me the hours I need to get all of my work done. They have got a box every Friday which I can put my work into, which they'll send back to my teachers. They'll mark it and they'll send it back to me. It just took a while to figure out the logistics of how it was going to work and how it wasn't. I found it quite frustrating and upsetting about all the insinuations that were made about why I was holding off, but I just had to make it work for me.

What are you studying at the moment?

EMMA WATSON: English literature, photography, art and history of art.

To what extent does your character mirror what happens in your life?

EMMA WATSON: It's really funny, because we get asked a lot about growing up and being on camera and growing up in the limelight and all those sorts of things. It's a really funny question to us, because we can't see ourselves from the outside, if that makes sense. It's a bit like looking at it from a different perspective. But in answer to your question, sometimes I barely have to act because I feel so close to my character and I just feel like I know her so well. I think we're quite similar in a lot of ways, so it's not trying so hard really. I'm quite lucky like that. It's nice that we've kind of grown up together. I think we're all a tiny bit older than our characters, so in a way it's nice because we're kind of experienced with what our characters are going through before them. We kind of know what it's like to have been through that experience and then we can apply it to what we're doing in the film. It works quite well, really.

What are your plans when the Harry Potter films are finished?

EMMA WATSON: I don't know what I'm doing [*laughs*]. You know, you can't really say what you want to do, because it's really not your choice. This business is completely unpredictable. You never know what films are going to be made, what work is out there. You've just got to ride it out and see what's out there, I guess. But ideally, I'd like to try some theater at some point. I'd love to do a period drama. I mean, there are loads of different things I want to do. I also really love to sing — don't worry, I'm not launching a singing career or anything, but I'd love to do something that has music in it. A lot of it also has to do with scheduling because, obviously, I've got the new two Harry Potters to do and juggling that with school is going to be challenging. You've just got to get yourself out there and audition for lots of different bits.

What's it like working with director David Yates?

EMMA WATSON: There is a different atmosphere with each director. With regards to their personality, they still set the pace of the day. But David Yates is quite laid back. I always felt like David had time to talk to us about what was going on and he always had time to listen to us and for us to talk about things.

In your opinion, does the character of Harry Potter have a dark side?

EMMA WATSON: You have to consider and you have to remember that this is a boy who has never known his parents. Who is living with the truth of their death, which I think is any one's worst nightmare. He's probably quite lonely; no one will ever understand what it's like to be him or go through what he's gone through. He's lost his godfather, which is the only other family member that he's had. He's world famous, everyone knows who he is and look at him as he walks around in the street. Considering all of that, it's a job that's he's actually sane and that he is a really nice guy and that he isn't more screwed up or more self-centered, or not just completely gone off the rails. He's a survivor. He's a strong guy.

You mentioned something about Harry being world famous. How has being famous affected you?

EMMA WATSON: I guess why it's always difficult for Harry was the fact that he lived all of his life as this normal boy, and then suddenly he came into it and found out that he's a wizard and that he was famous and it was just something he had to deal with. In a way, it feels kind of easier for me, because it almost feels like I've never known anything different. I was so young when I first started doing this that it kind of built up quite gradually as well. I've kind of learned as I went along, just from experience and just to bulk up my confidence in myself, and being able to deal with fame. I've also just been really well looked after.

I have to say, Warner Bros., just from the very beginning, have really taken care of us. Not just as the kids from Harry Potter, but as individuals and as people they're really fond of. The fact is that we had a kind of a family that they genuinely care about as people, and we're not just looked at as, I don't know, vehicles or something. That just really helps. Dan, Rupert and I have really strong families around us as well, who have taken care of us and, I think, that's what keeps all three of us sane. Just having a really strong base and a really strong identity outside of the films. We know we're worth something apart of what everyone thinks of us. We have very strong identities than just what people write about us in the press. We can laugh about it. Some of it's frustrating, some of it's annoying, some of it's freaky, some of its scary to us. But to be fair, we've been treated pretty well by the press.

LIFE WITH AND AFTER RON WEASLEY

Rupert Grint comes of age, both inside "Potter" and out

Originally written in 2009

Rupert Grint, who's played Harry's best friend Ron Weasley in all the *Harry Potter* movies, maintains a relatively low profile. You're not likely to see him baring it all on a Broadway stage, as *Potter* portrayer Daniel Radcliffe has done in the play *Equus*, nor will you see him popping up in movie after movie, as you will with many of his more famous *Harry* castmates (think Gary "Sirius Black" Oldman or Alan "Severus Snape" Rickman, who between them have made some 100 films).

But that's not to say that Grint doesn't take his acting seriously. Although 2001's *Harry Potter and the Sorcerer's Stone* was his first movie, the young actor had appeared in several school plays. And in addition to acting, he enjoyed reading books — including the adventures of a certain budding wizard and his friends.

"Before I knew there was going to be a film, I was the biggest *Harry Potter* fan," he says. "I read all the books. Ron was always my favorite character, because I feel like I relate to him, like we've both got red hair, we both like sweets, we've both got lots of brothers and sisters — I've got one brother and three sisters — and we're both scared of spiders!"

Going to audition to actually play Ron left Grint "really nervous. Even when I left the audition I was nervous. I went to meet the producer and the director and read another bit of the script, and then I went to do the screen test at the studio. Then, later, I was with Emma [Watson, who plays Hermione], and they took us into [director] Chris Columbus' office and he told us that we were going to be in the film. I was so excited I nearly fainted."

Making the first film, he adds, was "really weird, but so fun. I had such a brilliant time. It was so different from what I normally did."

The plan was always to follow the same core trio of actors as Ron, Harry and Hermione grew up, with Grint, Radcliffe and Watson "aging" before audience's eyes. Grint, who was 13 when *Sorcerer's Stone* came out, will be 23 when the second part of the concluding film, *Deathly Hallows*, is released in 2011.

"You get a glimpse of the early films every now and then and we've changed quite a bit," Grint muses. "Looking back at all the films, it just seems like one long film. Feels weird looking back about the early ones, how young we were and how much we've changed now. We've really enjoyed it. It's been a really good part of my life."

With the films' success has come greater public recognition, of course, but the young actor says being recognized usually doesn't bother him. "It's not too bad, actually," he says. "It's only been in the last few years where I get recognized a little bit more. The hair does sort of stand out. But they're always really nice, so it's not really a problem."

Enter *Thunderpants*

Grint's first non-*Potter* flick, 2002's *Thunderpants*, found him playing the best friend of a boy (Bruce Cook) whose problems with intestinal gas lead the Grint character, Alan A. Allen, to invent the titular Thunderpants, part of a space suit strong enough to contain Patrick's emissions. Patrick ultimately becomes an astronaut. "Making *Thunderpants* was a lot different from making *Harry Potter*," Grint understates. "*Harry Potter* is a very big production, and *Thunderpants* was much smaller. It was really a lot of fun."

While not making much of a splash at the box-office, the film did garner some decent reviews; *Time Out* called it "peculiarly quaint," while *Empire* declared, "This is a film that plays to its target audience without apologies to those who turn up their nose at such juvenile stuff." All told, not a bad reception, and for anyone pining for the sight of a young Grint wearing huge spectacles and a bizarre, *Napoleon Dynamite*-ish perm, this is the film for you.

His next non-*Potter* role, however, had a much more adult theme. *Driving Lessons* (2006) gave Grint his first lead as 17-year-old Ben Marshall, who takes a job looking after a fading, alcoholic actress (Julie Walters, who coincidentally plays Ron Weasley's mother). Along the way he learns a lot about life, including intimacy with the opposite sex in the form of Bryony (Michelle Duncan, *Atonement*).

"*Driving Lessons* had such a low budget," he recalls. "We just filmed it round London. It was really simple and I enjoyed it. We didn't do too many takes — usually just about two takes. About five scenes a day. It's such a different way of working; quite cool. And it was nice to be in such an atmosphere — not full of magical creatures, dragons and stuff like that!"

He adds that he was quite pleased to learn that Walters was joining the *Driving Lessons* cast. "It was really nice when I heard Julie was going to do it, just to have a friendly face," he remarks. "I was on screen the whole time and it was a bit scary. So it definitely made it much easier. And she's great anyway. She's really funny."

In fact, he says, it was difficult for him to keep a straight face. "All the argument scenes were really hard when I had to be serious and stare her right in the face," he laughs. "I've got a bit of a problem with that, anyway. I've got a bit of a reputation with the *Harry Potter* films to be a bit of a laugher. I don't know why it is. I just laugh in stitches sometimes. It's a weird feeling."

Reviews this time were again mostly positive, with the *San Francisco Chronicle* cheering: "With the aid of a charmingly offbeat story and a jolly good dialect coach, the stars leave you thinking, 'Well done.' Their spirited performances help cover up glaring holes in the plot," and the U.K.'s *Guardian* singling out Grint's performance as "attractively played."

His next non-*Potter* picture, *Cherrybomb*, due for release later this year, tells the story of teenagers Malachy (Grint), Luke (Robert Sheehan) and Michelle (Kimberley Nixon) as they embark on a wild weekend of drink, drugs, shop-lifting and stealing cars. But what starts out as a game turns deadly serious when the three discover that they can't get off the wild ride they've set in motion.

"Usually, Malachy doesn't get the girl," Grint says. "Luke is more of the ladies' man, but he's a bit more dodgy. Malachy isn't a geek — he's a bit of a thug — but he starts off as basically a good kid. He goes to work, he has a good relationship with his parents, but he's got some bad influences, so he gets into a bit of trouble."

Grint got a "little love scene" that's even more adult than the one he had in *Driving Lessons*, "which was quite awkward to film, with the whole crew watching," he says. "I don't think it's quite up there with Dan's *Equus*, but it was quite a surreal experience, especially as we were sharing the bed with half a dozen camera crew. It was a new thing for the two of us —

though, weirdly, I remember Kim and I doing a crossword in between takes. That definitely took our minds off the deed."

He adds with a grin that he hopes that when he films his eagerly-anticipated kissing scenes with Emma Watson's Hermione in *Deathly Hallows*, "I'll have a stack of crosswords at the ready.

Only having one week of rehearsals for *Cherrybomb* was an eye-opening experience, he adds. "On *Harry Potter*, we do a scene every few days, and this was like 12 scenes a day. It's a much tougher shoot, really, and quite tiring, but it's good to be at this much faster pace. I prefer it to the waiting around. You're always moving about. And at least I'm playing such a cool, different character that I've never done before. It's nice to get to act like you're more confident, even for a little bit."

In the midst of all this, Grint came up with a rather singular vehicle to drive around in: an ice cream van. Explaining that he's always had "an interest in the ice cream industry," he says that driving a van with a kitchen and freezer at the back is "really cool."

Yet another Grint film, *Wild Target*, is due this year as well. The comedy, about an uptight hitman (Bill Nighy, Davy Jones of the *Pirates of the Caribbean* films) who falls in love with one of his intended victims (Emily Blunt, *The Devil Wears Prada*), features Grint as Tony, the hitman's apprentice.

Potter and Beyond

Now the actor's immediate acting future consists of doing press tours for *Harry Potter and the Half-Blood Prince* and the two *Deathly Hallows* films. "Because we've been doing it so long, it's quite easy to slip back into it, really, because we know the characters pretty well," he says of himself and his young castmates.

In *Prince*, Ron Weasley nearly dies after he drinks Professor Slughorn's (Jim Broadbent, *Indiana Jones and The Kingdom of The Crystal Skull*) poisoned mead, a gift the professor was meant to pass on to Dumbledore (Michael Gambon) in an assassination attempt gone wrong. Ron had already been poisoned in one sense — "He gets poisoned quite a bit in this film," Grint laughs — because he ate Romilda Vane's chocolate cauldrons (also meant for someone else, this time Harry) which were spiked with love potion. Harry rushes his friend off to the potion's professor for a quick fix, only Ron goes from a bad predicament to a lethal one in mere moments.

"That was a really fun scene," Grint remarks. "But the whole film is gonna be massive. It's gonna be really cool. I was a bit disappointed when Quidditch didn't make it, but I mean… it's such a big book, there's so much to fit in I can understand why they pared it down."

Ron spends much of the *Deathly Hallows* swinging from one heroic deed to the next, saving Harry several times and, as previously noted, developing his romance with Hermione. For the epilogue, set 19 years in the future, Ron and Hermione are married and have two children, who along with Harry and Ginny's and Draco Malfoy's kids will be attending Hogwarts.

"It's going to be weird when it's all over," muses Grint. "I've really enjoyed it and part of me will miss it. But it'll also be good to be free. Ron Weasley has become a big part of my life, and not just because we've both got ginger hair! I've been so proud to play him and loved every second of being part of this world. I'm really looking forward to filming the last two films and being back with my 'Weasley family' and, of course, to seeing my good friends Emma and Dan."

And once *Potter* is in the rear-view mirror for good? "I don't really give it much thought, to be honest," he says. "But I think I do feel like continuing acting and I'd like to see where it goes from there, really. If it doesn't work out, I've still got the ice cream van."

TOM FELTON & THE TWO SIDES OF DRACO MALFOY

In *Half-Blood Prince*, Tom will have his biggest role to date in a Harry Potter film

Originally written in 2009

It's often said that a hero is measured by his villain, and while in the case of Harry Potter his evil counterpart is undoubtedly Voldemort, it would seem that Draco Malfoy is rising to be a fairly strong runner up. Thanks to actor Tom Felton's portrayal of the Hogwarts devotee to the dark arts, Malfoy has definitely become a hissable villain.

It's a point that his real-life alter ego, Tom Felton, wouldn't argue with. "My opinion of him?" he asks rhetorically. "Not a very pleasant one, I assure you. I think of him as a misled only child who's been slightly bullied into his state of mind, if you will. But overall, he's a nasty bit of work. A bit of a slimy, troublesome character who's not really up for any good and certainly not for the benefit of anyone else. Maybe he's misunderstood by others, but by the same token he doesn't do a great job of trying to convince them otherwise, does he?"

Tom must be doing something right in his portrayal in the sense that there are indeed fans who look at him negatively in real life; as though he really is the kind of dark and evil character that Malfoy represents. "It has happened, especially with the younger generation," he laughs. "Sort of six or seven down, age wise. Very early on, some people took very seriously how I was making Harry's life not pleasant at school and they would plead with me not to pick on him. They can get rather off put by seeing my face. They seem to associate me with something rather negative, which I can only take as a compliment, really, I suppose. So if I can convince them, then I can consider myself at least a good actor. But I don't know if they were taking it to the next level or whether they were actually confused about whether it was real life or film. I tried to reassure them, that nothing was real and that me and Daniel were quite good friends, but it didn't seem to sink in with them."

IN THE BEGINNING

Tom was born Thomas Andrew Felton on September 22, 1987 in England. Growing up, he found himself drawn to music and was a part of no less than four choirs, the first when he was only seven. Throughout his life he's continued his interest in singing and in recent years has even gone so far as to post some music videos on YouTube in which he plays guitar and provides vocals.

"A friend of mine," he offers in explanation, "a good musical friend of mine, moved away about a year and a half ago and she was always very keen to hear new music. And we just figured the best way to do that was to put it onto YouTube under an alias, obviously. But it didn't stay hidden very long and now it's very much sort of in the public domain. So it was never intended to be an advertising spin by any means, but, yeah, they are original songs and obviously not sort of developed by any means, but just sort of little early draft, if you will. Just a bit of fun. But it seems to have a positive response, so I'm enjoying it."

He also enjoys fishing. At the age of 11 he began working at a fishery, which triggered a lifelong fascination with fishing itself. In fact, Tom is able to draw a certain parallel between two of the great loves of his life, fishing and acting. "Patience," he muses. "Patience is required heavily in fishing and much the same with the film set. Some days it doesn't go as fast as you would have hoped or you would have expected. But it's all about keeping the energy and not only being patient, but just enjoying every minute of it. Because sometimes it can be quite easy to sort of slump back if you have an hour or two to wait, and it's important to make the most of the time with the cast and crew while you're still there.

"Unfortunately," he adds, "these days the fishing actually has taken a sort of back seat. I seem to spend more time with a guitar in hand than a fishing rod. So I haven't really been fishing for a while. My brothers' really keen still and I'm sure we'll be back out before you know it. He's going twice as much as he used to, so he's keen to get me back out there. But I think I'm taking the odd year or two off and I'll get back to it in the latter stage of life."

His acting career began when he won a role for an advertising campaign, beating out 400 other actors. This was followed by several other campaigns, including those for Commercial Union and Barclaycard. He finally got the chance to start doing some actual acting in 1995 when he provided the voice of James in a television series called *Bugs*, which was followed two years later by the feature film *The Borrowers*, in which he played the part of Peagreen Clock. Two years after that he starred opposite Clive Owen in *Second Sight*, and in the same year portrayed Louis T. Leonowens in *Anna and the King*.

MALFOY ARRIVES

It was, of course, in 2001 when he really came to the attention of the public as Draco Malfoy in *Harry Potter and the Sorcerer's Stone*, where his portrayal connected with audiences. Naturally this was followed by the Harry Potter sequels *Chamber of Secrets*, *Prisoner of Azkaban*, *Goblet of Fire*, *Order of the Phoenix*, this summer's *Half-Blood Prince* and the forthcoming two-part *Deathly Hallows*. Not surprisingly, acting remains his true love, and he emphasizes that there are both positives and negatives in making a movie, though the former definitely outweighs the latter.

"The bond between the cast and crew is always a good one," Tom enthuses. "Each day you're subconsciously getting closer and closer, but you don't realize it until it's time to say goodbye and you think, 'Oh wow, it was only a few weeks ago that I didn't know this person.' And I really enjoyed Harry Potter because of the longevity of them. I mean, I've been on some films where it's four- or five- or six-weeks filming, and as fun as it is, you never really get the chance to know anyone. And on Harry Potter, I've had a chance to really sort of be there throughout the entire shooting of it. And, really, it's magical to see the whole thing come together from start to finish. Obviously, I haven't seen the final product, but the actual filming process itself, how it was done and just the bonds that were made along the way and the people I've met... well, you've got new friends and have them afterwards as well, really.

"It's a struggle to find something negative about filmmaking," he admits. "I could go so far as to say early hours sometimes. Obviously, the schedule is quite demanding in the respect that you might be out of your house from seven o'clock in the morning to eight o'clock at night for a few weeks. But that's hardly beyond the calls of duty by any standards, really. As long as you're patient and you appreciate what's in front of you while it's happening, I think it's easy to have a great time."

Of course, one fact that Tom as well as the rest of the Harry Potter cast and crew will have to face — and not very far off in the future, relatively speaking — is that it's only a matter of time before the Hogwarts Express makes its final run.

"I'd love to continue on acting," says Tom in terms of what he sees ahead of him career-wise. "I hope I get to do something between this and the next film, but basically, I want to keep going on that front. By the same token, I'm keeping all angles open, really. I've been intrigued to do other things. I mean, music has always been a passion of mine and nature and so forth. I'm not really ruling anything out."

THE WRIGHT STUFF

In her evolution as Ginny Weasley, Bonnie Wright is moving closer to Harry Potter's heart

Originally written in 2009

It may have happened without her realizing it, but Bonnie Wright is gradually falling in love with Harry Potter. Okay, maybe that's not exactly true, but her big screen alter ego, Ginny Weasley is, as will be evidenced in the sixth film of the series, *Harry Potter and the Half-Blood Prince*. Although she really wouldn't say much about the romance itself, Bonnie was more than willing to talk about her life and career, and the experience of being a part of the unique phenomenon that is Harry Potter.

Born on February 17, 1991 in London, England, Bonnie made her acting debut in the first Harry Potter film, 2001's *The Sorcerer's Stone*. Besides appearing in each subsequent film in the series, she has also been in the 2002 TV movie *Stranded* and 2004's *Agatha Christie: A Life in Pictures*, in which she played the younger version of the mystery writer. What will happen with her career after the Harry series is finished is anyone's guess at this point, though a behind the scenes role actually appeals to her.

How did you get into acting?

BONNIE WRIGHT: My first role was in *Harry Potter and the Sorcerer's Stone*. Before that, I had always enjoyed taking part in school plays, but I never considered pursuing the hobby seriously. Then I heard that they were making the Harry Potter books into films and my brother had read the first three. He said, "Oh, I think you're really like Ginny, so why don't you go for the part?" I said, "Okay, well, how do I do that?" And then my mom rang up the publishers and then she got to know the number and then they asked me to come along for an audition. This was with just the casting director, and then they asked me again with Chris Columbus and everyone. And then a while after I got the part, which was quite odd. And here I am!

Do you think starring in these films has made you a different person than you otherwise might have been?

BONNIE WRIGHT: I don't think I would be really different if I weren't involved in it. It has had influence in my decisions about what I wanted to do, but because I wasn't interested in acting before, perhaps it changed my mind about what to do. But I'm still not quite clear about what I want to do. I'm really interested in acting, but I still want to get in to college to study for a degree. Maybe something involving art, because I'm really interested in the film industry now. Maybe something behind the camera and not so much in front of it. Maybe more in costume or set design and things like that.

Do you have a favorite subject in school?

BONNIE WRIGHT: Art, design technology, English and music. I'm driven by the creativity within them.

How would you say you and Ginny are similar and different?

BONNIE WRIGHT: There aren't many things alike about us, really. I've got red hair, and we're the same age, but we don't have a lot of personality traits that are the same. I'm not shy and Ginny is quite shy. And I don't love Harry. *And* I don't have magical powers.

Do you think the Harry Potter films are continuing to get darker?

BONNIE WRIGHT: I think they all have become a lot darker and the more you get to see Voldemort, the more forward things are pushed. *Order of the Phoenix*, for example, kind of involves the government side of the magic world and is more politically aware, so, you know, that has made it become much darker. Also the relationships in the film have grown up a lot. Everyone has grown up together as a pack.

It almost feels like they're becoming more like movies for adults.

BONNIE WRIGHT: I think people always mention that children can't watch them anymore, but I think that they can, because the characters are still in school, although not in a usual school environment. But children can still relate, I think. If they kept it really family, kind of a friendly film, they wouldn't be able to keep a lot of the big parts of the films, which are dark. Everything isn't happiness. Nothing can always be just happy. There is an evil sorcerer, isn't there?

What's your favorite part of being on set?

BONNIE WRIGHT: Being on set in the middle of a really intense scene is what I love best. But every day holds a challenge, whether it is on or off set; preparing for a scene or completing my school work.

Are you being offered parts outside of Harry Potter?

BONNIE WRIGHT: I'm definitely interested in doing different acting and things, but obviously Harry Potter takes so much time of the year that there's almost no time for doing other roles. But I would be interested, definitely.

How do you think you'll feel when you're done with the films?

BONNIE WRIGHT: I think it will be sad when we finish the last one, but we'll have been doing it for about ten years. That's going to be a large chunk out of all of our lives. And a really special time.

Half-Blood Prince, *of course, shows a new evolution in the relationship between Ginny and Harry...*

BONNIE: I think it really shows she's not the little sister anymore; she's becoming herself. When I read the book, I wasn't expecting it at all. It was nice. I liked how it came through, as obviously in the first book she showed a liking towards Harry.

DRESSING THE HOGWARTS STUDENT BODY

For costume designer Jany Temime, each Harry Potter film presents a new challenge that must be met

Originally written in 2009

French-born Jany Temime was entrusted with the task of making sure that the costumes in each of the Harry Potter *films have brought with them a distinction that separates them from the films that have preceded them. It's a challenge that she has risen to repeatedly for each of the films. In the following Q&A, she discusses some of her efforts on the* Harry Potter *films, offering an inside look at the thought process that went into their making.*

What was challenging costume-wise on the new film?

JANY TEMIME: It was challenging, because the children were no longer children. They were teenagers, almost adults, to be honest. They have reached an age where first they need to have a much more definitely style than they perhaps needed to have in the past. I'm not saying there were lots of intrigue between them, but they had to look good and they had to look attractive. It was no longer that you could put anything on them and they look fine. Nobody wants to be funny or ridiculous, they all want to look good. On this film, it was like dressing 20 adults, but still keeping a young way and also keeping the style, because they do have a style and they do have a style that the audience is expecting them to have.

Anything new in particular in terms of costumes?

JANY TEMIME: There have been a whole series of new costumes, which were a lot of work as usual. In this movie, Quidditch is brought back and we introduce a new design to be worn by the seeker and the goalkeeper, Harry and Ron.

Quidditch is a very dangerous game. We wanted to have something a little bit stronger in terms of the look, Padding has been introduced because of the age of the players and the danger, because they go a lot further when they are 17 or 16 years old. They dare much more, so the game, being more dangerous, needs more protections. There is padding that will protect the shoulder and back. The cape is something that you wear to fly. It has a hood, because we are wizards. The additions have an inspiration from American football, but it's not from American football completely, because the shoulder had to be able to move when they were flying. We thought of maybe introducing a helmet, but we thought that might be too much during the match. However, when they are training, they will wear it. They will look very frightening. We also have the new Quidditch outfit for Slytherin. It is in silver, and it has some beautiful black and silver on green. It's a lot more silky. They look much bigger and very cool. All of it, I think, looks fantastic.

These films have changed and evolved as they've gone on. Would you say that challenge extends to the costumes as well?

JANY TEMIME: Constantly, because nothing is more difficult than sequels, because you have to keep a certain style, yet you have to innovate. You have to innovate in order to keep the public alert and entertained, and at the same time you need to give them what they expect.

Working with different directors on the various films, does each bring their own desire and look to that particular film?

JANY TEMIME: That was something that was very exciting about the films, but this time we have the same director in David Yates, but we love him. He's wonderful, very creative and really a dream to work with, so that was fine. We had an excellent new director of photography, which was also amazingly artistic and very challenging.

Looking back at some of the earlier films, what are your feelings about the costumes? For instance, Alfonso Cuaron's Azkaban *was the first one to shake things up in terms of the look of the series, right down to the costumes themselves.*

JANY TEMIME: For that film, we darkened the colors and included a hood with the house colors inside, so you immediately knew which house each student belongs to. To encourage individuality, we gave everyone a choice of singlets, jumpers, cardigans and other variations on the uniform. And with the Quidditch uniforms, the idea was to make them more modern, resembling gear from a sport like rugby or football. So we introduced stripes and numbers. And because the Quidditch sequence takes place in the rain, we had to use a very modern waterproof fabric, and that in itself gave the uniforms a more contemporary look.

Wasn't there also a difference in the way Michael Gambon's Dumbledore compared to Richard Harris'?

JANY TEMIME: Alfonso wanted Dumbledore to look like an old hippie, but still very chic and with a lot of class. His previous costumes had been quite heavy and majestic, but we took some silk and tie-dyed it so when Dumbledore is walking around his robes float behind him. It's a much lighter look, which also gives the character more energy. And for someone like Peter Pettigrew, we went with a 1970s era suit and wove silver hairs and a threaded tail into it. His look is frozen in time and has become very threadbare and worn.

When looking at Goblet of Fire, *it's obvious that there were a number of interesting opportunities for costume design.*

JANY TEMIME: When we were creating the look for Mad-Eye Moody, we were inspired by Spaghetti Westerns in creating his black coat. Moody is a warrior. The man has no house, no home. He literally lives in his coat. We had a team of people who spent a week aging and distressing the coat to give it a lifetime's worth of wear. And for the look of Rita Skeeter's wardrobe, I was inspired by the 1980s — strong colors, very angular and specific for the story she's investigating. For instance, when the Triwizard contestants face their challenge with the dragons, she's dressed in a snakeskin kind of material with scales. When she attends the diving challenge, it's no accident that her outfit is a poisonous, sickening green.

Obviously, you also created distinct looks for the different schools that were in the competition.

JANY TEMIME: Yes, exactly. The Beauxbaton girls are sophisticated and self-aware, so I draped them in the most sensual and feminine fabric I could find, a delicate silk in the blue color of the French flag. The fabric clings to their form, in complete contrast to the restrictive uniforms the Hogwarts girls wear. The Durmstrang boys radiate a masculinity the girls have never seen before with their rough, almost primitive, thick wool clothing, heavy boots and wool coats.

Goblet of Fire *also featured the Yule Ball, which required numerous costumes as well.*

JANY TEMIME: We prepared over 300 costumes for the Yule Ball alone. First, we designed the boys' evening attire. Each has a white or black tie and fancy waistcoat. Harry wears a very classic black waistcoat. The Slytherins have white ties, because they regard themselves as posh. Designing the girls' dresses took several months, during which 100 dressmakers and wardrobe artists handmade the gowns. The girls were so excited about what they were going to wear. It was as if they were going to a real ball! Hermione's dress had to be really special. I wanted it to be a fairy tale dress, something that would make all the children gasp when she entered the room.

And in Order of the Phoenix, *a character like Umbridge brought with her so much ... pink.*

JANY TEMIME: The color of her costumes was predetermined by the book: pink, pinker and pinkest. Every time we see her, she is in a different shade of pink. As she gains power, the color gets stronger and more atrocious until she winds up in the deepest shade of cerise. Also in that film, working with Evanna Lynch [Luna Lovegood] was very interesting. She was very specific about certain details. I made earrings for her that were red radishes, and she insisted that they had to be orange. That's how well she knew the character. We wanted to make sure that Luna's costumes reflected a girl with very individual tastes and her own special interests, but not so completely different that she would not fit in with others.

Have you been signed for the two-part adaptation of Harry Potter and the Deathly Hallows?

JANY TEMIME: Yes, and that is a challenge, too. It has to be, because it's the end. You have to do the finale in the best way you can. It's very challenging for me. I'm quite afraid, actually, because I always felt that doing a number five or s number six, you could always do better next time. Now this is the last one, so I've got to do my best. This is the end. It's always difficult to style a finale, because it is the last one that people will always remember.

ANIMAL TRAINER OF HOGWARTS

Forget Doctor Dolittle, it's Gary Gero who talks to the animals on the Harry Potter films

Originally written in 2009

You can call him an "animal coordinator," "animal supervisor" or "animal trainer," but the bottom line is that Gary Gero loves what he does, eliciting performances out of all sorts of animals, among them the furry and feathered cast members of the Harry Potter films. His career began in 1973 with the movie version of Jonathan Livingston Seagull *(where he was credited as "bird trainer"), and continued with such efforts as* Never Cry Wolf *(1983),* Ladyhawke *(1985),* The Crow *(1994),* Homeward Bound II: Lost in San Francisco *(1996), the live-action* 101 Dalmatians *(1996),* Doctor Dolittle *(1998) and every Harry Potter film with the exception of* Order of the Phoenix.

You've been with this film series from the beginning. Does the challenge get easier as the films go on?

GARY GERO: On this one, it got easier as we went. We've had a few new challenges on each show, but the fundamental animals, the stock cast, just get another year's worth of experience with each show. And they learn the crew, the approach to things. And the truth is, as the films have gone on, we've been amping down. This show and the next show, we're a little slower than we had been. The emphasis now has been more on people. They've seen all the magic and we're down to the people stories and less involvement with the animals.

Going back to the beginning, how tough was it to get the kids to interact with the animals? Kids are either very curious or very afraid when it comes to animals.

GARY GERO: These guys were incredibly professional for little guys, and it had a lot to do with Chris Columbus as well. He's magic with kids and brings the best out of them. They were just little pros from the get-go, and it's been great fun watching them growing up in front of us. And they loved the animals; couldn't get enough of them. They're all part of the family now, and the animals all know them.

Has it been the same owls, cats and so on for all of the films or have they changed as things have gone on?

GARY GERO: Everything's the same except for Hagrid's dog, Fang. We're in our second generation of dog on this one. The cats are still the same. Cats live longer, but these big old dogs have got about six years of working life and then they retire. But the cats live on and so on, going about 20 years. We'll probably be adding a new Mrs. Norris, possibly in the next year, just to take some pressure off of the original and maybe get a little more spontaneity with a young cat. They still work like crazy and love to, but it might be fun to go a different way. The owls are all the same. Owls can live 40 or 50 years, so they're just barely mature now. We went through a couple of generations of Scabbers the rat, of course, and we're on our second generation of toads. We've had lots of miscellaneous animals come and go.

With all these different animals, which of your "students" have been more difficult than the others?

GARY GERO: Probably the most straight-forward were the cats. I mean, cats are cats and there's a little different approach with them. This breed of dog is a challenge. They're smart, they've got energy, but they're just a different kind of animal. They can be aggressive and they just have funny innate social things that are engrained in them. And having them work with little kids was interesting the first year. They're just all business and they've been bred for hundreds of generations to be aggressive dogs. So it's really inside the dog. One of the challenges was keeping them low-key and working out that the whole thing they all have in their nature.

What kind of dog is it?

GARY GERO: A Neapolitan Mastiff. But the biggest challenge, I think, was the owls. Now they've got eight years' experience and they know most everything, but the snow owls especially are really dim and they have such complicated behaviors to learn. It literally took 20 times longer to teach these owls to do things than it would to teach a raven or a crow. They are really, really slow. Training-wise, that was the biggest challenge, I would guess. But after the third show, they had it all figured out. I think we've still got 20 owls here.

Thank goodness they live as long as they do.

GARY GERO: Oh, please. Maybe I'll retire by the time we need new ones. Little barn owls are pretty smart, but the other larger owls are dim, to say the least. They're very nice and they're so attractive and so interesting — you never get tired of looking at them — but they're slow.

In the first film, there are those sequences where dozens upon dozens of owls are dropping off letters at the Dursley home. Was that CG or did it involve real owls?

GARY GERO: There are some animated owls, but most of that is duplication by computer. We shoot lots of owls against blue screen and they put them wherever they want to in a scene. If they don't have the footage they need in the end, they do animate a few animals, which we don't like. I remember we shot gangs of crows at Hagrid's hut up in Scotland — we did 10 or 15 crows flying around, and they duplicate those and added many more that way.

Do you do a lot of blue/green screen work?

GARY GERO: We try to do it live. With the exception of those flocks of birds, most everything has been live. But as time has gone on, we're doing more and more of our work on blue screen — not just Harry Potter, but other films as well. They're shooting a background plate somewhere; animals are being shot on blue screen and the two images are then put together.

How do you feel about that?

GARY GERO: It's fine. The animal behavior is what's important to us. In the old days — meaning 10 or 12 years ago, given the way technology is changing — what's on the screen is pretty much what you did, and you had to pull it off and tell the story in real time and real life. It's different now. I've been doing this for fortysomething years and I'm not liking it too much, though it really gives you the opportunity to enhance the bottom line, because you can do things, even with a live animal, that appear on screen in ways you never could do live, because you can manipulate things in the computer. It enhances the performance, but there's an artificial element to it. You don't have to really pull it off live anymore. They very quickly go to, "Ah, we can do it on the computer." It's getting affordable. As much as 10 years ago, it was so expensive. Ten years ago, to build an animated creature and use it was $100,000 a shot and so forth. At the same time, we were feeling pretty smug about that, thinking, "We'll never be out of business, because they can't afford to do it. Of course now it's getting cheaper and cheaper.

So you find yourselves having to adapt?

GARY GERO: We're all taking computer classes to keep us employed when they put us out of business. But, knock wood, it's going to be a long time before they can replace an animal performance completely.

Harry Potter and the Deathly Hallows – Parts 1 and 2
Copyright and Trademark Warner Bros. Discovery

CHAPTER 7: *HARRY POTTER AND THE DEATHLY HALLOWS PARTS 1 & 2* (2010; 2011)

PART 1

Voldemort and his Death Eaters are living at Malfoy Manor when Severus Snape appears to tell them that Harry would be moved "Saturday next" to the home of someone in the Order that has been given all manner of protection. Knowing he can't defeat Harry with his own wand, it being a twin to Harry's, Voldemort takes Lucius Malfoy's wand to try and kill Harry during his move. The Order has given other members a Polyjuice potion to turn them all into exact likenesses of Harry Potter. This way, Order members flying off in different directions give the real Harry a chance to escape. But the Death Eaters fly in and attack and Mad Eye Moody is killed. Voldemort tries to overtake Harry who is with Hagrid on his flying motorbike, but the boy defeats the evil wizard and gets away.

This gives Harry, Ron, Hermione and the others a chance to get to the Burrow, the Weasley home, where Bill Weasley and Fleur Delacour are about to be married. Before the festivities can start, though, Minister of Magic Rufus Scrimgeour gives Harry, Ron and Hermione bequeathments from Albus Dumbledore; Hermione gets a copy of stories, The Tales of Beedle the Bard; *Ron gets a Deluminator and Harry is given the Golden Snitch he caught in his first Quidditch game. He is also awarded the Sword of Gryffindor, which has been missing for years.*

The ceremony begins, but is interrupted with news that the Ministry has fallen to Voldemort and his Death Eaters and Minister Scrimgeour has been murdered. Death Eaters immediately arrive to destroy the area and burn the Burrow to the ground. Harry, Ron and Hermione manage to transport to London, where they fight more Death Eaters when Hermione Disapparates them to Grimmauld Place so they can make plans to find and destroy the Horcruxes that give Voldemort his power. Ron figures out that the mysterious R.A.B. is actually Regulus Black, Sirius's brother. He had stolen Salazar Slytherin's locket, but then local thief Mundungus Fletcher was forced to give it to Delores Umbridge. They are certain she keeps it in her office at the Ministry of Magic.

The only way for them to get the locket is to slip into the Ministry. This involves taking Polyjuice Potion and follow others to the entrance to the Ministry. Once inside they are quickly split up. While Harry is free to roam the halls, Hermione winds up in a courtroom right under the nose of Umbridge, while Ron finds himself dealing with rain in Death Eater Yaxley's office. The three reunite in the courtroom, and seeing that Umbridge is wearing the locket they stun her, paralyse Yaxley, and grab the locket. Now that the Death Eaters are on alert and the dementors are set free, they rush to the chimneys to escape. There is a problem when Yaxley gets hold of Hermione on her way up the flue so Hermione Apparates them to the forest. During that process Ron is injured and needs time to heal. They find it impossible to destroy the Horcrux with their magic and realize they need to find something powerful enough to do the job. At this point they start taking turns wearing it so they can keep it safe until they can kill it. As each of them puts on the locket, the evil within it starts acting on them, particularly Ron, who becomes paranoid and believes Harry and Hermione are carrying on a secret affair. Ron starts a fight with Harry and won't listen to Hermione's reasoning, so he leaves and the remaining duo have no choice but to continue their search. After apparating a couple times and setting up new camps, Harry remembers that he didn't catch his first Golden Snitch with his hand, he almost swallowed it. Once he holds it against his lips it reveals a cryptic message; "I open at the close." While Harry is making this discovery, Hermione realises that what she originally thought was an eye printed in her book, **Beedle the Bard,** *someone has actually drawn in. She shows it to Harry and he remembers that Xenophilius Lovegood, Luna's father, was wearing it at Bill and Fleur's wedding.*

They apparate to Godric's Hallow. Once there they decide to go through the graveyard to see if Harry's parents were buried there. While looking Hermione finds a grave marker that also has the curious symbol and Harry finds his parents. After telling each other Merry Christmas they start walking down the street and come to the house in which his parents were killed and where Harry survived the Avada Kedavra killing curse. While looking at the destroyed house they notice someone watching them. Harry believes it to be historian Bathilda Bagshot, she leads them to her cottage and, once she gets Harry by himself, she reveals herself to be Voldemort's snake, Nagini. Harry fights off the snake and Hermione gets them out of there. In doing so the curse she cast backfired, accidentally destroying Harry's wand. That night the Patronus of a doe leads Harry to a frozen lake that has Gryffindor's sword on the bottom. Harry goes in the water to get the sword and is almost killed when the locket pulls him away from the sword and away from the opening he had made in the ice. At the last minute of Harry's air, someone jumps in and pulls him out along with the sword. As luck would have it, Ron is the one that did the saving thanks to his Deluminator which helped him get back to his friends so he could continue the search with both Harry and Hermione. Harry has Ron destroy the locket since it affected him the most. Once the two of them get back to their camp Harry calls to Hermione who unleashes her anger on Ron for leaving them. Once things settle down, Hermione comes in to talk to the other two about going to see Xenophilius Lovegood to find out what the mysterious symbol means. He tells them of the Deathly Hallows: the resurrection stone, the cloak of invisibility and the elder wand, the most powerful wand in the world. The owner of all three Deathly Hallows becomes the Master of Death. Unbeknownst to the trio, Luna has been taken hostage and her father made a desperate deal to turn the three of them over to Voldemort for her return.

As the house is being attacked the trio manage to apparate to the forest, not knowing that they were landing in the midst of a group of snatchers. Once the three are caught, Harry's scar is discovered and they are taken to Malfoy Manor instead of to the Ministry. There,

Bellatrix sends the boys to be locked in the cellar, where they meet up with Luna, Ollivander and Griphook. In a vision, Harry sees Ollivander informing Voldemort of the elder wand's location – buried with Dumbledore in his tomb. As Bellatrix Lestrange takes great pleasure in torturing Hermione upstairs to find out who stole the sword from the dark witch's vault at Gringott's Bank, in the basement Harry calls upon who he keeps seeing in the mirror shard for help. As he turns to look at the others, Dobby appears. Harry and Ron direct Dobby to take Ollivander, Luna and Griphook to the Shell House for safety. Harry and Ron then meet Dobby by the stairs and they set out to save Hermione. A fight breaks out and Harry grabs a wand from Draco as Ron and Hermione get wands from others. Bellatrix gets ahold of Hermione and forces Harry and Ron to drop their wands. They hear a squeaking sound and look up only to discover Dobby unscrewing a chandelier above Bellatrix and Hermione. As it falls Dobby and Hermione join Harry and Ron. They begin to apparate, but not before Bellatrix throws a knife that hits Dobby in the stomach. They get to the beach by Shell House and there isn't anything that Hermione can do to help Dobby.

Harry, without using magic, buries Dobby on the beach at the Shell House where Bill and Fleur live. It is a seaside cottage that was Bill's Aunts, now being used by the Order as a safehouse. Elsewhere, Voldemort enters triumphantly into Dumbledore's tomb to claim the elder wand.

PART 2

After giving Dobby a loving send-off, Harry goes to Griphook. He asks the goblin to get him, Ron and Hermione into Bellatrix Lestrange's vault at Gringotts, believing a Horcrux to be hidden there. Griphook will do it but his price for doing so is the sword of Gryffindor. With his own wand destroyed, Harry gets good news from wand maker Ollivander; the two wands the young wizard took from Malfoy Manor belonged to Bellatrix and Draco. Draco's wand has changed allegiance to Harry, recognizing him as its new master. The other they are told to treat carefully due to its owner.

Using a Polyjuice Potion to disguise herself as Bellatrix and Ron as a nondescript wizard, they get into the vault as Harry and Griphook sneak in under the cover of Harry's invisibility cloak. They discover that the Horcrux in the vault is Helga Hufflepuff's cup. Before they can get away with it, Griphook takes the sword and tells them that he said he would get them in, but had said nothing about back out, and he leaves the trio to Gringotts' security dragon. They jump on the back of the captive dragon and it climbs out of the vault area into the bank itself and then flies away with them on its back. When the dragon starts flying lower, they jump off into a lake. Harry has a vision of Voldemort in the vault incensed at the theft and escape. The dark wizard will suffer no failure. He tells Nagini that he must keep him safe. As it shows the aftermath of the dragon escape, most of the Goblins are dead, including Griphook and the sword vanishes.

After having another vision, Harry identifies that another Horcrux, that of Rowena Ravenclaw, is hidden at Hogwarts. The trio apparate to Hogs Mead where Aberforth Dumbledore calls them in to get them away from those searching for Harry, Ron and Hermione. After trying to convince them to give up, the former headmaster's brother sends for Neville to take them into Hogwarts. It was a new passage into the school because Snape had sealed all the others. Neville Longbottom, no longer the scared nervous little boy, bravely took the lead and enjoyed surprising the other students with the three of them. Harry told them that they were looking for something small and easily concealed associated with Ravenclaw. Luna thinks of the lost Diadem of Ravenclaw.

Headmaster Severus Snape has created a near prison in Hogwarts, and when he discovers they've been spotted nearby, he threatens to severely punish any student or staff who helps them. When he asks for anyone who has information to come forward, Harry himself steps out and tells him how bad his security measures are. Snape pulls his wand to fight with Harry but Professor McGonagall pushes Harry out of the way and duels with Snape, who escapes. McGonagall rouses the students and staff still loyal to Dumbledore, and has Filch take Slytherin house to the dungeons.

As Harry is on his way to Ravenclaw house, Luna stops him and convinces him to talk to the ghost of Helena Ravenclaw because no one alive has seen it. Helena is hesitant to talk to him at first, but Harry finally convinces her that he wants to destroy it once and for all, if she will only tell him where Voldemort had hidden it. Helena tells him "If you have to ask, you'll never know. If you know, you need only ask." With that Harry knows it's in the Room of Requirement.

Ron and Hermione make their way to the Chamber of Secrets and retrieve several fangs from the Basilisk that Harry had killed. With those in hand, Hermione destroys the cup with one of them. Voldemort feels the destruction of the horcrux and holds the elder wand up, firing off a very strong curse that destroys the shield McGonagall and the others had put in place to defend the school and give Harry as much time as possible to find the Diadem.

Just as Harry finds the Diadem, Draco, Blaise Zabini and Gregory Goyle confront him in the Room of Requirement. Ron and Hermione join the fight, with Ron chasing them around the corner and seeing Goyle launch a Fiendfyre curse that goes out of control, burning all it comes in contact with. He eventually dies in the fire. Harry and the others rescue Draco and Zabini and Harry destroys the diadem with a Basilisk fang just prior to Ron kicking it back into the Room of Requirement as the doors are slamming shut. That left Harry and Voldemort's snake Nagini as the two remaining horcruxes.

The evil Lord meets with Snape and tells him that the elder wand was not responding to him correctly. He also told Snape what a faithful servant he had been, but since he was the one that killed Dumbledore, Voldemort can't control the elder wand without killing Snape. He hits Snape with a curse and orders Nagini to kill him. Mortally wounded, with the last of his strength, Snape gives Harry some tears of memories and tells Harry to take the vile to the Pensieve. In the memories, the boy discovers that although he, Snape, hated Harry's father for being a bully, Snape dearly loved his mother. Over the years he worked with Albus Dumbledore as a double agent against Voldemort and his Death Eaters, as well as to protect Harry from attacks by the dark Lord. Dumbledore knew he was dying and gets Snape to promise to kill him so he can get complete trust from Voldemort. Snape had been helping Harry the whole time, especially when he conjured the Doe Patronus to lead the boy to Gryffindor's sword. When Voldemort tried to use the Killing Spell to destroy baby Harry, it was his mother's love that sent the curse back at him, destroying his body. But at the same time, Harry became a Horcrux himself. Voldemort is driven to kill Harry once and for all so everyone will see him as the most powerful wizard.

During the raging battle in and around Hogwarts, Fred Weasley, Remus Lupin and Nymphadora Tonks are killed. Connecting to the minds of everyone engaged in the battle, Voldemort tries to shame Harry into meeting him in the Forbidden Forest so he can meet his fate and die. Harry stops in a small clearing in the woods, takes out the Golden Snitch, says he's ready to die, and again puts the snitch to his lips. As he watches, the snitch revolves several layers to the hollow center and the Resurrection Stone floats out for Harry. As he grasps the stone his mother and Father, Remus, and Sirius join him in the clearing. After their words of encouragement Harry drops the Resurrection Stone and starts walking to where Voldemort is waiting to kill him.

Finally having the boy before him, Voldemort says "the boy who lived, come to die." He then casts the Killing Curse at Harry. His body falls, but a part of him meets up with Dumbledore in a kind of limbo at a very clean King's Cross Station. Voldemort had actually killed the part of his spirit within Harry, freeing him of Voldemort's connection. Dumbledore tells Harry he has two options: accept his death and catch a train to move on, or return to his body and take on Voldemort. Harry, of course, has no problem with his choice.

The Dark Lord sends Draco's mother, Narcissa, to see if Harry is truly dead. When she sees that he is still alive, she asks him if her son is safe. Harry lets her know that he is. She then turns to Voldemort and announces that Harry Potter is dead. Voldemort has Hagrid carry Harry's body to Hogwarts to show everyone that he is dead. Instead of the people at Hogwarts losing hope, Neville gives a speech that encourages everyone because Harry was still in their hearts and the battle was still worth fighting. Neville pulls the Sword of Gryffindor from the Sorting Hat and Harry drops from Hagrid's arms and runs into the castle while Voldemort is trying desperately to hit him with more spells. In the shock, Voldemort is abandoned by most of his Death Eaters, including the Malfoys.

A vicious battle ensues. Ron's mom, Molly, gets the best of Bellatrix, killing the lunatic witch. Neville comes to after being struck by a spell from Voldemort and picks up the Sword of Gryffindor. As Harry is fighting with Voldemort, Ron and Hermione are trying to kill the snake Nagini with Basilisk fangs but fail. The snake is preparing to kill the two just as Neville shows up with the Sword of Gryffindor and beheads it. That's the last Horcrux and Voldemort feels his beloved Nagini die as he once again is human with no more Horcrux. Voldemort is human and Harry knows it. They again take up their duel and Harry defeats Voldemort, acquires the elder wand, and watches Voldemort melt away into pieces. This time, the Dark Wizard is truly dead. While walking along the bridge to Hogwarts Harry reveals that the elder wand didn't respond for Voldemort because it never belonged to Snape. It was Draco who disarmed Dumbledore not Snape, and when Harry disarmed Draco at Malfoy

Manor it then belonged to Harry. He then breaks it in two and throws the pieces into the gorge below the bridge.

It's 19 years later; husbands and wives Harry and Ginny, and Ron and Hermione deliver their own children to platform 9 3/4. Little Albus Severus Potter expresses concern about the Sorting Hat placing him in Slytherin house, but his dad allays the boy's fear by telling him the Sorting Hat will consider his own feelings. As the children board the Hogwarts Express, the now adult trio of Harry, Ron and Hermione see them off.

The challenge inherent in Harry Potter and the Deathly Hallows *was probably obvious from the moment people were introduced to the world of Harry Potter. Everything that had preceded it was leading up to what would have to be a climactic battle between the boy wizard and his sworn enemy, Voldemort. On the film side of things, there was the additional challenge of turning it into what would feel like an organic two-part adventure.*

As far as David Yates was concerned, his personal challenge stemmed from the fact that at one point he was actually working on three Harry Potter films at the same time: he was busy tweaking Harry Potter and the Half-Blood Prince, *shooting* Deathly Hallows Part 1 *and prepping* Deathly Hallows Part 2.

DAVID YATES (director, *Harry Potter and the Deathly Hallows Part 1* and *Part 2*): It's amazing, but it was fun, actually and, fortunately, because this was my third in a row at that time, it felt very natural and normal to be working at that pace. What also makes it easier is that they're all part of the same story. They're all part of an unfolding saga. If you're a carpenter working on a particular piece of wood, it's just a bit of wood you're working on at that particular time. I used to work in television where I would relentlessly go from one project to another, because I'd be asked constantly to do different things. I've had that rhythm right through my career.

I've gotten very good at kind of parachuting into something, looking at it and then diving back into something else. It gives you a really healthy perspective on things sometimes. I don't think any of them have been short-changed.

I think what you get good at is that you instinctively know where you need to be, where your attention is needed most, because there is a plethora of things that you can get bogged down in that are important, but not necessarily the absolute crux of what a scene is about or a moment is about. So you get very used to saying, "The scene is really this, and that's where we need to spend our time and attention." And I've got such a lovely team of people I've worked with for four or five years, so I have many people who are really paying attention to the detail around all of that, and I can concentrate where I feel the mojo of the scene is, as it were.

Taking a look at the history of the James Bond films, there was a period where one director, John Glen, helmed four films in a row and the result was a kind of sameness that set in. This naturally leads to the question of whether there was a risk of the same thing happening with David Yates taking on the last four films of the Harry Potter saga.

DAVID HEYMAN (producer, *Harry Potter and the Deathly Hallows: Part 1* and *Part 2*): We were very conscious of that. I think you'll see that *Order of the Phoenix* and *Half-Blood Prince* are very different in spirit, and I think the very nature of *Deathly Hallows* and the fact that they're out of Hogwarts on this very clear sort of path to the final confrontation between Harry and Voldemort in itself provides a different color. So there was no real concern on our part. But there was an *awareness* of it, absolutely.

EMMA WATSON (actor, "Hermione Granger"): Having David stay on was a good thing, because it's such a huge undertaking and there are so many people involved. When David came on board, I think it was overwhelming for him to be the new guy, because we'd been there for so long, and all the crew had been there for so long, and he was the new guy and he was the one meant to be in control and in charge, and that was pretty hard. I think for anyone coming on board for the last one, or *Part 2*, it would have been so hard. So having that constant kind of father figure was really important.

DAVID YATES: You've just got to make sure the film works to the best it possibly can on its own terms. Of course the fact that you finally get to see Harry's duel with Voldemort, the fact that you see what happens to some of these other characters who the audience has grown up with and liked very much, the fact that you resolve all of this, gives it, in its very DNA, a really rewarding and incredibly satisfying arc. Fundamentally it's all in place, so you just have to make sure that the ride is as enjoyable and rich as possible. The material itself has allowed me to tap into different aspects of myself. *Death Hallows* is so different from *Half-Blood Prince*, and very different to the last two movies. It's a road movie — it's got much more variety, it's much more about the emotional states of these characters growing older and it's more nuanced than either of the previous films. And then there's Jo Rowling's writing; there are so many routes you can take, and so many rich things to pick off the branches as it were, and it feels like it's evolving. *Part 1* has got its big action set pieces, but it's much more about the delicacy of the relationships between the three characters, who are refugees on the road. *Part 2* is big, epic — they're almost back to Harry's fantasy roots as it were, so there's enough variation in the journey over those four pictures.

DAVID HEYMAN: The novels themselves are quite different. As I say, most of *Deathly Hallows Part 1* takes place outside of Hogwarts, though we move to Hogwarts for the last portion of the last act of the movie. Up until then, we're on the road. The first part of it we're on the road the entire time. But that brings up an important point: Hogwarts itself does not make it magical. I think the thing we are most drawn to is the relationship between the three kids, and that remains and sustains through all the movies, in particular the last two. In a way, what's so interesting about *Part 1* is the dynamics between the threesome. For example, this horcrux they're carrying around affects each of them and that's wonderful. In terms of the magic, there's plenty of it. There's the opening sequence of *Part 1* where you've got seven Harrys, which is incredibly fun and magical. Then we have a wizard wedding, which is kind of magical. All along the way, when they're on the run, they're in a tent that on the outside seems small, but when you go in, it's substantially larger. Jo's world, even when they're not at Hogwarts, is infused with magic, so that's not really an issue.

EMMA WATSON: I think the first one is more really high tension, really focusing on the relationship between the three of them, the dynamic in their friendship, and what it feels like to be out of Hogwarts and on the run. It's a lot more slow-paced, and the last one is really breakneck speed, the whole thing, I think. The audience won't breathe for two hours; it's very intense. Lots of action, very exciting, amazing visual effects, it will be mind-blowing. The first one is more psychological.

DAVID YATES: Ultimately you make these decisions every day, so all of the films are going to have a certain sensibility that come from me as a director, which is inevitable. However, I was trying slightly different gear shifts in each one. *Order of the Phoenix* I always felt was slightly more intense and emotional; *Half-Blood Prince* I've tried to go with a very expressive look, a beautiful look, and to create something very elegant. But it's great fun as well and much more fun than

Order of the Phoenix was and much more playful. There's much more comedy. And then part one of *Deathly Hallows* is the rawest and most real-world of the films I've made in the series up to then. I very consciously ran away from Hogwarts and tried to find a reality we hadn't explored to that extent before. Hogwarts has always been a big feature of these movies, so it feels very different, simply because the enormous character of the castle and Hogwarts *isn't* present. It feels quite grown-up, which I like very much, and it feels quite emotional and scary.

The other thing is that the cast was much older, were on the road and we were away from this magic school. It's very much the real world and that's quite fun and brings its own dynamic. And for the concluding part of the story, for *Death Hallows Part 2*, that's when we get very operatic and very expressive again. And oddly elegiac. So each film has a different gear shift, but ultimately, it's still filled with things I like to do. They're all connected and they're all part of the same unfurling story, but I was hoping for a slightly different rhythm to each one. *And* we get to see magic in the real world.

STUART CRAIG (production designer, *Harry Potter and the Deathly Hallows: Part 1* and *Part 2*): Being in the real world does tend to make things grittier. There are several settings, some of which are real and some of which were built theatrically on a soundstage. But one modifies the other, really. Yes, it has a gritty reality, but nonetheless reality often doesn't give you a good strong theatrical silhouette, and isn't always as simple and direct as you would like it to be. So in the real forest, we spent a lot of time actually adding odd tree trunks and eliminating certain other things — so it was real, but it was a selective reality. And on the sets, we built on soundstage, we made them as real as possible, to the extent that we went to the original forest and took impressions of bark textures and copied them absolutely, and brought in small undergrowth and vegetation that matched those things.

So it was a question of bringing two worlds together, but inevitably the use of location gave it, while not a documentary look exactly, an utterly credible, authentic look.

DAVID HEYMAN: I think the interaction with the Muggle world is exciting, too. In a way, what we liked about that is that it makes you look around and you can imagine the magic in your world. That's actually one of the things that works with Jo's books as well. Even though Hogwarts itself has magical qualities, it is a school like many of the schools that we've all been to. It may not look the same, but we've all had teachers we've gotten along with and those we haven't. it's all grounded in relatable institutions and relationships and so by placing that magic in the Muggle world, it highlights that. The very fact that magic may be around any corner, makes it that much more magical. We were having quite a bit of fun playing with that, a little bit in *Six* and a little more in *Seven*, I think it's really, really good.

J.K. ROWLING (author, *Harry Potter and the Deathly Hallows*): While each of the previous Potter books has strong claims on my affection, *Deathly Hallows* is my favorite and that is the most wonderful way to finish the series.

While there had been consideration given to the idea of splitting a Rowling novel into two films previously, most notably with Harry Potter and the Goblet of Fire, *it was pretty much a foregone conclusion that there was no avoiding the idea with* Harry Potter and the Deathly Hallows, *though the most obvious question was exactly where that split would take place.*

EMMA WATSON: When they told me they were splitting the last book into two films, I thought, "Why didn't I see that coming?" Obviously, there's so much material, that last book is so enormous, how on Earth were they ever going to fit that into one movie? I mean, it's just impossible. On the one hand the thought of it was overwhelming, with me thinking, "Oh my God, I'm now making three more *Harry Potter* films and not two." It just felt like a huge undertaking, but then again at the same time, as a huge fan of the books myself, I was happy to see that we were going to do it justice, and that stuff wasn't going to be left out. We were going to stay very, very faithful to Jo's story. But then, on top of that, there was an enormous pressure. It's the last chance I was going to have to play Hermione; this would be the culmination of ten years' worth of learning and experience; this is meant to be the apex of my performance as that character. Hell yes, I felt the pressure!

DAVID BARRON (producer, *Harry Potter and the Deathly Hallows: Part 1* and *Part 2*): Before we started, we all talked about where we thought it might break. Steve Kloves then went off to write it and see what felt natural. He came up with something that we hadn't previously considered and then we sort of had it like that for a while and we all changed it. I think that film one is more of a road movie, because they get to leave behind everything they've ever known before. Harry leaves Privet Drive, then they go to the Burrows and are forced to leave there because it's no longer safe. They go to Grimwald Place and the same thing happens, so everything they've ever known, other than Hogwarts, which they don't get to until further down the journey, they're forced to leave behind pretty much as soon as they get there. So it's a bit of a road movie and it's a film about faith and the loss of faith, because Dumbledore has sent them on a mission that Harry is aware that he's not fully equipped to carry through, but Ron and Hermione have faith in him. They assume Harry must know and Dumbledore must have told him what he has to do. That faith in both of them is eroded and culminates in Ron leaving the group so that the three become two for the first time, and faith is restored when he comes back and they carry on with their mission. Still, they don't know what they're doing, but they have faith that they'll work it out. And the second film, a large part of the second film is the final battle. Harry meets Voldemort for the final time, from which there can only be one victor. It's a road movie and the final fight. It doesn't split exactly like that, but I think that it's generally the way you can describe them.

DAVID HEYMAN: Once the decision was made to turn the final book into two films, you obviously need to find the right end point in the book halfway through. Each film up to that point had been different from the one that preceded it.

DAVID BARRON: It's crucial that they feel distinct, even though you're never going to be able to separate them entirely in the sense that *Part One* is the beginning of the end and *Part Two* is the end of the end, even though stylistically they should feel like two very different movies. Think of the first part of the book. They don't arrive at Hogwarts until the final denouement of the first part. In some respects, the first part of the book feels like a road movie. They're harried and harassed and they're trying to travel and hide themselves in the Muggle world with only the flimsiest of charms to keep them out of the sight of the enemy. That in itself is a very different feeling from anything we'd had before.

DANIEL RADCLIFFE (actor, "Harry Potter"): The first part is very different from the second. The first part is an exploration of character and how these characters react to one another in a totally different environment. Had we made it into one film, we'd have to cram so much in there and actually have to skip over some things. And in the seventh book, there are a lot of things you can't afford to skip over. The second part of it starts out as a heist movie and turns into a war film. There are many different phases to the book, but the progression is so natural and exciting that I don't think too many people were distracted by the fact that the film does move from so many different environments and so many different kinds of tones and feels to it.

EMMA WATSON: The first film is high tension, really focusing on the relationships between the three of them, the dynamic in their friendship and what it feels like to be out of Hogwarts and on the run. The second part moves at breakneck speed and it doesn't let the audience breathe for two hours. Lots of action, very exciting, amazing visual effects — the first one is more psychological.

DAVID BARRON: I think each of the two parts have to feel like different films. David Yates wouldn't want to make four films the same. It's very important to us that they are very different films, and it would be to the audience. Jo, again in speaking to the way she approaches the books tonally, always makes them different, which is why they're always exciting to read. It's not that difficult to make the films different, because we start with source material that is the same, but different. It's the same with David Yates. He very definitely wanted to make films that feel very different and are standalone films, even though you can look at *Order of the Phoenix, Half-Blood Prince* and *Deathly Hallows* as the beginning of the end of the franchise, really. Things started to gear up in *Order of the Phoenix*, they take a big step further in *Half-Blood Prince* and come to the final conclusion in the two parts of *Deathly Hallows*. But they all feel very different.

DAVID YATES: Helping with the feeling of difference is the fact that cast was still evolving in terms of performance. For example, in *Hallows Part 1*, something happened to Emma and she became so ignited. She had so much more interesting things to do in the first part of the movie than she ever had to do in *Order of the Phoenix* or *Half-Blood Prince*. She came to the table, read the script and said, "Wow, this is so cool, I get to do stuff for this I've never done before," and that kind of opportunity and that kind of challenge brought out something in her that I think is just fantastic.

EMMA WATSON: David Yates asked Steve Kloves to write a lovely scene at the beginning, which is not in the book, but I feel is very important for Hermione's character, which is where you see her wiping her parents' memories in order for her to go on the adventure with Ron and Harry, because she obviously knows that Voldemort could try and use her parents as a device to get to her in some way. They might be in harm's way for her helping Harry, so she has to wipe their memories so they can forget she ever existed. All the photos around the house of her disappear, and her parents don't know who she is, which is a tough thing to see and a tough way for the film to start. But it's obviously really important to see the sacrifice she has to make and the fact that she's really committed. She knows what she has to do, and she's totally there for Harry. She's also really independent — she's a woman now, and she has real conviction in her choices, and her decisions. It's pretty cool.

DAVID YATES: And Dan the same — Dan had to dig a bit deeper and go to a deeper level for some of the scenes in this, and *Part 2* is particularly Dan's movie. And what's great for Rupert is that he's always been the funny guy, and the audience naturally, instinctively every time Rupert comes on screen, they want to smile, they want to laugh. But Rupert got the opportunity to explore a darker side of that character, a more intense and serious side of that character, which he absolutely loved. He does the comedy really well, and we all know him for that and like him for that, but he does the serious stuff incredibly well. That was heartening and exciting to see him enjoy that challenge and to rise to it. So *Deathly Hallows* allowed all three of them to step up a plate or two, which is great. We were all challenged.

RUPERT GRINT: The romance between Ron and Hermione really starts to happen in *Deathly Hallows*. I was really worried about that, because it just felt like it was wrong. But David Yates was really good about it; he gave us a long chat before we kissed and it was fine. Kind of a fuss about nothing.

DAVID HEYMAN: What I think Jo did so brilliantly is that it's *not* an action-filled climax. it really comes from the very best place, which is from emotion and character. I think that's where Jo really succeeded brilliantly in the seventh book. There's that whole sequence with the figures from Harry's past, those who have died at Voldemort's hands, who are standing by him as he prepares. It's just beautiful. That's the strength of these films and the books — for all the magic, fantasy and visual effects, what people really connect with are the characters.

DAVID BARRON: The biggest pressure on us was to make sure that we delivered the emotional story and didn't get tied up with giants and hordes of Death Eaters and other things. A balance had to be found, because you had to get a sense that it's a battle to end all battles as far as our magical worlds are concerned. But the key thing is that we have spent eight films at that point leading up to Harry and Voldemort's final meeting, and the emotional element of that and their physical battle couldn't be overshadowed by 10 million Death Eaters. We had to be careful. There was a balance to be found there.

TOM FELTON (actor, "Draco Malfoy"): These battles took the Harry Potter films to another level. I mean, there's absolutely no way that these films could be classified as children's films. The appeal is to so many different people on so many different levels.

DAVID YATES: Paying off 10 years of stories *is* a massive challenge, but you can't think about it in those terms. You've just got to try to make sure the film works to the best it possibly can on its own terms. But of course then it *is* resolving that whole, huge journey in a way; ultimately, you're coming to the end and you're finally seeing what happens. Besides all of the other stuff, all the fun stuff, all the battles, all the other things, you actually finally get to see Harry duel with Voldemort in the end. The fact that you actually discover that Harry's mother's love protected him when he was an infant, the fact that you see what happens to some of these other characters who the audience has grown up with and liked very much — loved very much. The fact that you've never resolved all of this gives it, in its very DNA, a really rewarding and incredibly satisfying arc. Fundamentally it's already in place, so you just have to make sure that the ride is as enjoyable and rich as possible.

JOHN RICHARDSON (special effects supervisor, *Harry Potter and the Deathly Hallows: Part 1* and *Part 2*): The whole ending was the challenge. Although we had the script, we didn't have a definitive way forward until storyboards and pre-vis and all those other decisions had been made, so I think we would try to work on it and figure those things out as we were still doing all the stuff for *Part 1*. The whole process of making the movie became, I think, more difficult as a result. The ending sequence was obviously difficult for special effects, because you're sort of reaching the climax, and the spells all had to be bigger and larger and better — the battle sequences and the destruction of Hogwarts; everything was more intense and larger than it had been on any of the previous movies.

I think my favorite shot is the beginning of Voldemort's attack on Hogwarts. We did a little sort of sequence, all centered around one shot, really, where the magical shield that's been protecting Hogwarts comes down, and all the Death Eaters and Voldemort attack. There are a series of explosions that blow up the courtyard and the front of the castle, which is predominantly all live-action and physical, although you're going to have a certain amount of CGI work added to it. David Yates and I talked about the look he wanted, and he wanted *destruction*. I showed him some footage from the World War II film *A Bridge Too Far* and, in fact, we tried to replicate that, with debris and bits flying, and walls coming down and people running. For me, it's one of the hero shots you do in a movie that looks good, looks real and gives me a kick at the same time. You can't really do that any other way than do it for real.

DAVID HEYMAN: Ending the story properly was and wasn't a burden. There's such anticipation for each and every one of these films, and people have such strong opinions about how they should be done, and what's right and what's wrong with them. We've lived with that throughout, and that's okay. That's great. I think it's non-constructive to think of the outside pressure — we put pressure on ourselves through every film to make the best film we can. And that's the way we approached *Deathly Hallows* — we want to make the best films we can. Chris Columbus is amazing at that — I learned a lot from watching how he dealt with that outside pressure. All he cared about was making the best picture he could. It wasn't about the outside world. He's a fan, I am a fan, David Yates is a fan. It's about making the best film we can with this material, and then if we make a good film, we'll bring the series to the right conclusion.

DAVID YATES: In a way, the last three films in the series that I made have just been the continuation of the story. They all ended with a promise of more to come; they all had that feeling of saying we're partway through this saga. Just personally, as a filmmaker and storyteller and an audience member, it's so much fun to reach that final climax, and we've spent three films building to it in a way, so that in itself makes it rewarding and satisfying — the fact that we're getting to the end.

DANIEL RADCLIFFE: What I love about the final battle between Harry and Voldemort is it's the moment that I'd kind of been wanting to happen for years, but that never had and I was actually glad it hadn't because I'd always wanted a moment where the magic is not enough. He just tries to kill Harry, physically, just by beating him up, and it would have been totally wrong to do it any earlier. So physically that was a challenging thing, but there were a lot of physically challenging things in the film.

DAVID HEYMAN: We made a little more of the Voldemort/Harry fight than in the book. In the book it's over like that! [*snaps fingers*]. We felt for film reasons we wanted to expand on that a little bit — with Jo's blessing, of course. The battle has two parts. There is the part before Harry is killed by Voldemort or we all think he is, but he's not really dead. So there's that first part, which is a big, epic battle where the castle, if you will, is under siege. Voldemort brings the perceived dead Harry back and then we make the final confrontation more focused on the two of them. It doesn't mean that there aren't other bits, but it's primarily about them.

DAVID YATES: I changed their final battle from the book. In the book, Voldemort turns up and there's a walk around the Great Hall, they duel and that's it. I thought it was more important to have them face each other away from everybody else.

DAVID HEYMAN: We knew we had to make a little more of the Voldemort/Harry fight than in the book. In the book it's over like *that*! [*snaps fingers*] We felt for film reasons we wanted to expand that a little bit — with Jo's blessing of course.

DAVID YATES: Harry lures Voldemort into the destroyed castle and I wanted them to have a big fight. I figured we'd waited so many movies for this, you just didn't want to sort of end it in the Great Hall with them circling each other. So we go off, we have a big fight and allowed them to express their sense of rage against each other and the hatred for one another. Voldemort has taken so much from Harry. Oddly, they're also kind of connected in a way through time, because of this journey that they've shared. So I developed a fight between the two of them that would be properly climactic and finally resolves in this big duel in the courtyard.

DAVID HEYMAN: The battle has two parts. There is the part before Harry is killed — for those who haven't read the novel, in the book he's killed by Voldemort or we all think he is, but he's not really dead. So there's that first part, which is a big, epic battle, where the castle is under siege. Voldemort brings the perceived dead Harry back and then we make the final confrontation more focused on the two of them. It doesn't mean that there aren't other bits, but it's primarily about them. Yes, we'd been building toward it, but I didn't think we'd want a 40-minute battle between Harry and Voldemort, because it would be boring.

STEVE KLOVES: The battle, as a battle, didn't particularly interest me, but I found my way into it because I knew David Yates and his team would come up with the scale and the spectacle. David and I talked and decided that it wasn't going to end like other action movies conclude. We didn't want to do spectacle; we wanted to tie character and emotion to everything that happened.

DAVID YATES: Ralph Fiennes was terrific at sort of finding some of that rage and anger and that frustration and that sort of bewilderment that this child has caused him so much pain and frustration over these stories. I actually love that relationship, because they're kind of twins in a way. Part of Voldemort exists within Harry, which he discovers in the last movie. And there's an odd symmetry between them. Harry has gone to the dark side before and understands the dark side; he knows it's very deep within him. And there's a moment in the final sequence that I really wanted to express that where Harry pulls Voldemort off of this precipice and they apparate and they go on this journey around Hogwarts together, fighting with one another and they kind of meld into each other. When you apparate, you kind of extrude and break up and conform and reconform into smoke initially. As they're fighting, they kind of become one another. So there's this really weirdly expressive moment where Harry becomes Voldemort and Voldemort becomes Harry just before they have their final showdown. It's that notion that they are the same inside; there's a bit that coexists and makes them the same.

DAVID HEYMAN: What I love about the Harry Potter books and films is that for all the fancy and all the magic, it's still about the characters. I think what David Yates did, which is really important, is root that final; conflict between Harry and Voldemort in very human qualities. It's really about the two of them as characters. There's a sequence where Voldemort is beating the ... sugar ... out of Harry. He's venting all of his frustrations at having not been able to kill this young boy. And there's also the flipside of Harry confronting Voldemort about *his* failures.

Beyond the battle between Harry and Voldemort, no doubt the sequence that fans of the novels were most looking forward to in Deathly Hallows *was the epilogue that featured a flash forward that showed the characters in the future with their own children, who they're getting ready to send off to Hogwarts.*

DAVID YATES: I love that epilogue in the book. There's something haunting and beautiful about seeing this circle-of-life thing. Pulling it off was a combination of makeup and visual effects. Special makeup gets you so far, but you need a combination of things.

RUPERT GRINT (actor, "Ron Weasley"): I quite enjoyed that — the kids he's got and all, and I like the way we're on the platform seeing our kids off to their first year at Hogwarts. That was a nice way of rounding it off.

DANIEL RADCLIFFE: I was concerned about the aging scene, and I was worried about how we were going to do it, but I have to tell you, the make-up looks fantastic. I'm very pleased with my make-up in the scene. Harry ages much more flatteringly than Ron does, but as soon as they presented Rupert with the fat suit, he was like, "Make it bigger!" But we had a great fun doing that scene.

NICK DUDMAN (makeup designer, *Harry Potter and the Deathly Hallows: Part 1* and *Part 2*).): To pull this off, we made body suits for the kids for the epilogue, because we had to age them. Which meant for the girls we made them slightly more woman-like, and we made Ron a little tubbier. We used makeup to very subtly take them to 35, which is nightmarish. It's the hardest thing we did, making it look realistic without being distracting. The trick was that the audience mustn't pick up on it; it would be the last thing that they will see. *No pressure there.*

DANIEL RADCLIFFE: That sequence was ... *interesting*. I think we made it very hard on ourselves, because we shot it at King's Cross for real and had to shoot it far too quickly, because it's a train station and people actually need to use that platform, so there were time constraints. Then we did reshoots on a set where we could take more time. There was lots of crying by myself and Emma and Rupert. The crew as well, because a lot of them had been there for 10 years. So there were lots of tears from everybody. I remember at the time being quite sort of inconsolable for, like, two hours.

With the conclusion of Harry Potter and the Deathly Hallows *everyone involved was able to walk away with a truly unique experience — for themselves and filmgoers around the world — that likely would never be repeated again for any of them. As such, the ending was an emotional affair.*

DAVID HEYMAN: The ending of the films was a mixed feeling. It's good in the sense that there are other things to be working on, and good in the sense that I'm very happy with the body of work, and really excited about new challenges, brilliant new challenges and having the time to take on new projects. That being said, the experience of Harry Potter has been unique. I suppose every experience is unique, but Harry Potter is very, very special. And just having had the opportunity to be involved with something like this, which is such great material, where there is a receptive audience, where we have, because of the support of the studio and the freedom from the studio to make these films, where they let us make the movies as we see them, an incredibly supportive environment.

EMMA WATSON: The very last scene we shot was a tiny scene of us jumping into a fireplace, but that would be visual effects. We were just jumping on a crash mat, but that was our last scene. It was really weird and very surreal. It felt like a moment in history. At the same time, it was kind of a relief, because my life got to be about Emma for a while and not Hermione, which is nice. I got to go and spread my wings a bit and try out some other stuff, which was great, but of course it was devastating in a way. I hadn't known anything else since I was nine-years-old, so it was pretty daunting.

DAVID HEYMAN: Part of my sadness about it all ending has to do with the people working on it. To have the opportunity to work with people, some over the whole 10-year period, and see these kids grow up, to have made friends in this way, to have this security and environment, is something special. And that's not to say there won't be other great experiences. There will, of course, but this one is very special — you've been a family for 10 or 11 years, and all of a sudden, the kids are leaving and the family is going its separate ways. It's really exciting to see what the future holds for everybody — even with the kids, it's a lot of pain. I've got kids and they're moving on and that's exciting both to see what's going to happen to them, and because the time becomes a little bit more your own. At the same time, the time with them is something you'd rather not end, and you wish you could hold on to every single moment of it.

DAVID BARRON: For the cast, the Harry Potter films are the most expensive home movies ever made, as they can look back and see their complete adolescence unfold on film. It's extraordinary as characters, actors and people, and it's kind of thrilling. The whole franchise, I think, is unique. I can't imagine there being anything quite like it again. There never has been before. Frankly, we're all really lucky to be a part of something that's so unusual and unique.

DAVID HEYMAN: There's not been another film series, eight films, in which the same cast, all the way through, grows up — and the audience has grown up with them, which is unique. And that is something that we haven't seen before. It's also a film series without movie stars per se — I mean there are people who are well-known, but there are no movie stars. The star is the material. The big star is Jo Rowling and the books.

Harry Potter and the Deathly Hallows: Part 1 *was released on November 19, 2010 in both the UK and the US. The combined budget for* Part 1 *and* Part 2 *was $250* million. Part 1 *pulled in $977 million at the global box office.* Harry Potter and the Deathly Hallows: Part 2 *was released on July 15, 2011 in both the UK and the US. Its global box office gross was $1.342 billion.*

BEHIND THE SCENES OF *HARRY POTTER AND THE DEATHLY HALLOWS*

SET VISIT TO HARRY POTTER AND THE DEATHLY HALLOWS

Chronicling the making of the Harry Potter films since the very beginning is something that I'd done, writing and editing a wide variety of special issues that have brought the stars and the creators up close to the fans. Eventually the tables turned as Harry Potter brought me to Hogwarts. Or at least London's Leavesden Studios, where each of the films have been shot.

This actually wasn't my first visit to Leavesden, having gone there back in 1995 to check out the filming of the James Bond film GoldenEye, *which introduced Pierce Brosnan as agent 007 to the world. Back then I was impressed with the efficiency of the operation and just thrilled to be seeing the James Bond production machine in operation. Flash forward 15 years to December 2, 2010, and I was more taken in by the sense of family that was apparent. Not really surprising considering that the vast majority of the people laboring there had been doing so for the past decade. There's a certain familiarity between them as they speak, wave to each other throughout the day and reference the fact that they've been through one heck of a journey together.*

What follows is a chronicle of that day on the set as experienced by myself and several other reporters from around the world.

ARRIVAL

Loaded into a mini-van, we were brought over to Leavesden, a former Rolls Royce cart factory that had been transformed into a movie studio. Upon entering, the first thing you realize is the tremendous size of this place: in some ways it feels like a community that just happens to have a roof over its head.

With filming of *Harry Potter and the Deathly Hallows Part 2* not scheduled to wrap for another four months, the sounds of production can be heard almost everywhere you turn. You also find that there are various props and pieces of sets in the most unusual places, reminiscent of a child who has neglected to put away his or her playthings.

The first stop is a fairly large tent, which, for the purposes of this set visit, has been set up with tables that house a number of large images from the production, including shots from the film, behind the scenes imagery and design illustrations. Also, behind glass are a number of Wizarding books the characters utilize, as well as copies of *The Daily Prophet* that were used during filming.

Images include Harry and Ron in Malfoy Mansion, where they are attempting to rescue the captured Hemione, who is being tortured. Pointing to a particular image, our host describes, "Towards the end of the first film, this is a scene where, basically, they've just escaped from the Malfoy Manor, back to Shell Cottage. This is after they've seen that Dobby has got the dagger in his heart, which is why they look so horrified." Other descriptions follow — many of them spoilers for *Part 2* — in some cases mapping out a sequence that we'll see filmed later in the day.

PRODUCER DAVID BARRON

Once the explanation of imagery is completed, we're joined by producer David Barron, who engages in a Q&A session with us.

How much of a light at the end of the tunnel do you finally see?

DAVID BARRON: It's still too far off to feel like we're almost there. We don't finish filming until the end of April [of 2010] and then we've got a years of post-production to edit and deliver two films. We know it's coming, but at this point the end of filming is a goal to be achieved. We're on day 178, so it's a long, long shoot. Getting to the end of the shoot is a goal to achieve; getting to the end of *everything* is something that will hit us when we get a little closer to that.

Just to follow that up, have you gotten to the stage where you've wrapped any of the key players?

DAVID BARRON: Gary Oldman is finished, who comes back as a ghost with Harry's parents when Harry runs into the forest to confront Voldemort. In the weeks and months to come, we'll be ticking them off one by one.

We're speaking of light at the end of the tunnel, but is there a part of you that doesn't want that? That would prefer to keep going?

DAVID BARRON: Oh, absolutely. If there were more stories, we'd be happy to stay here and do them, because this is as good as it gets. David Heyman and I often say to each other, "It's a real shame; we'll never have it this good again." We work with fantastic material that people love, we're making films – unless we go pretty much go off the rails – where there's an audience that's very forgiving. They want us to make the films and they want to see them, which is a very rare circumstance to be in. We're working with great material, the best cast, the best designers and there's never quite enough money, no matter how much you've got, but enough to make a pretty good go at delivering the stories on film, and with a group of people we all really like and enjoy working with. I don't think we'll ever get it quite as good again, I don't think. So it's a mixed feeling, because the excitement of actually starting something new is something to look forward to, but it will be a huge wrench to give this up and walk away from here.

Every film brings with it the pressure to try and make a great film no matter what, but when you have a final film, where you've got seven movies leading to that final battle, how much pressure is it to deliver?

DAVID BARRON: There *is* pressure. I think the biggest pressure is to make sure that we deliver the emotional story and don't get tied up with giants and hordes of Death Eaters and other things. Which we have to do. A balance has to be found, because you have to get a sense that it's a battle to end all battles as far as our magical worlds are concerned. But the key thing is that we have spent eight films at that point leading up to Harry and Voldemort's final meeting, and the emotional element of that and their physical battle can't be overshadowed by 10 million Death Eaters. We had to be careful. There's a balance to be found there, so there *is* a tiny little pressure there [*laughs*].

Was there much that you had to leave out of the book?

DAVID BARRON: You can't leave that much out of this book, which is why it's two films rather than one. When we first got the book, oh my God, it was so huge — but we started off with the DNA of this series of one book, one film. We wanted to be true to that DNA and we also didn't want to give anyone the opportunity to say, "Warner Bros. can't resist one last dash to the till." That absolutely wasn't the case. They gave us the option of deciding how, creatively, we wanted to approach the final book. We tried really hard to fit it all into one film, but you just can't. Steve Kloves at one point said, "We can possibly make three films," but we didn't. We're not really leaving things out. Things get compressed more than left out, because you can't really leave anything out.

Having the same director for the past four films — what were the risks inherent in that and what has been the pay-off?

DAVID BARRON: The risk always is that you have four films that feel like they've come from the same place, but David Yates is very keen that that not be the case. He wanted to make four different films, there's no mileage for him to come back and remake the same film. The stories just lend themselves; they're very different stories. This last book is split into a road story and the big fight, so they're very different in tone. I think the benefits for us is the shorthand that someone like David now has in understanding the world. Part of our job — David Heyman and mine — with a new director is that whilst giving them free reign and full creative freedom, we actually keep them within the parameters of the world that exists. They're *not* fantasy films. Sometimes I think people come and think of a fantasy film with the visual effects and the magical world. There are very physical restrictions you can do. Imagination can run riot, which is great because that's where the great vision comes from, but at the same time it has to be within the premises of the world that exists, because they're not one-off films, they are part of a singular story.

The advantage for us is that it's a lot easier with a director who's done it before, because there's a lot to learn. I came in on the second film and by then everybody else had done only one film, but nonetheless I felt like I was miles behind everybody else because they knew so much more than I did. For a director, it's the same thing. Mike Newell said when he first started [on *Goblet of Fire*] that he didn't dare look up from his desk for the first three months because the landscape was so enormous that it was a bit scary. He picked away at it until he'd built his mind-map of the world. You use that as the basis from which to build your own film. David Yates had to do that for the fifth film, but by the time we got to the sixth, he had all of that inherent knowledge. As a result, seven parts one and two were a joy, because he knows much more than we do.

When you put it all together, it's been this unprecedented journey to watch these kids go from 10 years old to 20 years old. Being a part of that, what is your feeling?

DAVID BARRON: It's never happened before and it probably never will again. Bond had 21 different films that are single, individual stories. But to tell a singular story in eight films, I don't think it's ever happened before. If it happens again, there will probably be quite a long gap before someone else finds material that is as rich as Jo's creation. It feels really great and I'm real proud of what we've done. The state of Florida is saying the opening of the theme park will regenerate tourism in Florida in an unprecedented fashion. The tentacles reach out a long way and we're very proud to be a part of it.

Once David Barron departed, producer David Heyman stepped into the tent to talk with us. His quotes have been filtered into the making of Deathly Hallows *section.*

FILMING

From the tent following the sit-down with David Heyman, we were ushered over to the soundstage area where a sequence was being filmed. Due to the set up, we weren't able to stand just off-stage. Instead, we watched what was being filmed on a number of monitors set up behind the wall of the stage.

There is one aspect of moviemaking that has always amused me. Between camera set-ups there is a certain chaos apparent from people milling about, having conversations with each other, grabbing a bite to eat or moving equipment. It's *extremely* loud. But then the warning bell goes off alerting everyone that the director is getting ready to call "Action!" and everything goes instantly silent. The temptation is to check your hearing to make sure that you haven't abruptly gone deaf, but in reality, it's just about professionals doing what they do best.

There's the sound of clapboards, followed by director David Yates calling for "Action!" An instant later, Daniel Radcliffe as Harry Potter and Rupert Grint as Ron Weasley run breathlessly into frame. It feels like we're watching this on TV, but the actions we're viewing are occurring live on the other side of the wall.

"We have to do something, Harry," Ron manages. "We can't leave her…" The "her" in question is Emma Watson's Hermione Granger, who had previously recorded a sequence in which she is tortured by Helene Bonham Carter's Bellatrix.

Daniel and Rupert are interrupted by Evanna Lynch's Luna Lovegood. "Ron? Harry?" Evanna, who has arrived with John Hurt's Mr. Ollivander, says.

"Luna?" asks a bewildered Harry.

"You look strange, Harry," says Evanna, turning to Hurt. "Mr. Ollivander, look who it is – Harry Potter."

"Harry?" replies a confused Hurt in character.

"Hello, sir," says Daniel.

At that moment, Carter's voice is heard, screaming. "What else did you take?"

Watson's Hermione replies, "We didn't take anything."

"Liar!"

Ron: "We have to do something.

Mr. Ollivander: "There's no way out of here. We've tried everything. It's enchanted."

The screams continue.

The strangest thing happens next when we hear the sound of Dobby the elf, but when he steps into frame, he's very much in the form of the actor who provides his voice, Toby Jones. As the rest of the scene, which has suddenly taken on a feeling of the surreal as Toby speaks his character's dialogue, plays out, Harry realizes that Dobby can use his power to help them to escape, and he does just that for Luna and Ollivander, while Harry and Ron press on to rescue Hermione.

A QUICK RIDE LATER

While preparations for the scene to be shot again are made — definitely a downside of life on a movie set, one sequence being shot over and over again — we depart the soundstage and board a shuttle that takes us to our next location. As we do so, we pass the hedges that serve as the entrance to Malfoy Manor, and we see Hagrid's hut after it's been attacked and burned down.

Moments later we enter another sound stage only to find ourselves standing in the lobby of Gringott's Bank. There may not be any goblins behind the counters at this particular moment, but as voices and footsteps echo (those footsteps covered, incidentally, by plastic booties so as not to scuff the floor) there is just a moment when you feel as though you've been transported into the Harry Potter films. There is such an incredible sense of detail here, from the ornate design, marble floors, functioning counter bells and ledgers (many pages of which have been filled out) to gold bullion that looks so real, the illusion only being broken by the fact that if they *were* real, they wouldn't be here and neither would we. Gringott's is the setting for a scene in which Harry, Ron and Hermione arrive in disguise in an effort to steal a Horcrux.

From there we're off to "the boathouse," where again, we're looking at a boat on the water. We know we're indoors, but it's all so realistic that for an instant you believe you're outside — although the illusion is broken by a large green screen to be used to extend the river. It's the setting for a sequence that's different from the novel in which Voldemort corners Snape and (SPOILER ALERT) kills him. It's all about the power of the wand — since Snape killed Dumbledore, that particular wand can only be used by Snape, but if Voldemort kills him, then that power will be available to the dark lord. Just before he dies, Snape removes his memories and transfers them to Harry.

MAKE-UP!

Next on the agenda is Nick Dudman, make-up designer for all of the Harry Potter films. As he speaks, we find ourselves being led through the makeup department which also houses a wide variety of creature models, including a full-size hippogriff and a werewolf. In some ways, it feels like we're in a museum housing strange and bizarre creatures.

Referring to the work being done in the shop at this particular moment, Dudman explains, "We're making body suits for the kids for the epilogue, because we're going to age them all. Which means for the girls we're going to make them slightly more woman-like, and we're going to make Ron a little tubbier; and we'll be using makeups to very subtly take them to 35, which is actually nightmarish. I think it's the hardest thing we're doing, to make it look realistic without being distracting. The audience mustn't pick up on it; it will be the last thing that the audience will see." He pauses for a moment and smiles while he adds, "No pressure."

When asked how he will feel when it's all over, Dudman offers, "We'll never do it like this again. To be in the same facility, even this leaking old building, for 10 years with the opportunity to do something and then a year later try and improve it, with a decent budget and time, is just never going to happen again. And we will all have to be rehabilitated, because when someone asks me to do a rubber nose on a movie, I'm going to be asking for six months and a crew of 40 [*laughs*]. And I don't quite know how I'm going to adapt."

Things wrapped up with Nick by our asking what the creature or person he'd want to take home with him, and what's the one he would redo if he had the chance?

"If I was forced to choose one thing to take," he replies, "I would probably take Buckbeak the Hippogriff... if I could wheel it out and put it in a truck and take it, I would. Although I love Aragog the giant spider, I just don't know where I'd take it. And if I was to do something over again...God, *everything*. Nothing's perfect. Probably early stuff. We got to do the goblins again, and I'm really pleased about that. I was pleased with what we did back then, but what we've done now is 10 times greater and the work is just so much better, because we've refined the processes. We've set a standard for ourselves that are much higher than before, so I feel like I have redone things already. I'm a makeup artist, so the animatronic stuff I find fascinating, but it's not the thing that fires me the same way as sticking the stuff on a human being and watching it performed. That's what I personally get a kick out of.

CHATTING WITH RUPERT GRINT

Following the conversation with Nick, we returned to the tent to have a little talk with Mr. Ron Weasley himself, Rupert Grint.

The romance between Ron and Hermione really blossoms now and there's the kiss. How tricky is this to pull off when you've known someone that long?

RUPERT GRINT: I was really worried about that, because it just felt like it was wrong, but once we were on set – David Yates was really good about it, he gave us a long chat before we did it, and it was fine, it was kind of a fuss over nothing. We just did it and there weren't that many takes. It was over pretty quick, too — it was nice.

Did you watch it back on the monitor?

RUPERT GRINT: Emma has, I haven't. I think I'll just wait until it comes out.

Were there the usual gags about not eating garlic before the kiss?

RUPERT GRINT: No, I didn't do that — we were quite considerate of each other.

What was the biggest surprise about book seven leading into the films – what were you not expecting that happens with Ron?

RUPERT GRINT: I don't know. I suppose the thing with Hermione — I knew there had always been something playing between them, but I honestly didn't think about the kiss or the fact that in this film they're quite couply at the end. It's strange, but I loved book seven. I thought it was really good.

Is there a happy and sad feeling about this all being over?

RUPERT GRINT: Yeah, I mean, in two ways — I'm looking forward to moving away from this and to see what's out there, because it has been like half my life, and I've loved every minute of it, but I'm ready to move on now. But I'm definitely going to miss it because of all the people I've come to love over the years, and it's been great fun. So I'm going to miss it.

Are you nervous at all?

RUPERT GRINT: Yes, because it's kind of stepping out into the real world — this is kind of a safe place, so it's going to be strange, but I kind of got a feel for it because I did two other independent films. That was completely a different world, so it was nice to have that experience, but I think I'm kind of ready.

Will you stay in the UK?

I don't know — to be honest, I haven't really thought of it because the end of this seems really far away still.

How have you matured as an actor over the past 10 years?

RUPERT GRINT: I suppose I've taken it more seriously and cared about the performance more than I probably did for the first few films, because it was just fun and not being in school, it was just an amazing experience. So definitely now I'm taking it much more seriously. But I'm really not aware, because I haven't really seen any of the other films since I did them, though I do feel a lot more comfortable on the set.

How strange is it to be on the set of a lower budget film?

RUPERT GRINT: It took a while to adjust to that, because it was really culture shock, everything was different, just the kind of pace they worked at. I was doing ten scenes a day on this one film I was doing called *Cherry Bomb* — and it was *so* quick. We finished that in four weeks, which is like the average big scene for a Harry Potter film, but it was really fun. I kind of enjoyed it — *Cherry Bomb* and *Wild Target* — and, yeah, it was good, they were both quite quick, six weeks or four weeks, but it was a good experience.

Do you have any other films planned?

RUPERT GRINT: Nothing really definite, but I'm kind of just concentrating on *Deathly Hallows*, really.

What would you do if no more jobs come along?

RUPERT GRINT: I don't know really, it's quite a scary thought. I'll have to wait and see — I've got a lot of other things; I still have the ice cream van, I suppose.

Are you able to separate film one and film two in terms of production?

RUPERT GRINT: It's quite confusing, because they're all intertwined — part one it's a very different feel from any other Harry Potter film because we're out of Hogwarts because nowhere is safe. That's the feeling — the locations were all relatively close to the studio, but they were all random places like in the forest, and some fields and stuff, in tents - it was quite fun, because you kind of felt like you were on the run, and me and Dan are looking pretty rough because we have stubble and long hair.

How do you control the stubble so it looks the same?

RUPERT: It's quite a trick — you have to plan ahead to plan for the stubble, but they did an experiment of sticking bits of hair on our faces, and it didn't really work. And I'm wearing hair pieces at the moment because there are two kinds of hair looks, a longer look and a shorter look — in the film we're kind of captured, and then we escape, and then we're in the battle scenes with all the fighting. But we're really enjoying it - it's been a very different experience.

Do you feel like you're making two films?

RUPERT GRINT: When we started off it was part one and it was quite clear, but now over the past few months it's kind of been part two here and there, and we've been all over the place, so it's been quite confusing; you have to really think about it.

There's a shot of you with make-up on your shoulder?

RUPERT GRINT: That was part one — when Ron gets flinched when they escape from the Ministry, and it looks horrible. It's like a big open wound, and it's kind of, very bloody, it's actually kind of gory, I was surprised they went that far with it.

Do you have any feeling about the fact that we're watching you literally grow up before our eyes over the course of these films?

RUPERT GRINT: It's quite weird and strange, because it hasn't really felt that long. It's really weird when you see the first two films, because they play them on TV and it feels like a different person when I look at myself. But it's been great, I've really enjoyed it.

In reading the last book, what did you make of the epilogue in terms of what happens to you?

RUPERT GRINT: I quite enjoyed it — quite the kids he's got, and I like the way we're on the platform seeing our kids off to their first year at Hogwarts. I thought that was a nice way of rounding it off. I've seen a few pictures of how they're going to make us when we're older — Ron kind of puts on a bit of weight.

What's your mindset, playing that role but as a 35-year-old? Will you do a different voice?

RUPERT GRINT: I'm not sure, really. I don't know how far we're going to go — it's going to be a quite heavy prosthetic; I'll have to see what I'll look like.

Is there one thing from the books that you never got to play?

RUPERT GRINT: From all the books — God, I don't know really. I can't think of anything. I don't know. The books all blur to me, I do kind of re-read them each time.

Did they ever do apparition classes?

RUPERT GRINT: No, this is the first film we kind of start apparating.

Do you think Ron would be a friend in real life – would you go to the pub with him?

RUPERT GRINT: I've always felt quite similar to Ron, I've always liked Ron, he's always been one of my favorite characters in the books.

Do you think you've become more like him, or he's become more like you?

RUPERT GRINT: I don't know. I think we've merged into one kind of person. It's weird, I suppose. I'd like to think I'm a little braver, but in this one he does step up and become more of a hero.

BACK TO THE SET

Once we were finished talking to Rupert, we headed back to the soundstage where the sequence being shot earlier was still going through several takes. When a break was called, we managed a quick interview with Evanna Lynch, who plays Luna Lovegood.

When all of that screaming is going on, you don't even flinch...

EVANNA LYNCH: Luna just never gets shocked. She's just so accepting of everything. Even if Dobby appears, she just rolls with it. She never worries, because, to me, she believes in fate and whatever happens she accepts you can't change it. She's able to focus on the little details, like the aesthetics of things, and can really get lost in those moments. But it *is* a real shrill scream.

Is that a mindset that you enjoy as an actor?

EVANNA LYNCH: Yes, definitely. Maybe it would be fun to be shocked, but I think it's more real for the character.

What is Luna's part like in Part 1*?*

EVANNA LYNCH: She doesn't have a big role in *Part 1* at all. She's kidnapped for half of it. They spend a lot of time at their house, and it was very exciting to go on that set only to discover that I'm not in that scene at all. It's really interesting when you meet her and her dad together, because it all makes sense. I love being on set with Reece. He's dressed in bright yellow. Compared to everyone else we already felt like outsiders. I'm far more involved in film two. Being in Ravenclaw, that becomes really significant because she knows about one of the horcruxes at Ravenclaw. This film is so inventive, one thing after the other, so many things happening. Every time Luna comes on, you just forget about the plot. She's not really in tune with what's going on or what's happening next. She's just there. I always find it a huge relief when she says something and for a few seconds you forget what's going on. That's what I get when I read the books. She helps Harry along.

Was she an easy character for you to find as an actress?

EVANNA LYNCH: Definitely. We're quite different and I would really aspire to be more like her, because I love that she can tune out. I learned a lot from her definitely, because you can't change anything. Sure people may die and that's really worrying, but getting upset about it will only make it worse. I love how she's really adjusted to death. She's more spiritual than the others. It's not going to ruin her life thinking about what's going to happen.

Veteran actor John Hurt, who plays Mr. Ollivander, was the next person we had the opportunity to interview.

How confident were you that the character would be back?

JOHN HURT: I had no idea the character would be back. I just thought it was a one-off until a friend said to me, "Hey, you're going to be in Harry Potter again." "Why?" "Well, I read the book," and that was the first I heard of it, but it's good fun.

How big is your role?

JOHN HURT: I'm not in a huge amount, really. I get called back into it because they need a wand and he's the wandmaker. Then things go wrong and he gets tortured and he's ashamed of himself, because he gives away something he shouldn't. It's got a real human touch to it.

Had you followed the series since you first appeared in it?

JOHN HURT: In bits. I love going to the cinema, but it's not really my sort of film. My children love it.

How do you find working with David Yates?

JOHN HURT: I think he's wonderful to work with and I can't wait to do another film with him.

Is it strange to you knowing that you're something of a sci-fi icon because of things like Hellboy, *this,* Alien, *etc.?*

JOHN HURT: Well, I certainly get recognized by people for *Alien*, because it is a huge, wonderful film.

How interesting is it to have been in the first Harry Potter film and now reunited with the kids who started too young?

JOHN HURT: That's very interesting, because they were half their age 10 years ago. Seeing Daniel now is kind of amazing. And to see someone who may never have been an actor — because it's not an easy game at all — who has come out of it fantastically is wonderful. Emma, of course, has gone off to university and Rupert was always kind of a born actor.

Our final conversation took place with Toby Jones, who, as mentioned earlier, is the voice behind Dobby the Elf.

Is being on set and acting out Dobby's part fun for you?

TOBY JONES: To me, it's a measure of the care the producers take. I've been taken on location and everything to do the voice. I've always been pleasantly surprised that people respond to me and send me mail in support of Dobby, when I feel only partly responsible because incredible visual effects create the reality of Dobby. So, in short, I'm as surprised as you are.

Have you had to wear a motion capture costume?

TOBY JONES: They don't do motion capture like that. I've done that on other films, but not on these.

Dobby has a huge emotional arc in this final chapter. Can you talk us through his arc in the two parts?

TOBY JONES: In *Part 1*, there's a bit of reintroducing dobby into the narrative, since he hasn't been around since film two. In the second part, Dobby is instrumental at a key moment of the plot.

How strange was it to be playing the death of this character?

TOBY JONES: I did act it out and they filmed me acting it out, how the rhythm would be and how the emotion would be. I felt very happy because every time I'm on the set, I feel totally included in the whole process, which isn't often the case when you're voicing a character. I feel very proud of that moment. We did it on the beach and I hope the audience likes it as much as I enjoyed doing it.

What's your sense of how valuable it is for you to physically be on the set and interacting with the cast?

TOBY JONES: When I got the part, I was doing this play I'd been doing for eight months on the West End. My voice was in shreds. Chris Columbus came to the play and said that I got the part, and because my voice was shredded, I could reach a pitch that I normally couldn't. So I had to shred my voice again to reach the pitch of Dobby.

And with that, the gates to Hogwarts closed, with all of us heading back to our hotel before the return trip home to America the following morning. A lot was crammed in to one day, but it was a rare opportunity to experience the magic — in all its forms — up close.

Harry Potter and the Deathly Hallows Behind-the-Scenes Interviews

DANIEL RADCLIFFE AND THE ROLE OF A LIFETIME

While discussing *The Deathly Hallows*, Daniel looks into the future as he reflects on the past

This was the final opportunity I and a number of other reporters had to speak to Daniel prior to the release of Harry Potter and the Deathly Hallows Part 2, *and, as always, he offered up the detailed and thoughtful answers he always did.*

There was a picture of you kissing a lucky fan at Movie Com? Would you ever date a Harry Potter fan?

DANIEL RADCLIFFE: I wouldn't date them because they were a Harry Potter fan — that I think would be the height of egomania, but yeah, it's something I kind of tend not to do generally, particularly at premieres. It can create something of a hysterical atmosphere, but if the person in question were able to see me as something other than Harry Potter, then I would have no problem — because, to tell the truth, most people are Harry Potter fans, so it's hard to avoid them. Even girls I've been out with in the past have liked the films, and loved the books. But it's certainly never been the focus of a relationship.

Recently I read a quote that said you weren't thrilled with your performance in Half Blood *– going into the next two films, how did you prep yourself to play Harry and get over those insecurities?*

DANIEL RADCLIFFE: It's part of your job to be highly critical of your own performance, I think, and I always have been — I've never been entirely thrilled with my performance, and I've never liked watching myself, but in that last film I just felt there was a lack of variety. So I think in the 7th film I've made the effort to be more expressive and give it more variety — not over the top, and hammy obviously — and I think, in a way I was fortunate to have that experience of not being entirely thrilled with my performance in number six, because it gave me the kick up the backside that I needed to psych myself up and get ready for the journey of the 7th film. In terms of my preparation, I think I was just more thorough when it came to each scene — not that I was ever complacent, I would hate to give that impression, because that's not really in me, in my make up. I became slightly more obsessive about my preparations for the 7th film, and for all the various scenes, and I found what works for me in terms of those big scenes. It works to sort of take myself off the corner of the set and almost work myself into a little bit of a frenzy where I stop being particularly aware of what I'm doing. Because the times you do your best work is when you're not really thinking about it. I think so anyway.

If you do all the preparation in advance, and you know the thoughts of the character, and you know the character and you know why he's there in that scene, and what he wants in that scene, and why he wants it at that particular moment - if you're aware of all that, and then you just put all that in the back of your mind, so it's in-built, and then you just let whatever happens, happen. That became my way of working on the 7th film that I didn't have on the 6th. I think the difference as well between number five and number six is that, five working with Gary Oldman, was something I didn't realize how much better I became when I worked with him. And so I think that on the 6th film I expected all that to carry on, but of course part of it is not having a sparring partner, because our characters have a wonderful relationship, but to have that person to act with, he brought something else out in me certainly, and I think in the 6th film I just expected that to continue, and after seeing it, I realized that it didn't to the extent that I would have liked. But in the 7th I worked harder to maintain some of the spirit and the feeling that I had working with Gary.

Can you describe Harry's emotional journey in the arc of this film, and also your own emotional journey?

DANIEL RADCLIFFE: As far as Harry goes, one of the major things in the *Deathly Hallows Part 1* and *Part 2*, but particularly *Part 1*, is the theme of faith, and his faith in Dumbledore being tested, because obviously in the 6th Dumbledore dies, he leaves Harry this mission, and he leaves him with almost no information with which to work on. Apart from three rather cryptic bequests in his will — which, to Harry, Ron and Hermione, seem to make no sense at the time, but gradually as the film carries on, they make more and more sense. So, for me, it's a journey in which you're hearing all this stuff about Dumbledore constantly, stuff you didn't know before, stuff that makes him doubt the man's integrity — something that he's never even questioned before. He questions what Dumbledore's motives were all along, and it's almost — it's always dangerous to throw around religious comparisons — a Job type of test of faith, and how far that faith can be pushed before Harry gives up. But ultimately, every time Harry finds himself in that dark moment where he thinks it's a worthless quest and he doesn't know why he's doing it, something happens which just allows it to continue on. As far as his relationship with Ron and Hermione goes, it's one of them gradually realizing that Harry has no idea what to do — he has no plan, he's just winging it. And so as they lose faith in him, he starts to become more paranoid and isolated and, I suppose, angrier, but it doesn't ever display itself as anger, it comes across as more of a desperation.

In terms of my own personal emotions, it was a very long film, it was very exciting, it was at times very hard work, but you know, that's why we do it and that's why we love it. I didn't have any of the more traumatic emotions that Harry had, but obviously as you said, towards the end it was very emotional, I think I've been quoted as saying we all cried, a lot, and we did, and since then it's been very odd. The first sort of month away was very strange, but luckily there were lots of times over that time that I saw people who worked on the films. I was at Pinewood the other day, prepping things for *Woman in Black*, and I bumped into at least 30 people, some of whom worked on the last film, but some of whom I haven't seen since the 3rd or even 2nd movie, and so I've always said, with *Harry Potter* it's like the Mafia – once you're in, you're never really out. I will know these people for the rest of my life, no matter where I go or what happens, so there is some sadness in leaving, but I've gotten now to the point where I'm excited about the future. I'm also very excited to see the films; the journey's not over yet in the sense that people still have to see these movies, and I'm excited to see what people think.

There was talk about different directors – what were the pros of having one director, specifically David Yates, handling those last four films?

DANIEL RADCLIFFE: Whoever directed the 6th film had to direct the 7th film, because though we obviously changed things around before, and that was great because it was what kept the series fresh and alive. We've been very good at talking perceived risks in terms of directorial choices — I don't think many people expected Alfonso to direct the third film, I don't think many people expected David Yates to come on for the 5th – but I think it would have been too much of a risk for someone to come on with such a distinct style. What we've been very lucky about, in terms of the directors is that they all brought their own style to it, but it's never been such that it becomes distracting and doesn't feel like it's not a continuation of the last movie, but the risk of that happening with the 7th – well, it's different enough already. It'll take people a bit to adjust to the fact that we're no longer in robes, we're no longer in Hogwarts, so if you had on top of that a totally different style of direction, that would have been distracting, and taken away from the movie. And specifically why I think David Yates is brilliant, and particularly for the last movie, parts one and two, is that David is a bit of a genius at plot. And I've always said, it's like he can see the whole film in one frame in front of him, and he will relate things in scene 350 — because we get far beyond that in scene numbers for these two films — to something in scene 8, and he will link it up beautifully has such an understanding of the arc of the story. On a film this big, you need someone with that kind of clarity of vision about the story, and about how he wants to tell the story, so I think it definitely was the right thing to do to have David stay with us.

How do you feel it worked splitting up the two films?

DANIEL RADCLIFFE: The first part is very different from the second – the first part is an exploration of character, and how these characters react to one another, in a totally different environment. When Jo was writing the seventh book – she referred to it as, "I'm writing the *Deathly Hallows*, and at the moment it's like a very weird road trip," and that's kind of how we saw it going in, and the second part sort of starts out as a heist movie and turns into a war film. There are many different phases to the book, but the progression is so natural and exciting, that I don't think too many people will be distracted by the fact that the film does move from so many different environments, and so many different kind of tones. I think that's what's going to make the film exciting and different from the other films,

Looking back on the arc of this journey, knowing what you know now, what one particular thing would you do a re-do on?

DANIEL RADCLIFFE: If I was young enough, I'd like to go back and do the first two again, because I do still find those kind of very embarrassing to watch. Something along those lines, but to be honest, I don't really look back on the films too much, because I probably would be sitting there going, "Oh God, there's so much I would want to change about what I've done." I genuinely think you'd struggle to find an actor who's truly happy with what he's done, and if you do, the chances are they aren't very good. I mean, it's hard to say, but I'm sure if I sat down and watched the films with you, I could point to every other scene, and I would ask to change something.

Are there any souvenirs took from the set?

DANIEL RADCLIFFE: The only thing I wanted was the glasses. I didn't want the wand, I definitely didn't want the broom, and I ended up getting two pairs of glasses — one lens-less, because often the glasses we wear on set are lens-less because of camera reflections. I've got them, from the 7th film, but I've also got the lensed version that we had from the very first film, I didn't even know they still kept them, but they did. I'm very happy and they're both in a private place.

Emma told us about this great party she threw – did you go?

DANIEL RADCLIFFE: Is this the dinner party they had? It was lovely, it was fantastic, Emma cooked and she was very impressive, and she was very much the hostess with the mostest. I never had a dinner party in my life, but the idea terrifies me; I would have been so intimidated by the idea of that. But, yes, she got the core of the young cast members, and we all went round to her house, and it was great, dripping with nostalgia, reminiscing about the early days, and how young and cute and innocent we all were. It was a really good night, because if you talk to me and Rupert, neither of us would have had the wherewithal to put together a party, so the fact that she did was really appreciated.

What was the hardest scene for you to film in Deathly Hallows?

DANIEL RADCLIFFE: I suppose getting beaten up by Ralph Fiennes in the second part was physically quite demanding, because what I love about that scene is it's the moment that I've kind of been wanting to happen for years, but that never has. And I'm actually glad it hasn't, because I've always wanted a moment where the magic is not enough, and he just tries to kill Harry, physically, just by beating him up, and it would have been totally wrong to do it any earlier than the seventh film. So, physically that was a challenging thing, but there were a lot of physically challenging things in the film. But I love getting involved in running up and down, and falling, and getting hit; I love all that. And I think, emotionally, all the stuff early on, in the first part with myself and Rupert, where we're fighting and hating each other. That was hard, because it's very hard to hate Rupert Grint, even in acting, and there are scenes where Harry goes and finds his parents' grave. There are so many deeply emotional scenes that it is hard to pick one, but if I got 50% of them right when I did them, then I'll be very, very happy. I mean, there are so many tough scenes in the film – and also to be honest, a lot of scenes I've completely forgotten about. You film something for 18 months, and if there's something in the trailer from the 1st month of filming, you think, "Oh my God, I've totally forgotten about that." I'm sure that when I see the film, I'll be able to give you a much clearer answer. But there were plenty of emotionally challenging scenes.

This is the end of an era, but if JK said I'm writing another book, would you want to star in that next movie?

DANIEL RADCLIFFE: Probably not, because ten years is enough. I think the films have reached a rather perfect and wonderful conclusion and to do anymore at this point would be gilding the lily, unfortunately. But I have had assurances from her that she will not be doing that.

What do you walk away with, as an actor and as a person, from the experience?

DANIEL RADCLIFFE: I will never be able to watch one scene in any of these films without immediately connecting it to the memory of that day on set, or to the memory of what was happening in my life. I walk away with a wealth of experience that actors who go to drama school would kill for in terms of the people I've been able to work with, and watch and learn from. And I walk away, most importantly, with a love of film, of film sets, and the most amazing group of friends anyone could wish for, and I'm not just talking about the cast, I mean, so many of my best friends are in the crew, and you know these are people I will know forever now, and I feel very lucky.

THE OTHER SIDE OF THE COIN

Tom Felton Reflects on Draco Malfoy

It's not surprising that when people think of actor Tom Felton, they instantly think of his on-screen alter ego, and Harry Potter nemesis, Draco Malfoy, and the thought isn't always a positive one. After all, there seems to have been very little redeemable about Draco through the 10-year history of this film series, although the actor sees things somewhat differently, as he explains in this exclusive Q&A.

Like everyone else involved with the films, Tom has the challenge of proving to the world that there is a career beyond Hogwarts, and he seems to be well on his way to doing so. He's already shot his role for next summer's *Planet of the Apes* reboot, *Caesar: Rise of the Planet of the Apes* and is getting ready to film the independent drama *Out of the Rough*.

Is this a weird time for you as the Harry Potter series comes to a close?

TOM FELTON: It's a very strange experience. It's kind of weird when suddenly they say, "Get your stuff and get out" [*laughs*]. It's quite a scary concept, especially since we've never known a world outside of Potter and as adults, it's kind of like stepping out on your own two feet for the first time. But it's been a fantastic thing for my whole life, something I can look back on and be proud of, but I'm hoping that it's not going to be what my whole life has been about. There are a couple of things out there that are keeping me very excited.

Have you prepared for the end in a sense?

TOM FELTON: I certainly have. It only really hit me in the last two years how lucky I am to do what I do for a living, and how I shouldn't take any of it for granted. The last two years have been basically working on different sides of it: auditioning, American accents, different regional accents, just generally trying to prepare myself. I know it's been a fantastic platform, Harry Potter, but there's no way any of us can possibly think it's a given now that we will have careers in the industry. I think it's all still something to work at, and these next few years are the critical years because you don't want to be looking back thinking, "I should have tried something more, I should have tried harder," so, yeah, it's important to me now that I give it my all, and if I don't succeed, then at least I know I tried my hardest.

I would like to get a sense from you of how the character of Draco has evolved over the course of the series.

TOM FELTON: In the first five films I think he was played kind of one dimensionally on purpose. Just to establish that horrible, slimy bully that I think goes to every school. But in the sixth film, like all good school bullies, you have to have a chance to see *why* it was he was like that. You meet more of his family, and you understand the pressures at home were beyond the usual pressures, so I'm hoping that at the end of the sixth film there was a little more empathy for Draco; that not everyone will still insist that he's a born evil Satanist or anything like that. I actually think there's a lot of good in him.

I sometimes think of Draco and Harry as two sides of a coin, with Harry having all the best possible influences around him, whereas poor old Draco gets the worst. He's conflicted, heavily conflicted. In the top part of the brain, if you will, he's trying to please family and make sure he makes his family proud like any kid does. But equally, I think deep down there's some underlying emotions – and I'm not even sure if he's aware of them. That's something that they were quite keen to do, the idea that we're not making much of what he does as conscious thought, it's all coming through the subliminal, and from the unconscious side of himself. So it's a real mixture, although generally speaking he's not the nicest kid in the world, but there's a heavy background to that and there's A good story as to why he's like that, so it's not unjustified.

When you look at Deathly Hallows, *what is the power of this story?*

TOM FELTON: It's all so much climax now with regard to all the love stories, and obviously for me, these battles are taking it to another level as far as Harry Potter goes. I mean, there's absolutely no way that these films could be classified as children's films. They're going to appeal to so many different people on so many levels – and I'm just excited to see the war, and to see the big fight.

How do you feel leaving Draco behind?

TOM FELTON: It's kind of sad in a way. It's been great fun playing him, and there are no two ways about it, I'm certainly going to miss playing the character. Equally, it's been a great learning lesson for me and I've had the opportunity to learn from so many actors on how to play him. I'm sad to see him go, but ultimately, I'm proud of what we achieved in the last ten years and it's always something to look back on. But saying that, if Jo wrote another book, I would never say no.

But Dan's said he's done even if she does write another novel.

TOM FELTON: But our roles are quite different. Young Daniel has been in there for literally ten years! No one actually takes the job more seriously and enjoys it more than Daniel — he's definitely someone you can look up to, and someone I've learned lots from. I have lots of respect for Daniel and why he wouldn't be so keen to carry on — I understand completely.

It seems nice that you've come out of this ten-year experience unscathed – everyone seems to have their wits about them.

TOM FELTON: We're very fortunate. We're all from great families who are very caring, and parent first rather than sort of being agents and managers first and then parents later. It's always been a priority, I think, for all of us to remain as normal, if that's the word, as possible, and keep normal friends around you and normal people instead of being swept away by it all.

APPENDIX: ODDS & ENDS FROM THE POTTERVERSE

In all of the material that has preceded, the focus has been squarely on the making of the eight films making up the Harry Potter *saga which encapsulate J.K. Rowling's seven novels. This appendix, as the title suggests, encompasses a variety of items, interviews and articles that didn't quite fit within the context of the "making of sections."*

SOUNDBITES FROM THE POTTERVERSE

Quotes from cast and crew members about different elements of Harry Potter's world.

DAVID HEYMAN (on what got cut from the books): It's really hard to cut things, because you're killing babies, as it were. But if you make the governing principle that which is relevant to Harry and Harry's journey — once you define the theme and what the journey is as it relates to that, and make everything about Harry, then a lot falls away. Not to say that Hermione and Ron aren't pivotal characters, they are and it's the three of them, but we have to mold it accordingly.

DAVID HEYMAN (on audience expectations): It's going to sound strange, but what one thinks when one is making the film is just making the best film possible. One can't think about the pressure of audience expectations, because if we do, we would be paralyzed. That's from one hand, but on the other, it's a real privilege working on something where, with a certain degree of confidence, there's an audience. The size of the audience may increase or decrease depending, but you know that each of the films is embraced. The least successful film did $795 million worldwide. So far, it's always done incredibly well. *Azkaban* sort of heralded a new beginning in the films, and 4 and 5 saw an upswing. Part of it is exchange rate, part of it is time of year and all sorts of things contribute to it. But there is an audience and I will probably never work on something again where there is that confidence and certainty of an audience awaiting. I'm trying to enjoy it. Also, because we've done it successfully for five films, Warners trusts us and is supportive every which way. They leave us alone and encourage us, they're not breathing down our necks and are very generous and even allow us to make the films we wanted to make and take some chances. Even though hiring Alfonso Cuaron, in retrospect, wasn't a risk, but it was. David Yates was also a risk.

STUART CRAIG (production designer, on Hogwarts): For fans who care to take a frame by frame look at the films, they'll see that certain things change from one movie to another. This is partly due to expedience, but also each director has different priorities and each film is a film in its own right. So if things change a little bit, I think that's fine. It's a magic place after all. Hagrid's hut, for example, grew a little extension between *Harry Potter* 2 and 3. It was moved slightly to a more glamorous location. Whether that's evident, I don't know. But changes come about because the directors all have profoundly different priorities, and different directors of photography are always looking to treat it in a different way. And so it's amazing how fresh the same territory can be. That's what kept me going: the fact that this new blood kept coming in each time and the whole thing was literally a new movie that regenerated itself.

STUART CRAIG (production designer on influence of the novels): What reads well on the page can often be very internal and emotional responses can be very effective. It can on screen, too. But also, what the movies require is some visual impact from time to time, as well as orchestrating. So your big moments are counterpointed with quiet, more intimate ones. And so there was always plenty still to do. Jo's descripts are very full and very complete and very detailed, but as I say, we also ramp up the scale of something retaining the spirit of it and hopefully showing Rowling's intention. I'm sure, for example, the whole of Hogwarts is bigger than it reads in the novel. And the lake is probably bigger. The horizon is the mountains of Scotland. The wider context isn't actually described very fully, as I remember, even in the early novels. But hopefully the movies have brought that. As far as we know, she approves — we hope so anyway.

STUART CRAIG (production designer on his favorite set detail): I like the upper reaches of Dumbledore's office; that kind of amuses me and gives me a good feeling. There are places up there where the cameras actually haven't been, and I kind of lived in hope we would take it up there. He has a telescope — a magical telescope — and there's a system of balances and counterweights and pulleys and ropes above that, and balconies and little windows, and tiny little stone staircases, which are built into the thickness of the wall. And they're all there on the set, waiting to be explored by an adventurous director and camera operator. At the beginning of every movie, I dragged them up there, but the scene is the scene and you shoot what you've got to shoot.

STUART CRAIG (on the production designer's role in a film): I think one of the designer's primary functions is to draw very sharp distinctions between the scenes — analyze what the purpose of the scene is and then exaggerate it, underline it, deliver it as forcefully as you can. So the World Cup Stadium is the biggest, most spectacular place, but finally also kind of a jolly fun place. And the graveyard in which Voldemort appears at the end of *Goblet of Fire* is tiny in scale, very creepy, because of what you *don't* see. It's surrounded by mist and shadow. In terms of spectacle, it's the total opposite to the opening of the movie, and in terms of mood also. As I say, I regard that as my job to make those distinctions. So that film opens large and ends small, but then the threat kind of hangs in the air. It isn't resolved and obviously everyone's left waiting till the next movie.

STUART CRAIG (production designer on how the look of the films changed over the years): Two things come to mind. In the beginning we had to, for practical reasons, shoot on a number of real locations that might have been better built, so Hogwarts is this amalgam of real places and invented places. It's kind of untidy if you don't shoot it carefully, so we've been able to improve and tidy up the world of Hogwarts and slightly reinvent things as we've gone on. We've managed to make things better, so there's an evolution of that kind.

But also, there has been a succession of cinematographers who have wanted certain things. Naturally, to do something different from their predecessors. So there's been a tendency that as the kids have grown up and the stories have gotten darker, the look of the films has literally gotten darker, more mysterious, more monochromatic and more threatening. The new cameraman this time has just had a ball with it. The design — my side of things — has gone hand in hand with that. We physically make darker sets. The most important thing is that these movies deal with death a lot so we're adjusting the palettes and the nature of the sets accordingly.

DANIEL RADCLIFFE (on the person most fun to work with): Michael Gambon, who plays Dumbledore, was always fantastic to work with. He's mad and I love him to pieces. He's a fantastic actor, but he's also always chatting and joking and laughing, right up to and including while we're doing our scenes. I think it's because he's Irish, and Irish people are often the best storytellers. I'm half-Irish, too, so I'm quite good at that myself.

MIKE NEWELL (on scenes from the novel left out of *Goblet of Fire*): I'm sorry about the Dursleys, actually. Also, in this story Harry has bad dreams which pre-figure what's going to happen to him. It's as if Voldemort is beginning to inhabit his dreams as he does in book five, *The Order of the Phoenix*. So right at the beginning, Harry has a bad dream, which is the beginning of the through story. But then we're off to the World Cup and everything rolls from there.

RELATIONSHIP BETWEEN DANIEL, EMMA, AND RUPERT

EMMA WATSON: Rupert and Daniel have seen me in every single state, at my most glamorous to me at six in the morning with no makeup. They do feel like my brothers, and we've been through all the ups and downs of this mad experience together. When I was younger, they used to tease me, and now they're quite protective. It's nice. I'm glad we have each other. I would have been so lonely if this was just about one kid.

DANIEL RADCLIFFE: Well, we don't get sick of each other or anything like that, but we see each other so much when we're working. I do see Emma between films, because she's become like a sister to me. She really is one of my best friends. That thing about Rupert is, we've known each other for a long time, but we don't know each other particularly well. He's a cool guy and very funny, but I've never really become that close to him. I think it's because he's actually a bit older than me, and when I'm off at school, he's doing his own things, so I don't know that we have as much in common anymore.

EMMA WATSON: People have asked me if I would date Dan or Rupert. Oh God, no! With them it's really a brotherly relationship. It would be like kissing your brother. It's just wrong, awkward! Very weird, not good.

RUPERT GRINT: We hang out when we're on location. We see each other and hang out, but when we're not filming, we don't, really, because we live quite far away from each other. But we get on really well and have a good laugh on set.

EMMA WATSON: Daniel and Rupert are the only other people in the world who will ever understand what it is like to have been through what I have been through. I think we have quite a special bond. Even if we hated each other and didn't get on at all, we would always have that. That's important to me, being able to talk to them about it and going through it all with them.

DANIEL RADCLIFFE: When you hang around with someone, work with someone, for 10 or 11 months, it's so intense you're bound to occasionally become irritated with them. I'm not saying we throw plates at each other, but sometimes things do become a bit tense. But with Emma and I, when we have arguments, we end up being even better friends, because we have the kinds of arguments that actually improve a friendship.

EMMA WATSON: Kissing Rupert on screen is going to be *soooo* awkward. I'm not even thinking about it. Luckily, Rupert is lovely. Girls would probably give their left arm to be in my position, so I'm not complaining. But we've known each other so long, it's going to seem strange. He's a wonderful friend, but he's not someone I would date.

FANDOM & FAME

DANIEL RADCLIFFE: I was in New York and I appeared on the show *TRL* on MTV. It was a freezing cold day and I looked out the window and saw a girl standing in the street wearing a towel wrapped around her — nothing but a towel! She was wearing a sign that said, "Nothing comes between me and Harry Potter!" And there was another time when I arrived at the airport in Japan and there were over 5,000 girls waiting for me. I don't like to say this, because it makes me seem arrogant, but someone told me that more girls waited for me than for Tom Cruise or Brad Pitt. I think it's the English accent.

EMMA WATSON: Getting typecast as Hermione is my worst nightmare. One of my biggest concerns about being in *Harry Potter* for so long is that I will get stereotyped and people will only be able to see me as Hermione and nothing else, because I do want to do other things. I want to try different roles.

RUPERT GRINT: My friends and the other kids have been great — they treat me normally. It's just the teachers who are a problem, because they tend to suck up to me a bit! [*laughs*]. Other than that, it's been great.

EMMA WATSON: My friends were, like, "I really want to see Dan or meet Rupert." They'd say, "I have so many questions," but when they come to the set, they just go, "Yeah, cool," or don't say anything. It's funny, Dan and Rupert are like my brothers, so I feel kind of protective of them. Get away!

DANIEL RADCLIFFE: Younger fans think I'm actually Harry Potter, which is fine. But there was one kid — he was the son of one of the women who did the makeup on the set. Apparently, the makeup woman, a lovely woman named Louise, had told her son if he didn't behave, I would turn him into a frog. And of course he believed that, so every time he saw me, he started crying. But in the end, she told him he was stronger than Harry, so eventually he decided he wasn't scared of me anymore.

EMMA WATSON: I've always loved school. Always. I love sports, I love learning, I love being with my friends, so whenever I'm not filming, I always go back to school. Whenever I get the chance, I always try to be there and stay involved with that part of my life and not forget friends, my old friends. I work really hard to keep in touch. With filming, I might be in Scotland for a month, which will mean I won't see my friends for a month. Or I work adult hours, so I don't get to see them as much as I'd like. Long days, long hours.

DANIEL RADCLIFFE: Do I have an action figure of myself? I don't have an action figure of me. A very short answer. Apparently, this time around, I've been told by Warwick Davis, who plays Flitwick, that they're great. I don't have any of them. One of Gary Oldman's kids gave me a Lego figurine of myself, which was so sweet. So I've got that in my bag at the moment. The first action figure that came out looked very odd. Lego is also very interesting to see, because that's my head if it was perfectly cylindrical and yellow. The merchandising in general is a very odd thing — and that's a long-winded answer to a very short question.

RUPERT GRINT: I wouldn't say getting recognized is embarrassing, but it's a bit weird at times, like when I'm in the supermarket with my mom and people come up to me. That's the sort of place it usually happens, really. It's usually fun and they're usually really positive and nice about the films. It's quite cool, I suppose, in a way.

EMMA WATSON: I started to realize on *Prisoner of Azkaban* that people were starting to care. It sounds crazy, but it never occurred to me that people would care what I was wearing. When that hit home, it was a strange moment. I think for me, fashion has always been something that is fun. I've always loved clothes and I think it is important how I choose to dress, because it *is* how I'm presenting myself to the rest of the world. I think it's worth looking good, but it's fun at the end of the day.

DAVID HEYMAN: Fame never impacted Daniel Radcliffe. He is amazing. And it's worth noting he's no longer a kid, but is a really great man. He's very down to early, he's very humble, he's very enthusiastic, he's incredibly curious — all those qualities he had in 2000. He hasn't changed at all. He's more mature, he's had more experiences, and he's got stronger opinions, and as a human he has opinions that are more sophisticated. He's formidable, but never is there any sense of, "I'm better than you" or "I'm amazing." He has humility. I think that's his parents in a large part — and I do think that the environment here has been one that encouraged that humility. You can't get away with anything on the *Potter* set, we've been there for so long. You'd get brought down to Earth pretty damn quickly.

EMMA WATSON: The media just decided, with absolutely nothing to go on, that they were just going to make up one way or another what I was doing about the films. I guess they got the idea that I wasn't going to complete the series, because I actually took some time to think about it. The press are a bit funny like that.

EMMA WATSON: The French newspaper *Liberation* claimed that the Harry Potter universe painted a degrading image of women. These things really upset me. Whoever wrote these words can only be an idiot. *Harry Potter* has helped change loads of stereotypes. Where else, in fiction, can you find a character as clever as Hermione, who is an absolute feminist and wants to be second to none? Gosh! It's true that they're children's books, but they cover most important subjects, like life, death, politics, the importance of friendship and the choices that need to be made. Harry Potter really makes children think; it's not just like any other production for teenagers.

DATING

EMMA WATSON: I love someone who can make me laugh, who makes me feel like I can be myself around them. Confidence is good, arrogance is not. Someone who is genuine, just interesting, someone I can relax with. It's bad, isn't it? You have such high expectations. People say to me, "Oh, it must be easy for you; there must be people lining up for you." It's *not*. I suppose guys are either intimidated by me, or they have their defenses up, or they're ready to knock me down a peg. I really like guys as friends and I have as many guy friends as girlfriends, but the dating thing is a real minefield. I don't find it enjoyable at all. It's stressful.

ON ACTING

EMMA WATSON: As an actress, I can act mad, I can cry, I can do pretty much anything, but when it comes to laughing, putting on a realistic laugh that doesn't sound fake, I really, really struggle with it. There'll be times when we're shooting something and they'll have to cut because Dan, Rupert and I would be laughing at something and they'll stop. But when they stand you there and say, "Action! I want you to laugh," it's impossible to laugh on the spot. You've no idea. So that's what I struggle with.

RUPERT GRINT: When I was a kid, I didn't want to be an actor. I wanted to be an ice cream man. I just always thought that it seemed like a really good job, because you have a cool van that you get to drive around in all day.

EMMA WATSON: I think that I've been lucky in some ways to have worked with different directors every time. That keeps it interesting, because every time they bring something new to it and they teach me something, I learn something from them. It's funny that it's just the kind of way it turned out — I've been playing the same role for four years [at the time of *Goblet of Fire*] but she's grown up, she's coming across new challenges. For instance, in the fourth one, I love to travel and I do travel and I love scuba diving. I only have that certificate, but there's some underwater sequences which they wanted us to do which we had to get special certificates so we could do scuba diving — just stuff like that I've never done before. Filming underwater is a bit of a new experience. Learning to waltz — difficult. I get to work with new actors every time, which is always great. Filming aside, I've been lucky enough that I've been able to travel and see new places because of this.

DANIEL RADCLIFFE (on planning to star in *Equus* on Broadway): I can't wait to work on *Equus*. On this I'll get to spend the first half of next year on it almost, which is great and I'm looking forward to it. [The show] *Extras* was incredibly fun to do. I was very nervous going into it, because they've done a whole series before this. So I got a taste of what it must be like to come into the Harry Potter films halfway through. It was a nice experience. But just to clarify, I don't pick roles specifically because they are very different from Harry Potter. You have to judge each role on what it is and who you'll be working with. It just so happens that the two projects that have come are very different from Harry, and that's a nice bonus, really.

Equus is a really intense, sexual and in some ways violent play, and some of the audience may be shocked. People may even possibly think that I shouldn't be doing it because of the Potter fans. But I think that would be a mistake. The person at the center of all the attention should always be the one to lead where the attention goes. Jo Rowling is actually very excited about it, which is great. I think it will be weird for her, because someone said that when she first saw my screentest for Harry, she said something about it being like she'd found the son she never had. So it's going to be very weird for her to see her long-lost son blind horses. I look forward to hearing what she thinks.

EMMA WATSON: Still acting 10 years from now? It's a question that's always really difficult. I can't say how I will feel or what I will be doing. I mean, they are mammoth projects, absolutely mammoth. They don't get any bigger than *Harry Potter* — in the length they take to film, in the post production afterwards, in the publicity. They're huge and all-consuming, so I really try and take it one film at a time. It is a bit overwhelming.

DANIEL RADCLIFFE: I *do* think there's a timetable to get as much work between now and the end of the Harry Potter series and the immediate aftermath of the series to prove to people that I can do other things, and that's why I'm constantly on the lookout for scripts and things to do. That's why I'm doing two things between *Harry Potter 5* and *6*. I do feel a need to say to people that I am capable of more than Harry Potter. Having said that, Harry Potter is a very demanding part, really challenging. I don't mean to make it sound that Harry is an easy ride, because it's not. Hopefully doing things like *Equus* and *My Boy Jack*, which is a World War I story about Rudyard Kipling and his son, and I did *December Boys* last year — hopefully all of this stuff should begin to let people see me in a different light.

EMMA WATSON: I'm very careful to separate me and Hermione. There's me as Hermione and being part of that industry, and there's me, Emma, and they're two very different people. I have my professional life here and I have my home life here and they're very far apart and you never mix the two, ever. There are so many brilliant things that I get offered to do, and opportunities and experiences that are great. But I still know that without it, I've got things to go back to. I still make the effort to see all my friends. I've got friends to go back to when I go home. There's always something to go back to.

RUPERT GRINT: I actually think that I've gotten more comfortable with the whole acting thing and more confident thanks to the whole experience. I mean, my first day on set when we were making *Sorcerer's Stone* was really quite scary, because I'd never done anything quite like it. It was my first real project. It was quite daunting, but as the years have gone by, I have become more comfortable in it. It's just gone on from there and been really good.

I think at this point it definitely feels more like just returning to work than that amazed feeling I had at the beginning. The first film was just really good, because it was a whole new world that was absolutely amazing and fun. Now it seems a little more routine, but I still really enjoy them, they're really good fun and it's a really good atmosphere on the set because, for the most part, it has been the same crew and the same cast for most of the films. It's just a really good place to go.

DANIEL RADCLIFFE: Growing up in front of the camera, the only character that I think has gone through it this much, and I didn't think of this so I can't claim to be that knowledgeable, is Antoine Coinel from Francois Truffaut. He takes a boy of 11 or 12 and goes into his late teens. Funny enough, that was one of the films that Alfonso Cuaron got me to watch as a reference to Harry. But I am aware of that idea that this has never really been done where a boy grows up into a man on screen. It is very odd and I try not to think of the significance, because it is quite scary, really. But it's a privilege, too.

EMMA WATSON: I definitely don't want *Harry Potter* to be the last thing that I do within this business, whether it's film or not. Originally, what I sort of used to love was being on a stage and reacting to a live audience. So maybe my calling is more in theater. But I don't know. There are so many wonderful things that you can do within it, so I'm just not sure. There are so many different things that I don't know where I'll end up. I'm definitely looking around and definitely interested.

DANIEL RADCLIFFE: I am a little hard on Harry. I think I have to be. People are hard on themselves normally, so you have to be hard on the character you're playing. You sometimes have to look at them in the most unsympathetic light. At the same time, what's great about Harry is that he is a flawed character; he's not perfect and is deeply flawed. There are touches of arrogance about him, which clearly his father, as we find out in *Order of the Phoenix*, did have. He's reckless, which isn't always a bad thing, but he possibly likes to make a bit of a martyr of himself. As I said, he's not perfect. But I think he's an incredibly human character and really endearing. And I think that's why they're so successful, the books and the films. He is a hero and a really good person, but he's a good person who is mired in self-doubt all the time. That's what most people are.

ON BELIEF IN MAGIC

RUPERT GRINT: I'm not really into magic. I remember that they once got a magician in and tried to teach us all some stupid little card tricks, but I was never really that keen on that — and I'd never be able to do it! Dan got pretty into it, though. I know he learned quite a few magic tricks, but magic's not really my sort of thing. I'm really into golf. I've done that quite a lot. I got into it because I've got a couple of mates who play and a lot of people on the set play as well. The twins, George and Oliver Phelps, play, so I've played with them a couple of times. My dad also plays, so I played with him a couple of times. It's a good way of chilling out.

ON J.K. ROWLING'S NOVELS

EMMA WATSON: It's imaginative and completely takes you into another world. It just lets your imagination run wild, and I think it's great for something that is described so specifically that you know *isn't* there — but it's written so brilliantly that you almost believe that it really is there. I was always a massive fan of the books, even before I got into the films.

ON GROWING UP

DANIEL RADCLIFFE: I think my growth has been similar to any teenager in a way, possibly heightened by a couple of things that have happened, such as I've had to grow up slightly faster because I've spent so much time around adults. Most people at the age of 11 or 12 usually relate to adults on two levels: either as a parent or a teacher. I was put into a role of co-worker, though I never thought of it that way, which is a very different way to look at adults. But I don't think it's hurt me at all. I don't think I've developed into anything I wouldn't have had I been in more of a usual environment for a young kid. So it's been an odd, amazing experience. Very strange at times, very surreal, but ultimately, it's been fantastic fun, which is all that really matters, I suppose. But I am aware of the idea that this has never really been done where a boy grows up into a man on screen. It is very odd and I try not to think of the significance, because it's quite scary, really. But it's a privilege, too.

SIMILARITY TO CHARACTER

EMMA WATSON: I guess I'm a bit of a feminist. I don't know. It's really important to stand up for yourself and Hermione's never afraid to take control of a situation or be the brains behind anything. She says what she thinks and she doesn't hold back. In many ways, she bosses the boys around, which I think is kind of cool. I think they need her. In my own life, there have been times when other people thought that they knew what was better for me, and that the better for me was not to think. But I'm not a rebel. I usually do what I'm told. If anything, I try to negotiate. I'm ready to fight for my rights, but I don't think it is worth playing the role of the teenager who wants to rebel against the world. I don't like it. It is overused. I know how Hermione feels. I'm a teenager and I know how it feels to want to be rebellious and irresponsible and carefree, which were qualities we saw in Hermione in *Order of the Phoenix*. But she'll always have a very serious side to her as well.

ANECDOTES

EMMA WATSON: You know how you have those really fancy screen chairs with your name on the back? Well, I've got this little one that says "Emma Watson" on it. I was in the middle of the set, just sitting there, sipping my drink casually, and then I think my chair was on a wire or something and I went straight over backwards on this chair and spilled my drink all over me. That was pretty bad.

THE HAPPY GIANT

Robbie Coltrane reflects on playing Hagrid

Life for an actor, particularly when one is starring in an adaptation of a popular book, is difficult enough in that it's a struggle to find one acting assignment after another, but for Robbie Coltrane, the Harry Potter films have added even more pressure. "I got a letter from a woman," he reflects, "and it started off very sweetly: 'I've been a big fan of yours for x amount of years,' and then she said, 'We're so glad that you're playing Hagrid, because it's going to be very, very difficult to get that blend between scariness and humor and millions of children throughout the world are relying on you.' So, I thought, 'No pressure there then,' and, of course, she was right."

As fans of Harry's world are well aware, Coltrane portrays the friendly giant Hagrid, who is the one who escorts young Mr. Potter to Hogwarts and becomes a close friend in each of the books and both films that have been made from them so far. And for the actor, if there's one question he's been asked above all others, it's how the filmmakers made it appear as though he is, quite simply, so huge on screen.

"I couldn't tell you that, because it would spoil the magic," says Coltrane cryptically. "I mean, it's like Orson Wells says, you know, 'Everyone knows that the lady doesn't really get cut in two,' and so I'm leaving that one. It really would spoil it. If you knew, you would agree with me, trust me. You would say, 'I know exactly why he hasn't told anyone.' You'll have to trust me on this one."

One of the challenges of playing Hagrid has been finding the balance between what is funny and what is terrifying. "He *is* very scary," Coltrane points out. "I mean, he's half a giant and the giants aren't very nice, as you will discover later on. So he has to have that edge to him, and they did it very cleverly. They said, 'When he kicks the door in and then says, "Sorry," that's real Hagrid.' He forgets how strong he is and that he could break your neck with a snap of his finger. But it's also quite clear in the writing when he's supposed to be funny. I mean, Hagrid's problem is that when he starts talking, he doesn't know when to stop. He actually gives away major plot lines, so that has to be an established part of his character. Otherwise, it just sounds like he's giving away plot lines. He had to sound very natural and his statement, 'I should not have said that,' became a bit of a catch phrase in the shooting, because he keeps doing it. But this didn't change my approach to the character. I mean, it was quite clear to me how the character should be played in the movies. And, of course, Jo Rowling and I are great friends. We talked on the telephone for hours like a couple of adolescents about everything.

"The books are about everything," he continues. "The books are about friendship and peer group pressure and how you discover your individuality and are you prepared to be unpopular. All of those things that fuel your childhood, really. The magic, in a sense, is not really what they're about, I would suggest. That's the icing on the cake, I think. Jo also gave me some clues to the character. She said, 'Imagine a Hell's Angel who gets off of his Harley Davidson but doesn't live up to the image. He starts with a cup of tea and talks about his garden.' I thought that was great, because I have known people like that. But if you say anything rude about their garden, they will take you out and beat the crap out of you. That's Hagrid, really."

As far as the actor sees it, if there is any particular pressure that has faced both *Harry Potter and the Sorcerer's Stone* and *Harry Potter and the Chamber of Secrets*, it's the criteria by which they are judged. Not only do they have to be viewed as movies in their own right, but they have to satisfy countless legions of Harry Potter fans.

"That's absolutely true," says Coltrane, "and children, as you know, are sticklers for detail. Terrible sticklers for detail. I mean, you will know if you've ever bought a child a toy that's not exactly the one they wanted. 'But this one has the white wheels.' 'It's the same as the other one.' 'It's not, it's got white wheels,' and, you know, they will know every single thing. That's scarier for [director] Chris Columbus than anyone else."

The one question that mystified critics have been asking, is just why is Harry Potter as popular as he is? Like most people, Coltrane can only offer his own feelings on the matter, as no one can truly identify why something becomes a phenomenon.

"I think it's because it encapsulates all of the good elements of drama and particularly children's drama," he proposes. "Children wonder what life is about, and a lot of the times, they wish they had new parents, but not really. It's that whole thing about them wanting to be scared, but not really, and it's got all the things in it that children worry about. You know, you want to be popular, but you also want to be yourself. There is always that tension, and then there's your relationship with authority. You want to be a good boy, but you don't want to be too good. You want to get on at school, but you don't want to be the teacher's pet. Jo Rowling gets all of that absolutely right. And besides that, they're just great stories."

THE MANY FACES OF VOLDEMORT

Portraying Ultimate Evil Requires Several Actors

Any truly memorable hero in fiction always has a villain to face off against: Superman and Lex Luthor, Frodo Baggins and Sauron, Luke Skywalker and Darth Vader. Harry Potter is, of course, no exception, with his ever-escalating face-offs with the mysterious Lord Voldemort.

But while Superman, Frodo, and Luke know (with some notable exceptions) who and what they're up against, Harry has a harder time of it. As readers of the Potter books and viewers of the movies can attest, Voldemort's appearance shifts fairly frequently, with several different actors taking on the role at various points in the saga.

In fact, Voldemort appears even before Harry himself in the series' first installment, *Harry Potter and the Sorcerer's Stone* (or *Philosopher's Stone* in Great Britain). The novel begins with a celebration by the wizarding world – the society of conjurers and spell-casters that exists hidden from the non-magical, or "Muggle," world – in the aftermath of the apparent downfall of the evil and powerful Voldemort, who after killing Harry's parents attempted to kill the then-one-year-old as well. Unfortunately for Voldemort (but fortunately for the series' legions of fans), his magic curse rebounded and destroyed his body, resulting in the famous lightning-bolt scar on Harry's forehead.

Once he reaches the age of 11, however, Harry's true calling is revealed: he has magical powers, and will learn to use and control them by attending the Hogwarts School of Witchcraft and Wizardry. Once there, he learns of the existence of the

Sorcerer's Stone, which promises eternal life – which the body-less Voldemort is very much interested in acquiring.

Harry later discovers that Quirinus Quirrell, the Defense Against the Dark Arts teacher, has been acting on Voldemort's behalf; in fact, during the story's climax, as Harry and Quirrell fight over the stone, Voldemort reveals himself on the back of Quirrell's head and speaks directly to Harry, threatening to kill him if he does not assist Voldemort in recovering it. Harry continues to fight against the possessed Quirrell before Voldemort escapes, resulting in Quirrell's death.

For the 2001 film, British character actor Ian Hart (*Finding Neverland*, TV's *Dirt*) played both Quirrell and the Voldemort apparition. Thanks to computer-generated imagery and Hart's ability to disguise his voice, the dual nature of the actor's performance was nearly undetectable.

As if all this wasn't confusing enough, Richard Bremmer, a veteran theatre, television and film actor, is also credited as the voice of "He Who Must Not Be Named," the code words for Voldemort. Although Bremmer was originally signed to portray Voldemort in the subsequent films, ultimately the role went to distinguished actor Ralph Fiennes (*Schindler's List*, *The English Patient*).

"I can only assume they wanted more of a Hollywood name," Bremmer says of the decision. "Originally, I was cast as Voldemort, but they changed it during the process and gave me the credit for He Who Must Not Be Named."

Bremmer says he enjoyed making the first film, but believes that financial and Hollywood pressures on the filmmakers led to his being pushed aside. "My children were disappointed up to a point, but it is the world we live in," he shrugs. "I have been in the business for 30 years now, so I'm not surprised by things."

Posing a Riddle

At any rate, the requirements for the role in the second film, *Chamber of Secrets*, went beyond Bremmer's talents. The character first appears in the book as 16-year-old Tom Marvolo Riddle, the last descendant of wizard Salazar Slytherin, one of Hogwarts' four founders. In the book, Tom resides inside a magical diary found by Ginny Weasley, younger sister of Harry's pal Ron Weasley and Harry's (eventual) love interest. Ginny expresses her deepest feelings and fears to Tom in the diary.

Not a good decision, as it turns out. At the story's climax, Tom reveals that when the letters in his full name are rearranged, they spell "I Am Lord Voldemort." Riddle reveals that he has grown strong on Ginny's fears, and eventually possesses her, using her to unlock the Chamber of Secrets to set free a basilisk, a monstrous serpentine creature that petrifies several Hogwarts students. Eventually Harry is able to defeat both the basilisk and Riddle.

The fact that Riddle's name turns out to be itself a riddle underscores author J.K. Rowling's occasional cleverness with names. Though she's said "Voldemort" is simply an invented name, it does include "mort," the French word for "death." That was much on Rowling's mind when she conceived the character, she says. "He regards death itself as ignominious. He thinks that it's a shameful human weakness .... His worst fear is death."

To portray the teenaged manifestation of the Dark Lord, the 2002 film's producers turned to actor Christian Coulson. "I hadn't read [the books] until I was told that I was going to audition," he recalls. "I had a few days to prepare, so I got the first two books and read them. After auditioning I read the next two, because I got involved with the whole *Harry* thing and enjoyed the first two so much."

Coulson adds, laughing, "By the time I was given the role I'd been auditioning for about six months, so at that point I think it was a relief for everyone I know, since they'd been watching me slowly go mad waiting to see if I'd got the chance to play it or not."

Voldemort does not appear in the third book, *Prisoner of Azkaban*, although his voice is heard when Harry passes out from the effects of a Dementor, one of the soul-sucking beasts who guard the wizard prison.

The Dark Lord returns with a vengeance in the next book, *Goblet of Fire*. The plot is set in motion when Ron Weasley's pet rat, Scabbers, is revealed to be Voldemort's underling Peter Pettigrew, who captures Harry and uses his blood to help the evil wizard regain his body and full power. *Goblet of Fire* marks the first time that Rowling employs a physical description of Voldemort, noting that he's "tall and skeletally thin" with a face "whiter than a skull, with wide, livid scarlet eyes and a nose that was as flat as a snakes with slits for nostrils." Voldemort's hands, she writes, "were like large, pale spiders; his long white fingers caressed his own chest, his arms, his face; the red eyes, whose pupils were slits, like a cat's, gleamed still more brightly through the darkness."

The 2005 film marked Ralph Fiennes' debut as the adult

evildoer. "I have no doubt children will be afraid of me now if they weren't before," he laughed at the time, noting his previous villainous incarnations, such as the Nazi Amon Goeth in *Schindler's List* and as the "Tooth Fairy" serial killer in *Red Dragon*, probably hadn't been seen by the series' younger fans.

In preparation for the role, Fiennes read the *Goblet of Fire* novel, but jokingly said, "I was only interested in my scene, and I had to go through thousands and thousands of other scenes which I did, dutifully, until I got to my scene and I read it many, many, many, many, many times -- and that was my research."

Despite his long list of credits, Fiennes says that playing someone who's pure evil has been a real challenge. "It's the hardest thing in the world to play pure, pure evil. I still don't know what it is. [The producers and I] just talked about different levels of psychotic madness in people, when you don't quite know what someone's going to do. They could do anything -- they could slash your throat, they could put their arm around you and offer to be your best friend, and the next thing you know they turn really nasty. That sort of terrifying thing you see and read about."

Voldemort Rising

For the fifth book, *Order of the Phoenix*, Voldemort again appears at the climax for a showdown with Harry, who spends much of the book going through extreme emotional stress which, Rowling says, was necessary to prove that her young hero is emotionally vulnerable and therefore human, as opposed to the cold, inhuman Voldemort. "Obviously there's a contrast between him, as a very human hero, and

Voldemort, who has deliberately *de*humanised himself," she says. "The question I was asked a lot early on was, 'Was Voldemort really Harry's father?' And of course, that's a STAR WARS question. He is not, in a biological sense, related to him at all."

In the book, Voldemort engages in a ferocious duel with Hogwarts headmaster Dumbledore. The Dark Lord attempts to possess Harry but finds that he cannot; Harry is too full of that which Voldemort finds detestable: love. Sensing that Dumbledore could win, Voldemort disappears, but not before his return to life becomes public knowledge.

Fiennes again assayed the part of Voldemort for the 2007 film. "I latched onto what was maybe crude psychology in working out Voldemort's obsession with Harry," he reflects. "Harry was loved by his parents, which Voldemort can't stand. He is, of course, a rejected person. It's quite basic: the rejected child who's emotionally been denied affection turns violent. You have to suggest there's more there, a life, a spirit, a mind. It isn't just a creepy voice and makeup."

In the ensuing book, *Half-Blood Prince*, Voldemort declares war, and begins to rise to power once more. Rowling includes a series of flashbacks to fill in Voldemort's history, including that he was the son of the witch Merope Gaunt and a Muggle, Tom Riddle Sr. However, Riddle abandons Merope just before their child's birth, soon after which she dies. Young Tom grows up in an orphanage before being taken into Hogwarts by Dumbledore. Although a model student, the young Riddle is revealed to be a hateful and spiteful child who eventually murders his father and grandparents.

In the book's main plot, Voldemort leads an assault on Hogwarts and seeks to slay Dumbledore. *Prince* ends on a sombre note. For the film, Fiennes' young nephew, Hero Fiennes-Tiffin, plays the young Tom Riddle Jr. and Frank Dillane plays the teenaged Tom. Evanna Lynch, who plays Harry's Hogwarts classmate Luna Lovegood in both *Phoenix* and *Prince*, said before filming began that she wasn't quite sure of how to approach Dillane.

"I saw him, but to go up and say, 'Hi'? He's *Voldemort!*" she laughs. "But maybe I will. He has a quiet, dark side, so people don't know him much yet. He doesn't say much. I'm sure he's a lovely boy. But he does have that aura."

As all fictional villains must be, Voldemort is finally vanquished in the seventh and final book, *Deathly Hollows*, which will be split into two films, coming out in November 2010 and July 2011. For his part, Fiennes is looking forward to continuing his exploration of the villain's psyche. "You've got to struggle not to play all the obvious notes," he says. "And with such extreme makeup, such an extreme look — that's the challenge. Also, the style of the movies is so strong. The movie itself is its own machine, and you've got to fulfill a function of a bigger machine. It would be good to keep the sense of some kind of real psychology going on, even with all the special effects and everything.

*Official Poster for the Stage Production
Harry Potter and the Cursed Child*

THE EXPANDING WORLD OF HOGWARTS

The film series came to a close in 2011, but there have been a number of means of keeping the world of Harry Potter alive over the years. Much of this has come from the creativity of fans and their frequent gatherings, theme park attractions and a studio tour. But perhaps the most important spin-off of all of them is the four-act two-part play *Harry Potter and the Cursed Child*, which originally ran on London's West End from 2016 to 2017, and then made the jump to Broadway in 2018.

Written by Jack Thorne, and based on an original story by J.K. Rowling, John Tiffany and him, it's set 19 years after *Harry Potter and the Deathly Hallows* and focuses on Harry Potter (who is serving as the Head of the Department of Magical Law Enforcement at the Ministry of Magic), and his younger son, Albus Severus Potter, who is getting ready to attend Hogwarts. Considered the eighth story in the series, the script was published in book form, but there has not been a novelization or any talk of film adaptation. *Yet.*

Wikipedia offers up this breakdown of the four acts:

ACT ONE: In the opening scene, set during the epilogue of *Deathly Hallows* in the year 2017, Harry and Ginny Potter send their son, Albus Severus, on the Hogwarts Express to begin his first year at Hogwarts. Harry works a desk job as the Head of Magical Law Enforcement at the Ministry of Magic, while Ginny is the editor of the sports section of *The Daily Prophet*. Ron Weasley and Hermione Granger also send their daughter Rose on the train. Hermione is now Minister for Magic, while Ron manages Weasley's Wizard Wheezes in Diagon Alley alongside his older brother George Weasley. On his first trip aboard the Hogwarts Express, Albus forms an unlikely friendship with Scorpius

Malfoy, the son of Harry's former nemesis Draco and his wife Astoria (née Greengrass). Unlike his father, Scorpius is very polite and very nerdy. The school is stunned when, in a break with the tradition of Potters being sorted into Gryffindor, Albus is sorted into Slytherin alongside Scorpius.

Both boys are bullied by other students over the next few years, Albus due to his perceived failure to live up to his parents, Scorpius due to unproven rumours that he is the son of Lord Voldemort. Scorpius's mother then passes away due to a fatal disease. Albus and Harry drift apart due to Albus's struggles with his father's shadow and Harry's uncertainty on how to deal with his son's problems. Albus also drifts apart from Rose, with whom he was close before meeting Scorpius. Prior to his fourth year, Albus gets into a fight with his father after being given the latter's baby blanket and a love potion from Ron. During the fight, Harry angrily says that he sometimes wishes Albus was not his son, and Albus spills the potion on the blanket.

Harry obtains a prototype of a more powerful version of the Time-Turner that allows one to travel into the past and change history. Simultaneously, Harry's scar starts hurting again, causing him to become concerned that Voldemort may be returning. Amos Diggory, who has become old and is cared for by his niece Delphi, asks Harry to use the Time-Turner to prevent the death of his son, Cedric. After overhearing Harry refuse to help the Diggorys, Albus is inspired to do so and convinces Scorpius to help him. The two escape from the Hogwarts Express to visit Amos, and they team up with Delphi to steal the Time-Turner from Hermione's office, in the Ministry of Magic, while disguised with Polyjuice Potion.

ACT TWO: Knowing that Cedric's death was the result of him winning the Triwizard Tournament alongside Harry, the boys use the Time-Turner to travel back to the first tournament challenge in 1994. The two disguise themselves as Durmstrang students in an attempt to sabotage Cedric to prevent his victory. The plan fails, and the disguises cause Hermione to become suspicious of Viktor Krum, a Durmstrang student, and go to the Yule Ball with Ron instead. As a result, Ron never experiences the jealousy fundamental to his relationship with Hermione, and the two never marry. Ron instead falls in love with Padma Patil at the Ball, and Hermione becomes a frustrated and mean professor at Hogwarts, teaching Defense Against the Dark Arts.

Meanwhile, Harry has nightmares about Voldemort as he grows suspicious that the wizard will return. A centaur named Bane tells Harry that a "dark cloud" is around Albus. Convinced that Scorpius is a threat to Albus, Harry tries to have the boys kept apart at Hogwarts by attempting to force Headmistress Minerva McGonagall to keep tabs on Albus using the Marauder's Map.

Albus and Scorpius' friendship is destroyed, but the two eventually reconcile after Albus steals Harry's old Invisibility Cloak from Albus's older brother James Sirius. Harry is persuaded to relent after a conversation with Draco and Ginny. Meanwhile, Albus and Scorpius make another attempt to use the Time-Turner to change Cedric's fate, this time by humiliating him during the Triwizard Tournament's second task. When Scorpius returns to the present day, however, Albus is not with him. Dolores Umbridge walks up to him and reveals that Harry is dead and Lord Voldemort rules the wizarding world.

ACT THREE: Scorpius discovers that as a result of his actions, Cedric joined the Death Eaters and killed Neville Longbottom, preventing him from killing Nagini and allowing Voldemort to win the Battle of Hogwarts. With Harry now dead, Albus never existed, while Voldemort was able to completely consolidate power and transform the Ministry of Magic into a dictatorial regime. In the new timeline, Scorpius became a popular Head Boy and Quidditch star, helping the staff and students torment Muggle-borns. Umbridge became the new Headmistress of Hogwarts and patrols the school with Dementors and a revived Inquisitorial Squad led by Scorpius.

A powerful dark figure called "The Augurey" leads the Ministry of Magic. With help from Ron, Hermione, and Severus Snape, now the final members of a dwindling anti-Voldemort resistance movement, Scorpius is able to use the Time-Turner to prevent the interference of Albus and his past self and restore the events of the original timeline, the alternate Ron, Hermione, and Snape sacrificing themselves to the Dementors in order to allow him to do so. Scorpius reunites with Albus, and the two boys are eventually found by their parents, as well as Ron and Hermione. Following these events, Harry scolds Albus for his actions, but the two nevertheless begin to reconcile.

Realizing the danger the Time-Turner poses, Scorpius and Albus attempt to destroy it themselves, but they are joined by Delphi. Scorpius notices that Delphi has a tattoo of an Augurey and realizes she was in charge of the Ministry of Magic in the alternate timeline. Delphi takes them captive, killing a fellow student in the process, and reveals her intention of restoring the alternate timeline.

After Ron reveals he saw Albus and Scorpius with Delphi while he was in Hogsmeade with Neville, Harry and Draco confront Amos, only to discover Delphi had bewitched him into thinking she was his niece. Delphi takes the boys to the final challenge of the Triwizard Tournament, but Albus and Scorpius prevent her from acting, and Delphi uses the Time-

Turner again to travel farther back in time. She inadvertently takes the boys with her and then destroys the Time-Turner to leave them stranded in time.

Searching Delphi's room, Harry, Draco, Ginny, Hermione, and Ron discover hidden writing on the walls describing a prophecy that will allow Voldemort to return. Draco questions why she would be so obsessed with Voldemort's return, as Ginny finds writing on the ceiling that claims Delphi is the daughter of Voldemort.

ACT FOUR: Albus and Scorpius discover they have been taken back to the night before Harry's parents were killed and assume Delphi is planning to kill Harry before Voldemort attempts to do so. Albus and Scorpius write an invisible message on Harry's baby blanket, knowing in the present, the blanket would become stained with a love potion and expose the message. The message reads: "Dad.Help.Godric's Hollow. 31/10/1981."

Meanwhile, Draco reveals the Time-Turner was actually a prototype for a perfected model owned by him, but they remain unable to rescue the boys due to their uncertainty over which time period they have entered. After Harry receives the message from the boys, he and his allies use Draco's Time-Turner to travel back in time to save them and stop Delphi. While waiting for Delphi, they deduce she intends to convince Voldemort to abandon his doomed attempt to kill Harry, ensuring her father's survival and allowing her to be with him.

Harry disguises himself as Voldemort using Transfiguration to distract Delphi; after a struggle, the group manages to subdue her. Rather than killing Delphi, it is decided that she will be given a life sentence in Azkaban Prison. Lord Voldemort then appears and is oblivious to the presence of

Harry and the group. The group allows the murder of Harry's parents to play out again, unwilling to risk the consequences of altering the past.

After returning to the present day, Delphi is sent to Azkaban. Albus and Scorpius now decide to be more active at Hogwarts, with Scorpius expressing interest in trying out for the Slytherin Quidditch Team and asking Rose out on a date. Harry and Albus visit Cedric's grave, with Harry apologizing for his role in Cedric's death.

There have also been productions in Melbourne, Australia and San Francisco, California, and what follows is a breakdown of some of the cast members for the various stagings.

Harry Potter: Jamie Parker (UK, NY), Gareth Reeves (Melbourne), John Skelley (San Francisco)
Ron Weasley: Paul Thornley (UK, NY), Gyton Grantley (Melbourne), David Abeles (San Francisco)
Hermione Granger: Noma Dumezweni (UK, NY), Paula Arundell (Melbourne), Yanna McIntosh (San Francisco)
Ginny Potter: Poppy Miller (UK, NY), Lucy Goleby (Melbourne), Angela Reed (San Francisco)
Draco Malfoy: Alex Price (UK, NY), Tom Wren (Melbourne), Lucas Hall (San Francisco)
Albus Severus Potter: Sam Clemmett (UK, NY), Sean Rees-Wemyss (Melbourne), Benjamic Papac (San Francisco)
Scorpius Malfoy: Anthony Boyle (UK, NY), William McKenna (Melbourne), Jon Steiger (San Francisco)
Rose Granger-Weasley & Young Hermione: Cherrelle Skeete (UK), Susan Heyward (NY), Manali Datar (Melbourne), Folami Williams (San Francisco)
Delphi Diggory: Esther Smith (UK), Jessie Fisher (NY), Madeline Jones (Melbourne), Emily Juliette Murphy (San Francisco)

Craig Bowker Jr.: Jeremy Ang Jones (UK), Joshua DeJesus (NY), Slone Sudiro (Melbourne), Irving Dyson Jr. (San Francisco)

Moaning Myrtle & Lily Potter Sr.: Annabel Baldwin (UK), Lauren Nicole Cipoletti (NY), Gillian Cosgriff (Melbourne), Brittany Zeinstra (San Francisco)

Polly Chapman: Claudia Grant (UK), Madeline Weinstein (NY), Jessica Vickers (Melbourne), Lauren Zakrin (San Francisco)

Vernon Dursley, Severus Snape & Lord Voldemort: Paul Bentall (UK), Byron Jennings (NY), David Ross Patterson (Melbourne), Andrew Long (San Francisco)

Rubeus Hagrid & Sorting Hat: Chris Jarman (UK), Brian Abraham (NY), Soren Jensen (Melbourne), Julian Rozzell, Jr. (San Francisco)

Albus Dumbledore: Barry McCarthy (UK), Edward James Hyland (NY), George Henare (Melbourne), Charles Janasz (San Francisco)

WRITER JACK THORNE BRINGS THE MAGIC — IN THE FORM OF *HARRY POTTER AND THE CURSED CHILD* — TO BROADWAY

"Absolutely terrifying."

Those are the words that Jack uses to describe the idea of attempting to follow up the epic Harry Potter book and film series with *The Cursed Child*. "But we had two very big advantages," he says. "One is John Tiffany and I had already made two plays before, so I knew him intimately and he knew me intimately and we could have a very honest relationship throughout the whole process. I think that honesty is *so* important. And then the other key advantage we had is J.K. Rowling, who happens to be one of the nicest individuals that ever walked the Earth. She was incredibly supportive and brilliant all the way through the process. She was a joy."

As to the power of *Harry Potter and the Cursed Child* he notes, "It's about the pain of history and how we deal with it. Harry has not overcome his childhood and it takes *his* child, who is unable to cope with being the son of Harry Potter, to overcome it. By the end of the play, he has got a completely different relationship with history.

"There are so many things," Thorne adds, "that we need to let go of in our past and Harry, who was an incredibly brave boy from the first moment we meet him, has to be brave in an entirely new way in this play. That was always the story we wanted to tell. What did that childhood do to the man that was made? And to the other people around him? To Hermione and Ron and Draco, and the rest? By looking at that, reexamining that, and having the *time* to reexamine that, we were able to tell a story about who Harry is and who he is going to become. Again, by the end of the play, I hope that the journey is one where we leave a character who's optimistic for the future and who he can be."

Through seven novels, eight films, and, now, a two-part play, the public's fascination with Harry Potter seems to be unwavering. The real question, of course, is *why*?

"It's a beautiful story," he offers matter of factly. "One of the things I like about Harry is he's *not* extraordinary and he's a wizard, but he's not an extraordinary wizard. He's not amazing at spells. He's very good on the broomstick, but he's not particularly academic. The secret to *why* he achieves and survives and ultimately wins is his trust in the people around him and his ability to love *despite* everything that's thrown at him. And his own innate bravery. I love both those things about Harry, and I think the world loves both those things about Harry. That, I think, is what the books celebrate and what we try to celebrate in the play."

ABOUT THE AUTHOR

EDWARD GROSS is a veteran entertainment journalist (*does that just mean old?*), who began his professional career in the mid-1980s, writing articles on film, television and comic books for such publications as *Starlog* (where he would become New York Correspondent), *New York Nightlife, Daredevils, Comics Scene,* and *Fangoria*. He would go on to be Editor-in-Chief of the magazines *Not of This Earth* and *RetroVision*, as well as Senior Editor of *Cinescape, Femme Fatales* and *Cinefantastique*. Other positions have included Executive Editor of *Life Story, Movie Magic, Film Fantasy, TV Magic* and *Superhero Spectacular*, all from Bauer Publishing; Executive Editor, US for Empireonline.com, Film/TV Editor for closerweekly.com, intouchweekly.com, lifeandstylemag.com and j-14.com; and is currently Contributing Editor to doyouremember.com and Senior Editor of *Geek* magazine. He has written or co-written more than two dozen non-fiction books on film and TV.

Twitter: @EdGross
Instagram: @EdGrossWriter
Facebook: ed.gross.923

www.ingramcontent.com/pod-product-compliance
Lightning Source LLC
Chambersburg PA
CBHW041125110526
44592CB00020B/2689